Muuto
Nottingham.
2002.

Constituting
Federal Sovereignty

THE JOHNS HOPKINS SERIES IN CONSTITUTIONAL THOUGHT

Sanford Levinson and Jeffrey K. Tulis, *Series Editors*

CONSTITUTING
FEDERAL SOVEREIGNTY

The European Union
in Comparative Context

LESLIE FRIEDMAN GOLDSTEIN

THE JOHNS HOPKINS UNIVERSITY PRESS
Baltimore & London

The Johns Hopkins University Press
2715 North Charles Street
Baltimore, Maryland 21218-4363
www.press.jhu.edu

Library of Congress Cataloging-in-Publication Data
Goldstein, Leslie Friedman, 1945–
Constituting federal sovereignty : the European Union in comparative
context / Leslie Friedman Goldstein.
p.   cm. — (The Johns Hopkins series in constitutional thought)
Includes bibliographical references and index.
ISBN 0-8018-6663-4 (alk. paper)
1. European Union.   2. Federal government—European Union countries.
I. Title.   II. Series.
JN30.G65   2001
321.02—dc21   00-011516

To Phil Goldstein, a world-class husband,

and Ben Goldstein, a world-class son

Contents

Tables

Acknowledgments

One does not complete a work of this magnitude without accumulating a great many intellectual debts. I thank all of the following for their collectively massive contribution to my learning, and note that none of them is responsible for any of my remaining errors. First, the European law specialists who attended the 1988 Salzburg Seminar on American law and alerted me to the importance of the ECJ, especially Laurence Gormley, Aidan O'Neill, and Sylvia Paisley. Second, Alec Stone, who generously invited me to attend the workshop on comparative member-state reception of European law that he organized with Anne-Marie (Burley) Slaughter, Martin Shapiro, and Joseph Weiler. Third, the faculty and staff associated with the Institut de Droit Public at the University of Lausanne, especially Maryl Tintori, Pierre Moor, Suzette Sandoz, Anouk Neuenschwander, and Christine Sattiva Spring, for their help in my research on the Swiss union. Fourth, Michel Troper and Francoise Michaut, both for their inviting me to the stimulating seminars of the Centre de Théorie du Droit at Université de Paris X, and for their own insightful conversations. And, finally, to the numerous colleagues, both at my own university and around the globe, whose helpful comments (face to face or via e-mail) have encouraged me along the way or kept one or another error out of the book. These individuals include Pia Caroni, Roland Ruffieux, Arnold Heidenheimer, Peter Russell, Ted Morton, Gary Jacobsohn, Karen Orren, Sandy Levinson, Jeff Tulis, Terrence Marshall, Alain Laraby, Greg Caldeira, Mary Volcansek, Bill Williams, Bill Funk, Craig Orren, Kurt Burch, Bob Denemark, Dan Green, Jo-Anne Kingsley, Hank Reynolds, and the anonymous reviewers for Cambridge, Routledge, and Johns Hopkins University Press.

Apart from my intellectual debts, I need to thank the University of Delaware Center for Advanced Study and the Unidel Foundation for the financial support that kept this project from taking even longer than it did. For permission to reprint segments of this work that appeared elsewhere, I thank *Studies in American Political Development,* MIT Press, and the Universities of Florida Press. My enormous debt to my family for putting up with me, my erratic temperament, and my absences during my work on this project is expressed on the dedication page.

Constituting
Federal Sovereignty

Introduction

Prologue: Who's Sovereign Now?

At the turn of the millennium, one must wonder whether the supposed rules of sovereignty still bind anyone. On March 24, 1999, the final tribunal of the British Law Lords rejected the (utterly traditional) claim of Augusto Pinochet that he may not legitimately be punished by either the United Kingdom or Spain on the basis of charges for crimes against humanity committed while he wielded purportedly sovereign power in his native Chile. On March 25, 1999, NATO forces began bombing Serbia without a declaration of war and without explicit United Nations Security Council authorization, in a self-appointed police action to punish Serbia for misbehavior within its own province, Kosovo. An *International Herald Tribune* subheadline characterized this attack by the NATO alliance as the "First in Its [fifty-year] History on Sovereign Land."[1]

During the final decade of the second millennium, numerous "police actions" and humanitarian missions guarded by armed force have been launched by more powerful governments, often but not always in the name of the United Nations, against less powerful governments, upon territory over which the less powerful government nonetheless continues to be called "sovereign." In December 1992, without permission from the Somalian government, the UN Security Council authorized the deployment of troops in Somalia for humanitarian relief efforts, which purpose was later expanded to include confiscating weapons, training civilian police, and rebuilding the Somalian infrastructure. Chapter 7 of the UN Charter permits the Security Council to use whatever force is necessary to check "threats to the peace," even overriding article 2(7) of the charter, which asserts that the UN will not interfere "in matters which are essentially within the domestic jurisdiction of any State." Such UN-identified threats in the nineties have included Iraqi repression of domestic Kurds and Shi'ites, Haiti's refusal to reinstate elected president Jean-Bertrand Aristide, Libya's refusal to extradite two of its citizens accused of bombing Pan Am Flight 103 over Lockerbie, Scotland, and civil wars in Liberia and Yugoslavia. These interventions have been controversial precisely because they violate the old rules of sovereignty.[2]

Moreover, in this same decade, the International Monetary Fund, an international organization that functions as a kind of quasi–credit union for governments and that tends to be dominated by a few wealthy countries that contribute most of its funding, has acquired a much more prominent public profile, as it bails out one national economy after another in the Southern Hemisphere, in Southeast and Eastern Asia, and in the former Soviet Union—each time visibly setting rules to which supposedly sovereign governments must agree to adhere in order to obtain the resources needed in their respective states. Even for wealthy states not in need of bailouts, the competitive pressures of a tightly integrated world economy have rendered quaintly anachronistic the old maxims about sovereignty that used to guide political theory. These traditional maxims include, for instance, "Sovereignty is . . . absolute and indivisible, inalienable and imprescriptible" (Jacques Maritain, 1969). And "Sovereignty means supreme authority; it stands to reason that no two or more entities. . . can be sovereign within the same time and space" (Hans Morgenthau, 1948).[3] Contemporary challenges to these older notions have become ubiquitous. Social theorist Jürgen Habermas, for instance, notes that "globally networked production relations" create imperatives that increasingly "call in question" the sovereignty of the nation-state.[4]

In Europe, in particular, the legal and political evolution of the European Economic Community (EEC) into the European Community (EC) and then European Union (EU) has problematized the concept of sovereignty. In 1992 Raymond Barre (at the time a member of the French Parliament and former prime minister defending before Parliament France's acceptance of the Maastricht Treaty, which was to transform the EC into the EU) argued that "the network of global forces subjects the exercise of formal national sovereignty to such constraints" that "real sovereignty" was no longer an available option. All that remained attainable, he argued, was regaining "a margin of maneuver and a possibility of influence," and for this would be required a multinational pooling of the functions that used to belong to kingly sovereigns, such as coining money, defense, and national security.[5]

Across the English Channel in the United Kingdom, Conservative leader Sir Edward Heath was proclaiming that "the traditional concept of national sovereignty is the doctrine of a period that has passed." And official publications of the Liberal Democratic Party announced in the same vein, "Increasingly, then, the concept of national sovereignty is outdated."[6]

To be sure, the contemporary willingness to abandon all-or-nothing conceptions of sovereignty remains contested. British analyst Noel Malcolm has objected, noting that such phrases as "pooled sovereignty" represent sloppy thinking and should be avoided: "A state either is sovereign, or it is not." But in the same essay he ends up implicitly acknowledging that the black-and-white distinction here proclaimed has already started to look quite a bit grayer in real-life politics. He defined sovereignty as a combination of (formal) legal authority and (in-practice-recognized) political authority over a defined territory and population, within a constitutional context of independence from other authorities. (Thus, for him, states within a federation like the United States are not sovereign, because they must answer to a higher authority). But he then acknowledged that the United Kingdom, by entering the EEC and agreeing to a decision process of non-unanimous voting and to a legal order that (under the *Costa v. ENEL* decision of 1964) permitted the European Court of Justice to rule unlawful any government's secession from the EEC, had already accepted the loss of the legal authority needed for its sovereignty. He concluded, "The next step would depend on [practical] political authority. If enough people do think . . . that the federal [EEC] authority is entitled to rule them . . . then of course it will be."[7]

Clearer thinking on the same subject has been provided by Murray Forsyth:

[In the European Community] a number of sovereign states . . . created a new sovereign body (in the special sense of a law making power) whose territorial sphere of authority overlaps but does not coincide with that of its constituent members. It is thus not a question of sovereignty being divided within one and the same political body politic, which is what the older theorists said was logically impossible, but rather of different but overlapping sovereign powers (the Union and member states) coexisting with one another [and each covering different "proper objects"]. . . . What [was] established was . . . a "nascent federal system."[8]

Even for European states that chose to remain outside of the EC during the late 1980s and early 1990s, economic pressures to avoid margin-alization moved countries such as Norway, Sweden, Switzerland, and Austria to adopt policies on their own that harmonized their laws, regulations, and currencies with those of the EC. Describing this process, Walter Mattli remarked, "Their national sovereignty remained intact *de jure,* but *de facto* it had lost much of its value."[9]

Meanwhile, independent governments to an increasing degree enmesh themselves in multilateral normative commitments, ranging from human rights declarations such as the European, or the American, Convention on Human Rights; to environmental accords; to free trade arrangements, such as the North American Free Trade Agreement (NAFTA) and the transformation of the General Agreement on Tariffs and Trade (GATT) to the World Trade Organization (WTO); to the 1991 Moscow Document of the Conference on Security and Cooperation in Europe (signatories of which included "virtually every European state, East and West" and which declared human treatment in each of the states a matter of "legitimate concern" in all the participating states.[10] These multilateral commitments are observably becoming more numerous at the turn of the millennium, although their rapid proliferation is not without critics.[11] Moreover, they are increasingly being enforced by "transnational" or "supranational" courts, whose rulings are obeyed, by and large, by supposedly sovereign entities.[12]

Thus, the world of the end of the twentieth century is one in which the classic accounts of state sovereignty as "absolute," "indivisible," and "inalienable," in the sixteenth-century terms of Jean Bodin, have given way to a new discourse.[13] One reads instead of "pooled sovereignty" in the European Union and of a "redistribution" of "portions of sovereignty" or of "shared sovereignty" between the territorial state and international bodies; or of "supranational regional regimes."[14] These late-twentieth-century developments pose a contrast to the friendly emendations of the classic theory concerning the now long-accepted notions that federal systems can divide sovereignty among central and subordinate units;[15] and that differing branches of government can share the sovereign law-making power with each other and with the constitution-making power—"the people."[16] These more recent developments are provoking the widespread recognition among political thinkers that a paradigm shift on the matter of sovereignty is currently under way.[17] One reads statements from political and legal philosophers to the effect that sovereignty needs "rethinking" or that the modern state has already evolved "beyond" it; that "an increasingly large number of commentators suggest the need to look outside existing theories of sovereignty"; or that it is "no longer obvious that the state system is the optimal way to organize political life . . . [and that] it is time to reflect on the nature of sovereignty, to make problematic . . . what has previously been taken as an analytic given."[18] Book titles of 1999 spoke openly of *A World without Sovereignty* and of *Questioning Sovereignty*.[19]

Granted, challenges to the concept of sovereignty are not entirely unprecedented; occasional political theorists in the past have pointed to problems with it. Years ago Hannah Arendt insisted that the "famous sovereignty of political bodies has always been an illusion"; Arnold Brecht asserted that people "cling to the magic" of believing that each sovereign state is free to regulate its own domestic affairs; and Harold Laski pointed out, "The orthodox theory of the state has proved largely without basis."[20] Nonetheless, the level of skepticism enveloping sovereignty at the end of the twentieth century is issuing from a much wider array of sources and seems dramatically more profound, in the sense that scholars and leaders of state now openly anticipate potential replacements of the sovereign state that prevailed for more or less three hundred years.

That new political developments produce new lines of thought about sovereignty is not surprising. Indeed, if there is any consensus that shows up in various histories of the notion of sovereignty, it is around the agreement that changes in political institutions accompany and are accompanied by changes in thinking about sovereignty.[21] (To attempt to unravel which precedes the other is to engage in the proverbial chicken-and-egg problem.)

Thus, previous moments—that is, fundamentally new phases, or stages—in sovereignty developments can be and have been identified. The age of the Greek polis was accompanied by Aristotle's analysis to the effect that political science is the architectonic science precisely because the polis (the political community organized in units of the size of one city with its surrounding countryside) shapes the way of life of the people as to matters of just and unjust, right and wrong.[22] Imperial Rome understood sovereignty by the maxim, "The will of the Prince has the force of law," since the people have transferred to him all their right and power.[23] The collapse of Rome gave way to the early Middle Ages, an era ruled essentially by relatively local warlords, who "sold protection and justice" and by relatively local Church bureaucrats who sold protection, justice, and salvation.[24] By the eleventh century, debates over sovereignty began to emerge from the conflict between Pope Gregory VII and the Holy Roman Emperor over who really stood at the peak of authority in Christendom. Since neither effectively ruled Christendom, these debates, which continued into the fifteenth century, had something of a mythical or legal-fiction quality, but they seem to have provided a terminology that shaped later European discourse.[25]

In the period 1550–1700 a decisively new moment in Western political history emerged.[26] On this newness political scholars agree, whether they attribute the rise of the modern state to any of a number of factors:

—changes in the technology of warfare combined with population shifts and concomitant economic changes, all of which strengthened the hand of kings vis-à-vis more localized authorities as sellers of protection and justice;[27]
—changes in people's understanding of, and related laws concerning, property;[28]
—Bodin's epoch-making insistence (in the wake of the Protestants' rejection of papal authority and Machiavelli's rejection of religious authority in general) that law proceeded not from God, nature, and immemorial custom—as in the medieval understanding—but from the will of a human political sovereign;[29]
—the epoch-making transformation of the world of diplomacy and of relations between religious and political authorities sealed by the 1648 Peace of Westphalia;[30]
—or even, most plausibly, to all of these.

The post-1700 modern "sovereign" state has been characterized essentially by the idea that it wields supreme authority, or a monopoly on the legitimate use of violence, over a particular territory. Although often called the *nation-state,* a more precise term for it would be the *territorial state.* The recent increase in intensity, however, of a variety of suprastate forces, and the rise to prominence of concomitant suprastate authorities, as described in the initial pages of this introduction, suggest that one should at least entertain the possibility that the modern world confronts the beginning of another such new moment in the reality of sovereignty.

This supposition that the twenty-first century is ushering in a fundamentally new phase in the sovereign state system has most recently been challenged by international relations theorist Stephen Krasner. In response to his own suggestion issued in 1988 that scholars "make problematic" the nature of sovereignty,[31] Krasner's latest book (1999) argues at length that the purported newness of deviations from the norms of sovereignty is much overstated. In this wide-ranging account Krasner demonstrates that the norms of sovereignty, which he refers to as a "bundle of attributes," have been violated from the beginning of modern sovereignty discourse and continue to be regularly violated.[32] There has never been a time when they were universally honored.

These attributes of sovereignty (per Krasner's analysis) have included (1) the holding of public authority within a territorial state that exercises effective control there; (2) the ability of the public authority to control transborder movements of goods, persons, and services; (3) mutual recognition within the international system of sovereign states as the sole entity authorized to act on behalf of the people within the territory of the state; and (4) the legitimate power to exclude external actors from interfering with domestic sovereign authority—that is, the ability to wield attribute number one as a monopoly. This latter attribute, the monopoly over legitimate authority within a given territory, Krasner called "Westphalian" sovereignty, and it is the primary focus of his book. Krasner effectively demonstrates that the idea that Westphalian sovereignty has universally characterized the state system since 1648 is a myth—one he terms (borrowing from Nils Brunsson) "organized hypocrisy" to convey the idea that it has involved a discourse, or an espousal of principles, that were systematically contradicted by actions (systematically, because the state system puts rulers in a position where they must please multiple, conflicting constituencies). The supposed autonomy of governmental authorities in "choos[ing] the institutions and policies they regard as optimal" was, Krasner documents, violated not only in the Peace of Westphalia itself, but also, repeatedly and in a myriad of ways, in the 350 years since. These have included voluntary treaties, forcible coercions of weaker states by stronger ones, dictation of policies for supposedly sovereign authorities as conditions of giving them economic assistance from foreign sources, and the wide array of colonial and quasi-colonial formations that have pervaded the world.[33]

Whether one prefers to think of the norms of sovereignty as incomplete scripts subject to improvisation when reasons of state so dictate, or as defeasible norms subject to violation when compelling reasons of state so dictate, or, per Krasner, as "organized hypocrisy," one should concede that numerous, open violations of these norms have transpired without having caused the perpetrators to be viewed as outlaw states. These violations of, or deviations from, the Westphalian sovereignty script are not something new under the sun.

However, the same cannot be said about the recent propensity of powerful states voluntarily to subject themselves to foreign, transstate powers with real and effective enforcement capacity, as has occurred both with

certain multilateral conventions and within the European Community/
Union. Regarding these, Krasner's effort to insist that the limitation on
sovereignty is not fundamentally new hits something like a brick wall. Regarding the European human rights regime, for instance, he acknowledged that "the existence of a transnational judicial body whose decisions
are directly applicable in more than twenty [sovereign] states cannot be
comprehended in terms of the Westphalian model." Moreover, he acknowledges that a formalized concern specifically with human rights, as
distinguished from minority rights, is distinctively a phenomenon of the
late twentieth century, as are the voluntary, multilateral conventions in
which powerful European rulers have, in effect, agreed to let outsiders
regulate their own exercise of power. What Krasner does not acknowledge is that his own fundamental organizing premise—his *grundnorm,* as
it were: "rulers want to stay in power"—simply cannot account for voluntary cessions of power from rulers of already strong states into the
hands of transstate authorities. Thus, Krasner also does not know what
to make of the European Community: "There is no commonly accepted
term for the European Union. Is it a state, a commonwealth, a dominion,
a confederation of states, a federation of states? Nevertheless, it exists."[34]

Rulers of states have in the past voluntarily limited their own power in
order to enter federated unions. One might perhaps stretch Krasner's
premise that "Rulers want to stay in power" to cover the case of federating unions of the past, as in the Dutch, American, and Swiss cases, to claim
that these involved relatively weak states whose cession of power to their
central union felt less like loss of power to a foreign "other" than conquest by a more alien power would have seemed. (This is essentially
William Riker's theory of why federations form.) However, Krasner's
premise simply cannot be stretched far enough to cover the late-twentieth-
century phenomenon wherein major powers like France, Germany, Italy,
and later the United Kingdom voluntarily ceded portions of their sovereignty to transstate or suprastate authorities. When rulers agree to suprastate federating formations, what Krasner says is primary—the rulers'
drive to retain their own power—becomes manifestly subordinate to
what Krasner says is secondary: "Being in power, they want to promote
the security, prosperity, and values of their constituents."[35]

If this self-subordination by major world powers into multilateral *enforceable* commitments continues, the world state system will be entering
a fundamentally new epoch. Since the modern territorial state does appear to be enmeshing itself in a variety of suprastate organizations, a close,

hard look at the processes by which formerly independent states voluntarily come to accept the authority of federal unions may prove enormously helpful for understanding current tendencies in the political world.[36] Such, in any case, is the aim of this book.

Federated unions of the past would seem to provide the closest parallel for understanding the patterns of these new formations. Thus, this book will provide an examination of member-state resistance patterns during the formative epoch—the initial several decades—of four federated unions, each in the modern Euro-American cultural tradition and each comprised of a voluntary union of independent states. These four unions include the contemporary European Union of 1958–99 and locate it within the comparative context of the American union of 1789–1859, the Dutch union of the seventeenth century, and the first half-century of the Swiss union that began in 1848.[37]

METHODOLOGICAL CONCERNS

These four unions were selected in accord with the following methodological concerns. The European Community (EC), which became the European Union (EU) after the Maastricht accords of 1993, is at the moment "the most advanced and even the only clear-cut example" of a supranational regional regime.[38] The fact that such suprastate regimes appear to be the wave of the future has, therefore, attracted enormous amounts of scholarly attention to the European Community.

Unfortunately, as Andrew Moravcsik's recent, extraordinarily thorough study of decision-making in the EC puts it, "The '$n = 1$' problem has traditionally burdened studies of European integration, which deals with the historical evolution of a single, exceptional institution."[39] He attempts to escape this problem by examining a multitude of decisions concerning the further tightening of the union, in effect addressing the following question: Why did the member states of the EC choose to pool their sovereignty (i.e., centralize their power at the suprastate level) to the degree that they have? Moravcsik does an impressive job of answering this question, but he does not escape the problem. He has told the story of why the EC centralized power, but has done nothing to demonstrate that the EC's story is generalizable to other suprastate formations.

I attempt to answer a different question. Once a multistate union has chosen to centralize authority (while retaining state-level authority as well) in a multistate, federated system, what forces will make state-level resistance to governance at the center more, rather than less, likely, and vice versa? Such a question can be answered only by comparing a plural set of multilevel governance systems.

Moravcsik's book eschews the comparative route (in contrast to this book) on the grounds that "comparisons between the EC and other regional integration schemes have proved an unwieldy tool to overcome underdetermination; so much varies across cases that the isolation of critical variables is difficult."[40] Indeed, he is correct as to the general comparative literature on federated governments. Some works in the comparative federalism genre like those of William Riker and Jonathan Lemco, in an effort to obtain a large *n* for social science purposes, lump together the study of ancient confederations of city-states, modern federations formed by voluntary aggregations of independent or quasi-independent states, modern federations formed by imperial or colonial conquest, and modern federations held together by military or party dictatorships.[41] As Moravcsik notes, it is highly improbable that generalizations formed from such unlike cases would prove useful for understanding particular federations.[42]

Even more limited federalism studies, which make it a point to eliminate dictatorships from the "federated" category, such as those of Wheare and Watts, have still included in their comparisons federations essentially formed by imperial or colonial conquest, where power was later devolved downward to the state or province level.[43] Again, such comparisons seem inapt if one's goal is to understand the level of cooperation that takes place among independent states that voluntarily join together in federated unions for certain purposes, while retaining governance authority for other purposes. This, by now, is the EC/EU situation and one that would seem to be best understood by comparison with like cases.

The Dutch, American, Swiss, and European unions represent four such voluntary unions in the modern world, not formed by imperial conquest nor by geographic lines imposed from a colonial power.

The Dutch union, which formed in the Union of Utrecht in 1579, united several provinces of the Netherlands that had revolted against the Spanish Hapsburg emperor during the 1560s. The union officially cast off King Philip of Spain in 1581.

The American union was formed by the Constitution of 1787 that was ratified by thirteen states in 1787–90. These thirteen British colonies began governing themselves independently with de facto committees even before the 1776 Declaration of Independence—according to Riker, as early as 1774.[44] The Declaration specifically described "these United

Colonies" as a plurality of states, indeed, "Free and Independent States." They fought the war for independence as thirteen militarily allied states, until the ratification of the Articles of Confederation in 1781. In principle, major Confederation decisions could be made by a vote of nine of the thirteen states, but the Confederation had no enforcement arm able to coerce a recalcitrant state. Thus, James Madison could assert as late as 1787 that the Articles were "nothing more than a treaty of amity . . . between so many independent and sovereign states."[45]

The Swiss union, like the American, evolved from an earlier confederation. The Swiss Confederation took a variety of forms over five centuries and by 1815 included the cantons that essentially make up modern Switzerland. These cantons were allied in a loose confederation between 1815 and 1847, rather similar to the American confederation of 1781–87. The Swiss union broke apart in a brief civil war in 1847 and then reunited under the Constitution of 1848, forming a federal union that has endured until the present.

These four voluntarily federated unions of the modern world are the subject of this book.

THE PROJECT: STATE RESISTANCE TO AUTHORITY IN FEDERAL UNIONS

This study begins with a puzzle. During the first four decades (1958–98) of the EC/EU, national member states accepted not only the interpretive authority of the European Court of Justice (ECJ) as the supreme arbiter of conflicts between member-state authority and central authority of the European Community, but also accepted the court's dictates that the treaties forming the community had constitutional status as supreme law in every member state and that European-level law had higher law status within every member-state, superseding any (even subsequent) national law to the contrary. Indeed, European member-state acceptance of this development advanced much more rapidly than state acceptance of the United States Supreme Court in that court's first several decades. Consider, for instance, the contrast described in the following illustrative quotes:

    1. "[The U.S. Supreme Court] has no appellate or other jurisdiction over this Court, and cannot, therefore, make a precedent for it" (Judge Benning, Georgia Supreme Court, 1854, *Padelford v. Savannah*).[46]

    2. "[The] assumption of jurisdiction by the Federal judiciary [to re-

view state actions for conformity to national law is] without authority and void. . . . [Only the several sovereign states have] the unquestionable right to judge of the extent of the powers delegated by the [national] Constitution" (Resolution of Wisconsin Legislature, March 19, 1859).[47]

3. "At present the constitutional character of the EC Treaties stands beyond doubt" (Koen Lenaerts, 1990).[48]

4. "All European judiciaries now accept European Court of Justice decisions governing conflicts between Community law and Member State law" (Henry G. Schermers, 1991).[49]

The pattern of respective acceptance of central federal authority described here runs counter to prevailing understandings of sovereignty. Most people consider the United States to have been a sovereign nation since 1787 and consider the states of the European Union to be sovereign nations today. Yet the detailed picture reveals a nominally sovereign but frequently state-defied U.S. government (1790–1860), and nominally sovereign European nation-states that are nonetheless regularly obeisant to the external, transnational authority of the European Union as set forth by the ECJ. This surprising picture suggests that "sovereignty" itself—at least by the beginning of the twenty-first century—is perhaps masking more than it reveals and might be well served by a dramatically new reconceptualization.

In order to advance toward such a reconceptualization, this study begins with a comparative analysis of the differing patterns of acceptance of federal authority between the early United States and the first four decades of the European Community. The goal of this analysis is to take a first step toward moving beyond the standard all-or-nothing conceptions of sovereignty in order to make better sense of this complex reality. Multiple, nonexclusive sovereignties have in fact been present in the West from the seventeenth century to the present; they did not disappear with the Middle Ages. Theorists beginning with Johannes Althusius in 1603, and extending through numerous American, French, Swiss, and German theorists of federalism in the eighteenth and nineteenth centuries, attempted to provide at least a juridical account of this reality.[50] They could not, however, have anticipated the complex arrangements of today, where, for example, purportedly sovereign Germany, itself a federal state, has willingly joined a larger "transnational" federation to which it has given some of its sovereignty.[51] Similarly, the Westphalian conception of the exclusiveness of governmental power over a given territory never operated to exclude such intermingled formations as colonies, protectorates, and commonwealths.[52] But again, colonial arrangements, whereby the strong formally ruled the weak, do not offer a real precedent for the EC/EU, wherein major world powers like France and Germany literally set up authorities outside their own borders, which they do not control, to exercise "supranational" authority over them on a wide array of issues.

Because federations and other forms of collective self-subordination by formerly wholly sovereign states appear to be increasingly likely in the world of the twenty-first century, the time appears ripe for amending current theory. The amendment offered in this book will not attempt to explicate with further precision the bounds and nature of legitimate authority within federal unions—that is, the goal is not to improve upon the juridical analysis of sovereignty in federations. Rather, the attempt is to analyze the phenomenology of the voluntary transition from sovereign, independent state to merely partially sovereign member of a federated union. What elements of the phenomenon render the transition smooth and nonconflictual? What elements make likely official and open resistance to the sovereignty transfer?

Chapter 1 describes the paradoxical pattern that emerges in a comparison of governmental assertions of sovereignty in the early United States and the early European Community, respectively. It then documents in more detail the respective histories of member-state resistance to federal authority in each of the unions. After this factual groundwork, Chapter 2 turns to potential explanations of this comparative paradox and the nature of this puzzling thing called sovereignty. The chapter extracts from the comparison of the American and European unions lessons about what causes states to act more rather than less sovereign within such unions; it both generates explanatory propositions and tests explanatory propositions already put forth by scholars who have looked at only the European side of the equation. At that point additional, voluntary federal unions that have formed in the modern Euro-American cultural context are brought into the analysis, to test and refine the propositions set forth. Chapter 3 examines the seventeenth-century Dutch union, and Chapter 4 the post-1848 Swiss union. Chapter 5 offers concluding reflections on what may be derived from this study for an enhanced understanding of the future world of suprastate commitments and suprastate constraints.

The Member-State Resistance Paradox: American Union (1790–1860) versus European Community (1958–1994)

THE PARADOX

An observer of the European Union familiar with the turbulent early history of the American union confronts a paradox. (Because much of that early American history has been neglected or forgotten, this paradox is not widely noted.)[1] In the United States, where the Constitution was ratified in 1788 and the government first took office in 1789, the Supreme Court—and to some degree the federal judiciary in general, as well as other federal authorities—was the target of an almost annual stream of open and official state resistance for seventy years. In stark contrast to the early federal history of the United States, the European Community, set up by the Treaty of Rome in 1957, with functioning institutions by 1958, experienced a much less rocky path to legal integration.

Originally and technically, there were three separate but overlapping European Communities, formed by three distinct treaties: the European Coal and Steel Treaty, which formed the European Coal and Steel Community in 1952; and two 1957 treaties, which set up organizations that began functioning in 1958: the Euratom Treaty of the European Atomic Energy Community, and the Treaty for the European Economic Community, or Common Market (the Treaty of Rome). By interpretive practice of the European Court of Justice, the three treaties and the three communities have been fused into one.[2] The resulting European Community took the title European Union at the end of 1993, as a result of the Treaty of Maastricht.

The Treaty of Rome is officially interpreted by one court, the European Court of Justice (ECJ), which was given a lower-level helper, the Court of First Instance, in the late 1980s. Occasions of defiance of the ECJ, in the sense of openly active resistance to or outright denial of the legitimacy of its authority, have been relatively rare. (Not that compliance with every mandate has been perfect, but noncompliance that results from inertia or passivity is not the focus here.)[3] While Europe has also seen instances of governmental resistance to the central community authority, the occasional outcropping of them (described below) does not approach the veritable parade of them experienced in antebellum America.

In short, the evident paradox is that the nominally sovereign government of the United States of America experienced several decades of overt and occasionally even violent official defiance of its authority by the member states of the American union, while the nominally sovereign member states of the European Union virtually from the start obeyed as a legitimate higher authority the dictates of the judiciary of their federal union. That which in ordinary understanding was less sovereign acted as more sovereign and vice versa.

Apart from its conflict with prevailing conceptions of sovereignty, the contrast between the frequency of overt and official state governmental defiance on the American side and the rarity and softness of tone of member-state resistance to the authority exercised by the EC, specifically by its Court of Justice, is puzzling for additional reasons. The contrast between the two unions becomes almost startling when one closely considers the relation between each federation's supreme court and their respective founding documents on each side of the Atlantic. Indeed, the differing member-state resistance patterns directly contradict what someone reading the two documents would plausibly expect. The federal Constitution ratified by the American states was tolerably explicit about where power would lie, whereas the wording of the Treaty of Rome (not to mention the probable expectations of its signers) turned out to be a far cry from what the ECJ managed to make it mean.

In the American example, there was the Supremacy Clause (Article 6, Clause 2), stating essentially that federal law, whether Constitution, statute, or treaty, was to be "the supreme law of the land; and judges in the several states shall be bound thereby, anything in the constitution or laws of any state to the contrary notwithstanding." Anticipation was surely that this clause would be among those upheld through the federal judiciary, whose power was described in Article 3 as "extending to all cases arising under" the national Constitution, national laws, or national treaties, as well as (inter alia) to all controversies "to which the United States shall be a party . . . ; between two or more states; between a state and citizens of another state; [and] between citizens of different states." Indeed, James Madison himself, who was later to change his mind for the notorious Virginia and Kentucky Resolutions,[4] publicly acknowledged before the Constitution was ratified that "in controversies relating to the boundary between [state and national] . . . jurisdictions, the tribunal which is ultimately to decide is to be established under the general [i.e., national] government." He added: "The decision is to be impartially made, according to the rules of the [national] Constitution. . . . Some such tribunal is clearly essential to prevent an appeal to the sword and a dissolution of the compact; and that it ought to be established under the general rather than the local governments, or, to speak more properly, that it ·could safely be established under the first alone, is a position not likely to be combatted."[5]

The first Congress in 1789, acting upon this widespread expectation, gave the Supreme Court jurisdiction to hear appeals from state courts of last resort when a state law had been upheld against a claim that it violated federal law. And, to most Americans at any given moment, the appropriateness of this jurisdiction was not controversial. Yet for seventy years—beginning with Georgia's steadfast refusal to carry out the first U.S. Supreme Court decision, *Chisholm v. Georgia* (1793), during the five years before it was overturned by constitutional amendment—particular states, on particularly intense issues, resisted this national authority. (State resistance or defiance, as the terms are used here, refers to actions by state governing authorities relying on their official capacities: formal public pronouncements by the governor, majority decisions of state appellate courts, or official legislative resolutions.)

By contrast, the European Community Treaties appear on the surface to be more or less run-of-the-mill multilateral treaties. The treaties contain nothing that looks like the American supremacy clause. They call for a Court of Justice to be appointed to apply the treaties, but this is not unprecedented for international treaties. What is unusual about the European Court of Justice is that, beginning in the early 1960s, its judges took a treaty and turned it, as well as any rules adopted under its authority, into judicially enforceable, higher law—law that takes precedence within each member state, even over subsequent national legislation or constitutional provisions to the contrary.[6] In effect, the ECJ transformed this international treaty into a higher-law constitution and thus transformed the

EC into a nascent federated polity. As a well-known ECJ scholar put it, writing in 1981,

> Proceeding from its fragile jurisdictional base, the Court has arrogated to itself the ultimate authority to draw the line between Community law and national law. Moreover, it has established and obtained acceptance of the broad principle of direct integration of Community law into the national legal orders of the member states and of the supremacy of Community law within its limited but expanding area of competence over any conflicting national law.[7]

Since Eric Stein wrote those words, the "areas of competence" of the then-Community, now-Union, have expanded even more substantially. They extend far beyond the technicalities of tariff adjustments to encompass, for instance, limitations on treaty-making powers of the member states;[8] authority to permit non-nationals to vote for European representatives and even for municipal officials in the country in which they reside (rather than in their country of citizenship);[9] and major aspects of environmental policy[10] and educational policy, including eligibility for non-nationals to compete for government-granted scholarships.[11] The EU now speaks for all the member states collectively in World Trade Organization (WTO) negotiations, and at meetings of the Organization for Security and Cooperation in Europe (OSCE).[12] A recent list of topics now covered by the EU Treaties and EU-level law included the following: "competition, intellectual and commercial property, public procurement, state aid, telecommunications, banking, financial services, company accounts and taxes, indirect taxation, technical rules and standards, consumer protection, health and safety, transport, environment, research and development, social welfare, education, and even political participation."[13]

Moreover, the Court of Justice announced that member-state judges have to make available the financial sanction of damages when their government fails to fulfill properly its obligations to private citizens under European Community directives.[14] In this way, the judicial branch of the EC gave itself a foothold, as it were, in the executive branch. Indeed, one dissident scholar characterizes the ECJ's jurisprudence as exhibiting "blatant disrespect for the unambiguous, state-sovereignty friendly language of several treaty provisions."[15] Another scholar characterizes the ECJ's foundational move, empowering private parties to participate directly "in the enforcement of the Treaty of Rome, a treaty of international law" simply as "without precedent."[16]

Far from resisting these judicially wrought changes, the member states have accepted and moved beyond them via the Single European Act of 1986–87, the Maastricht Treaty of 1992–93, and the Treaty of Amsterdam of 1997, tightening their union in a variety of ways. For instance, they have agreed to restrict their veto power on the main decision-making body of the EC, the Council of Ministers, and move to a less centrifugal, weighted majority voting system on an increasingly wide array of topics. (The veto system developed informally under pressure from France's Charles DeGaulle in the mid-1960s. It was officially restricted by the Single European Act, which specified that certain topics would be decided by a "weighted majority" voting system instead. The Maastricht Treaty then moved several more topics from the veto system to the weighted majority voting system, and the Amsterdam Treaty, which took effect in the spring of 1999, then moved an additional sixteen topics to that system.)[17] The Maastricht Treaty included a provision authorizing the ECJ to impose at the request of the Commission a fine on member states for failing to comply with a prior ECJ judgment regarding a violation of Community law. Moreover, the 1997 Treaty of Amsterdam added certain areas to ECJ jurisdiction that had been carefully excluded in Maastricht.[18] While there has been ample political controversy over these various tightening moves, including two negative national referenda, the basic constituting of the European Community as a legal entity, with the ECJ wielding supreme legal authority, succeeded with remarkable ease.

Thus, a comparison of the founding documents makes it appear that the American states should have known what they were getting into when they ratified the Constitution, whereas the first six EC states signed up for a much weaker union than the ECJ later imposed on them.[19] This fact is a second reason for finding the relative resistance pattern puzzling. (The six states that joined the EC in the 1970s and 1980s—the United Kingdom, Denmark, Ireland, Greece, Spain, and Portugal—are not the focus of this work; these countries entered the EC already cognizant and presumably accepting of this supranational legal system.)[20]

Third, the comparative level of member-state resistance within the two unions is paradoxical from the perspective of cultural, linguistic, and ethnic homogeneity versus heterogeneity; the EC/EU is far more heterogeneous on all these dimensions than the pre–Civil War American union. Moreover, the European states have far lengthier traditions of independence than the few years of independence of the American States during the Revolutionary War and the quasi-independence under the Articles of Confederation.[21] All these cultural elements, at a common-sense level at least, would seem to predict much more resistance to federal authority on the European side than the American.

Currently prevailing understandings of sovereignty, a comparative look at the founding documents of the two unions, and a consideration of cultural heterogeneity in the two unions—all three render this situation contrary to what one would expect. As thus laid out, the mystery that is the point of departure for this study has at least two dimensions: first, why were the American states so restive under central authority, and, second, why have the EC states been so relatively placid?[22]

One perhaps should hesitate even to begin an answer because the unions being compared vary so widely: not only in degree of internal heterogeneity but also across time and culture and across type of political institution (a federal nation-state versus a union of nation-states). Still, there is a core similarity that begs for analysis: both cases involve federal unions wherein a major ingredient of the cement of union has been a federalizing court. Both the U.S. Supreme Court and the ECJ are widely recognized by legal scholars as courts of extraordinary political power—arguably the two most politically influential courts the world has known. While conclusions concerning such complex, multifaceted situations must perforce be somewhat speculative, the daunting quality of the questions need not preclude a thoughtful discussion.

A quantitative overview of these contrasting pictures is presented in Tables 1 and 2. Six different kinds of defiance of the authority of the central government on the part of antebellum American states are listed in Table 1, with each followed by the number of incidents for that type that occurred between 1793 and 1859. In an American union that began as thirteen states and numbered thirty-three by 1860, a total of nineteen different states participated in these incidents, several of them as repeat players. While prior to 1860 most American states at any given moment did recognize the legitimacy of the U.S. Supreme Court's power to take appeals from state supreme courts on questions of federal law, individual state resistance to the federal judicial authority began immediately and continued until the Civil War (1861–65), which confirmed federal authority by force.

The story summarized numerically in Table 1 is essentially as follows: American states, intermittently but in a steady and not regionally concentrated stream, resisted federal authority when feelings in particular states on particular issues ran high. Indeed, that a particular state at one time explicitly endorsed federal judicial authority was no guarantee that some issue in the future would not arouse passions strong enough to evoke resistance by that same state to federal authority. The range of issues that provoked such resistance was wide and variegated. Tax laws, debtor laws, controversies over land ownership, embargo laws, laws concerning Native Americans, laws concerning the banking system, laws concerning judicial procedures, laws regulating speech and press, fugitive slave laws—all at one time or another provoked state denial of federal judicial authority.

By contrast, in Europe (as summarized in Table 2), only three member states out of the original six have formally expressed any defiance of community authority. Moreover, that resistance has not been expressed as outright disobedience, except in the case of France and two short periods involving the German Supreme Tax Court and Finance Ministry, respectively, both of which were quashed by higher authorities within Germany. Nor has the European brand of defiance approached the actual violence, threats of forceful resistance, or explicit threats of secession witnessed in antebellum America. It has tended to be more in the nature of either—in Italy and Germany—theoretical line-drawing (as in, "You have not gone too far yet, but if you cross certain lines there'll be trouble . . .") or else as unofficial evasion (the latter of which is outside the scope of this work).

A categorization of the European incidents of defiance is presented in Table 2 (the letters attached to each category match as closely as possible the equivalent categories in Table 1). Because the European Community (unlike the American) contained no cases of outright legislative rejections of the legitimacy of central union authority, Table 2 includes even leg-

Table 1. Incidents of State Governmental Defiance of Central Authority in the United States, 1790–1859

Type	Number
a. Defiance of specific federal court interpretation of law	32
b. Rejection of authority of federal courts to interpret law	22
c. Defiance of the evident meaning of federal law	32
d. Formal acts of nullification of federal law	21
e. Defiance of a federal court order	20
f. Authorization of forceful resistance to federal enforcement	7
g. Openly permitting violent resistance to federal authority	2
h. Threats to secede from the union	2

Table 2. Incidents of Member-State Defiance of European Community
Authority, 1958–1994

Type	Number
a. Defiance of ECJ interpretation of EC law	9
b. Rejection of ECJ doctrine that EC law is supreme over national law	
Halfway measures	2
Formal rejections	1
c. Defiance of evident meaning of Treaty of Rome	3
e. Government refusal to comply with ECJ decision	5
j. Announcement that in theory national sovereignty sets limits to European	
law and claiming power to draw the line	5

islative gestures toward such rejection: in both France and Belgium one house of the legislature voted (once) to enact such legislation. These are given the value of one-half in Table 2, but no such examples are included in Table 1, because the United States presented many full-blown rejections of central authority.

Table 2 does not include what I consider to be merely instances of imperfect compliance.[23] While compliance with European Community–level law has not been perfect, there has been little blatant, explicit defiance of the American sort. In the United States, for instance, the Supreme Court declared, in *McCulloch v. Maryland* (1819), that no state could impose a tax that targeted just the national bank. Immediately thereafter, Ohio's state auditor, backed by the governor, insisted on enforcing precisely such a tax, in the face of a federal court injunction forbidding his action as unconstitutional (category *e,* Table 1). Moreover, he authorized his assistant to enter the national bank "by force if necessary" and withdraw all its assets (category *f,* Table 1). This defiance of the federal court order by the state executive branch in turn stimulated the Ohio legislature in 1820 to pass resolutions declaring its refusal to be bound by *McCulloch v. Maryland* (category *a,* Table 1) and rejecting as invalid the rule (formalized in section 25 of the Judiciary Act of 1789) that federal courts may determine how the federal constitution applies to state powers (category *b,* Table 1). In support of this rejection, the Ohio legislature reasserted the Kentucky nullification resolutions of 1798 and 1799 that insisted on the state's ultimate authority to decide the constitutionality of federal law (category *d,* Table 1).[24] It is these types of explicit and defiant rejection of federal authority that are included in Tables 1 and 2, rather than incomplete or less than prompt compliance, both of which are probably endemic in large and complex societies as well as difficult to quantify.

In a similar vein, certain scholars would find more incidents of category *j* in Table 2; they draw somewhat speculative inferences from the fact that Belgium's Cour d'Arbitrage has asserted, as a general matter, that there are fundamental member-state constitutional rights that limit the rules of international law within Belgium.[25] However, in issuing this statement the Belgian court spoke in general terms of international law as such (in contrast to the constitutional courts of Italy and Germany, whose rulings ascribed to category *j* in Table 2, focused specifically on the law of the EC); there is nothing to prevent the Belgian court from ruling, at some future date when the issue is directly posed, that EC/EU law is *sui generis* and therefore not subject to these limits that apply in general to international law.

Even if one allows for differing totals that result from differences of analytic approach, however, there does appear to be consensus among legal scholars attentive to the ECJ that this court has been remarkably successful in vastly expanding central authority in the EC/EU and in attaining legitimacy for that authority. As such, the European picture stands in stark contrast to the American, and the difference fairly cries out for explanation. Before that explanation is attempted, however, a more detailed account of member-state resistance to federal authority in each union will be provided, specifying in more concrete terms the basic picture so far delineated.

State Resistance to Federal Authority in the United States

In order to document these claims about state behavior in the early American union, this section will provide a more detailed chronology of state resistance to federal authority in the first seven decades of U.S. history. As Table 3 makes evident, this resistance focused with particular vehemence on the Supreme Court's authority to oversee state courts' interpretations of federal law in cases alleging a clash between state and federal law.

The closest European parallels to these repeated American state rejections of Supreme Court authority were the two outright refusals by the French Conseil d'État to obey the Article 177 mandate to refer cases to the ECJ in 1968 (*Semoules*) and in 1978 (*Cohn-Bendit*). After 1978, a mere two decades into the European Community, such outright refusals ceased.

This U.S. Supreme Court authority, as noted, had been reinforced by legislation from the First Congress setting up the federal judiciary and was clearly indicated in the constitutional text by the combination of Article 3's grant of appellate jurisdiction to the Supreme Court for all cases "arising under" federal law and the Supremacy Clause's mandate that "judges in every state" be bound by federal law against contrary state law. Despite the clear constitutional and statutory mandate, Supreme Court authority to declare state law void was repeatedly denied and flouted by state governments until the Civil War.

Table 3 reveals not only the frequency of American state rejections of federal authority but also the regional diversity and the issue diversity that characterized these conflicts of authority. The table does not show a single regional split over one issue, such as slavery; instead, the pattern over seventy years is one of a wide variety of issue stimuli with the long-term constant of a scattered but nationwide contest over the locus of sovereignty.

As detailed in Table 3, denials of the legitimacy of federal authority occurred almost annually, except for the years 1841–49 (during which only one instance of state resistance took place, in Massachusetts, in 1846). This apparently dormant period of state resistance to federal authority resulted from the domination of the Supreme Court by pro–states rights justices. That the Court was less friendly to central power than its predecessor naturally made it much less likely, in general, to offer occasions for state resistance.

But this dynamic broke down to the extent that the controversy over slavery became a national issue. Slaves ran to northern states for freedom; southern masters wanted them recaptured; Congress in 1793 (acting on the authority of Article 4, Section 2, Clause 3 of the Constitution) enacted a Fugitive Slave Act that made recapture relatively easy. Federal, state, or local judges or magistrates, upon testimony from the person claiming ownership, could issue a writ certifying a given black person as a fugitive from servitude, which writ would then authorize taking him or her South, by force if necessary. As antislavery feeling in the North heated up, some states passed laws to provide procedural protections, such as trial by jury, so that free blacks would not be kidnapped with the use of this federal law. Some of the laws also forbade state officials to aid in the capture of persons accused of being fugitive slaves.[26]

In *Prigg v. Pennsylvania* (1842), the U.S. Supreme Court ruled that the

Table 3. Chronology of State Resistance to Federal Authority in the United States, 1790–1872

KEY

a = defiance of specific federal court interpretation of law
b = rejection of authority of federal courts to interpret law
c = defiance of the evident meaning of federal law
d = formal acts of nullification of federal law

e = defiance of a federal court order
f = authorization of forceful resistance to federal enforcement
g = openly permitting violent resistance to federal authority
h = threats to secede from union

Year	State	Type of Resistance by State Government	Subject Matter of Dispute	Defiant Branch of State Government
1790	N.C.	c	Legislators' oath to obey U.S. Constitution	Legislature
1790[1]	N.C.	a, b, e	Land title dispute with British subjects	State supreme court, legislature
1793–98[2]	Ga.	a, b, e	Right of creditors to sue states	Executive, legislature, courts
1794[3]	Pa.	g	Federal tax on whiskey	Executive
1798[4]	Pa.	b, c	Libel charge against British subject	State supreme court
1798	Va.	c, d	Alien and Sedition Acts	Legislature
1798	Ky.	c, d	Alien and Sedition Acts	Legislature
1799[5]	Ky.	c, d	Alien and Sedition Acts	Legislature
1803–9[6]	Pa.	a, b, d, e, f	Property dispute, federal judicial authority over states	Legislature, governor, courts
1808[7]	Mass.; Conn.	d; d	Embargo Act of 1807	Legislature; legislature
1812–13[8]	Mass.;	c;	Federal use of state militias in War of 1812	Supreme court, legislature, governor;

Year	State		Issue	Branch(es) of government
1814[9]	Conn.; R.I.; Vt.	c; c; c	Federal use of state militias in War of 1812	Legislature, governor; Legislature, governor; Legislature, governor
	R.I.; N.H.; Vt.; Mass.; Conn.	d; d; d; d, e; d, e		R.I., N.H., and Vt.: delegates at Hartford Convention; Mass. and Conn. legislatures
1815[10]	Conn.	c; e	Enlistment of Minors Act of 1814 (War of 1812)	Legislature, courts
1815[11]	Va.	c	Federal statute allowing financial penalties via state courts	Appellate court
1815[12]	Va.	a, b, e	Land title dispute, federal judicial authority over state courts	State supreme court
1817[13]	Mass.	a, b, e	Customs law, federal judicial authority over state courts	State supreme court
1819–20[14]	Ohio	a, b, d, e, f	Tax on national bank, federal judicial authority over state courts	Governor, legislature
1821[15]	Va.	a, b	Anti-lottery law, federal judicial authority over state courts	Legislature
1821, 1822, 1823	Ky.	a, b, d; a, b, d; a, b, d	Land titles, federal judicial authority over state laws	Legislature, executive, and courts (legislative defiance in each year listed)

(continued)

Table 3. (*continued*)

Year	State	Type of Resistance by State Government	Subject Matter of Dispute	Defiant Branch of State Government
1824, 1825[16]		a, b, d a, b, d		
1823[17]	Ga.	a, b	Federal judicial authority over state courts	Legislature
1824[18]	S.C.	a, b, e	Regulation of free blacks, federal judicial authority over state laws	Legislature, executive
1824[19]	Ind.	c	Fugitive Slave Act of 1793	Legislature
1825[20]	Ky.	a	Timely execution of debts	Popular convention
1826[21]	Pa.	c	Fugitive Slave Act of 1793	Legislature
1827[22]	Ga.	b	Federal judicial authority over state laws	Governor
1828[23]	Ky.	a	Land titles	Kentucky Court of Appeals
1829–30[24]	Ga.	c, d, e, f, g	Cherokee Indian property rights/ federal treaty	Legislature, governor, courts
1830[25]	S.C.	d, f	Federal tariff	Legislature
1830[26]	N.Y.	b, e, e	Interstate controversy	Executive
1831	Ga.	e, e; f	Cherokee Indians/federal treaty	Governor; legislature
1832[27]	Ga.	a, b, e, f	Cherokee Indians/federal treaty	Governor, legislature
1832	S.C.	c, d, f, h	Federal tariffs	Legislatively convened popular convention, legislature, governor

Year	State	Code	Issue	Branch
1833[28]	S.C.	d	Federal Force Act of 1833 (to enforce tariffs)	Legislature
1833[29]	Ala.	g	Creek Indian property/federal treaty	Executive
1834[30]	Ga.	e	Judicial authority over state (criminal) laws	Legislature, governor
1837[31]	Mass.	c	Fugitive Slave Act of 1793	Legislature
1838[32]	Conn.	c	Fugitive Slave Act of 1793	Legislature
1840[33]	Vt.	c	Fugitive Slave Act of 1793	Legislature
1840[34]	N.Y.	c	Fugitive Slave Act of 1793	Legislature
1846[35]	Mass.	c	Troop recruitment for Mexican War	Legislature
1850[36]	Ga.	h	Number of slave states	Legislature
1850[37]	Vt.	a, c	Fugitive Slave Act of 1850	Legislature
1853–56[38]	Ohio	a, b	Tax exemption to corporation; federal judicial authority over state courts	State constitutional amendment (to override U.S. Supreme Court); executive
1854	Conn.	a, c	Fugitive Slave Act of 1850	Legislature
1854[39]	R.I.	a, c	Fugitive Slave Act of 1850	Legislature
1854[40]	Ga.	b	State sales tax, federal judicial authority over state courts	Judge of state supreme court, dicta on own behalf
1854–59[41]	Wisc.	a, c, e; e	Fugitive Slave Act of 1850	State supreme court; executive branch

(continued)

Table 3. (*continued*)

Year	State	Type of Resistance by State Government	Subject Matter of Dispute	Defiant Branch of State Government
1855	Mass.	a, c	Fugitive Slave Act of 1850	Legislature
1855[42]	Mich.	a, c	Fugitive Slave Act of 1850	Legislature
1855[43]	Ohio	a, b	Tort law, federal judicial authority over state courts	State supreme court chief justice and state appellate court
1856[44]	Calif.	a, b, e	Alien rights, federal judicial authority over state courts	State supreme court
1857	Ohio	a, c	Fugitive Slave Act of 1850	Legislature
1857	Maine	a, c	Fugitive Slave Act of 1850	Legislature
1858	Vt.	a, c	Fugitive Slave Act of 1850	Legislature
1858	Mass.	a, c	Fugitive Slave Act of 1850	Legislature
1858	Wisc.	a, c	Fugitive Slave Act of 1850	Legislature
1858[45]	Kans.	a, c	Fugitive Slave Act of 1850	Legislature

Sources

[1]Warren, "Attacks," 4; Ashe, *History of North Carolina*, 122; Powell, *North Carolina through Four Centuries*, 228–31.

[2]McDonald, *Constitutional History*, 49–50; Kelly, Harbison, and Belz, *American Constitution*, 166–67.

112–14; Kelly et al., *American Constitution*, 254–57; Campbell, *Slave Catchers*, 10–11; *Prigg v. Pennsylvania*, 16 Peters 539, 550–55 (1842).

[22]Warren, "Attacks," 166–67.

[23]Ibid., 20–27.

[24]Ibid., 167–68; McDonald, *Constitutional History*, 103–5; Kelly et al.,

[3] McDonald, Constitutional History, 94–96.

[4] Powell, Languages of Power, 121–24; Warren, "Attacks," 4–5.

[5] Ibid., 17–18, 129–48.

[6] Kelley et al., American Constitution, 186; Powell, Languages of Power, 249–55; Tipton, Nullification, 39–41.

[7] McDonald, Constitutional History, 98–99; Kelley et al., American Constitution, 150–53; Powell, Languages of Power, 230, 239–48.

[8] McDonald, Constitutional History, 99; Powell, Languages of Power, 287; Kelly et al. American Constitution, 153.

[9] Tipton, Nullification, 25–27; Kelly et al., American Constitution, 150–53; McDonald, Constitutional History, 99–100; Powell, Languages of Power, 287–89.

[10] McDonald, Constitutional History, 99; Powell, Languages of Power, 287.

[11] Powell, Languages of Power, 295–96, 301–2.

[12] Warren, "Attacks," 6–12; McDonald, Constitutional History, 100–101; Powell, Languages of Power, 296–309.

[13] Warren, "Attacks," 12.

[14] Ibid. 15–16; McDonald, Constitutional History, 102–3.

[15] Warren, "Attacks," 16–19.

[16] Ibid. 20–27; McDonald, Constitutional History, 77.

[17] Warren, "Attacks," 20, 166.

[18] Ibid., 19–20; Kelly et al., American Constitution, 258.

[19] McDougall, Fugitive Slaves, 65–67; McDonald, Constitutional History, 112–14; Kelly et al., American Constitution, 254–57.

[20] Warren, "Attacks," 20–27.

[21] McDougall, Fugitive Slaves, 65–67; McDonald, Constitutional History,

American Constitution, 210–11; Bobbitt, Constitutional Fate, 109–14.

[25] Kelly et al., American Constitution, 214–16; Tipton, Nullification, 32–33.

[26] Friedman, "Countermajoritarian," 397 n. 257.

[27] Bobbitt, Constitutional Fate, 109–14; McDonald, Constitutional History, 105–6; Warren, "Attacks," 168–75; Kelly et al., American Constitution, 211–12.

[28] McDonald, Constitutional History, 106–9; Tipton, Nullification, 36–39; Warren "Attacks," 175.

[29] McDonald, Constitutional History, 108–9.

[30] Warren, "Attacks," 174.

[31] McDougall, Fugitive Slaves, 68.

[32] Ibid., 65–66.

[33] McDonald, Constitutional History, 112; McDougall, Fugitive Slaves, 65–67.

[34] McDougall, Fugitive Slaves, 65–67.

[35] McDonald, Constitutional History, 113.

[36] Campbell, Slave Catchers, 17.

[37] McDougall, Fugitive Slaves, 66–70; Campbell, Slave Catchers, 44–47.

[38] 3 Ohio St. 342; Warren, "Attacks," 179–82.

[39] McDougall, Fugitive Slaves, 66–70; Campbell, Slave Catchers, 44–47.

[40] Warren, "Attacks," 175; Padelford v. Savannah.

[41] Warren, "Attacks," 182–85; Ableman v. Booth.

[42] McDougall, Fugitive Slaves, 66–70; Campbell, Slave Catchers, 44–47.

[43] Warren, "Attacks," 178–82.

[44] Ibid., 176–77.

[45] McDougall, Fugitive Slaves, 66–70; Campbell, Slave Catchers, 44–47.

procedural protections were unconstitutional in that they interfered with the procedures mandated by Congress (which had to be supreme under Article 6, Clause 2), but that the refusal to let state officials help in the federal project was constitutional, as a sovereign prerogative of the states. Thus from 1842 to 1850 the northern states busied themselves with laws taking their officials and their jails out of the slave-catching business. Activity that would have been blatant defiance of the 1793 federal law had now been declared legal. Since federal judges were very sparsely distributed around the country, this now-lawful state activity succeeded in making slave capture both difficult and expensive, so northern state governments had little incentive to resist congressional authority in more legally questionable ways.

Southerners, because of their dilemma, eventually pushed through Congress the Fugitive Slave Act of 1850, which created a plethora of federal commissioners who would serve to certify accused blacks as fugitive slaves. Now that the federal government had put in place another efficient slave-catching mechanism, northern states again had incentive to resist federal authority by passing laws that gave procedural protections to the accused, and they proceeded to do so in substantial numbers after 1850.

Throughout this period from 1790 to 1860, acceptance by a given state of the legitimacy of federal authority on one occasion failed to serve as a guarantee of acceptance of federal authority on future, more controversial occasions. For instance, Virginia denounced Pennsylvania in 1809 for the latter's resistance (in all three branches of its government) to U.S. Supreme Court authority to serve as the "impartial tribunal . . . to determine disputes between the General and State governments," and then Virginia itself actively disputed that role for the Court in the years 1815 to 1822.[27]

An enhanced picture of these incidents of defiance can be provided with a close-up on another well-known episode that exhibits the kinds of concrete actions that fill the abstract categorizations of Table 3.[28] The Georgia legislature in 1829 passed laws nullifying—not on interpretive constitutional grounds, but as an act of purported sovereign power—the federal treaties with Cherokee Indian tribes (category *d*, Table 3). The state basically passed legislation allowing whites to use violence to seize Indian property. Then, asserting its own jurisdiction over Indians, Georgia proceeded to arrest, try, convict, and sentence to hang for murder an Indian, Corn (also known as George) Tassel. *Tassel v. Georgia* was appealed to federal court (on the grounds that under the treaties, Indian courts, not state courts, had jurisdiction over Tassel) and the U.S. Supreme

Court subpoenaed the governor of Georgia, George Gilmer. Governor Gilmer informed the legislature that he would resist with force any attempt to enforce the subpoena (categories *e* and *f*, Table 3). The legislature then ordered the governor and every official of the state to disregard any federal process served on them (category *e*, Table 3). Tassel was executed.[29]

The next year, Gilmer's successor, Governor Wilson Lumpkin, was served two federal writs from two different Cherokee Indian cases, *Cherokee Nation v. Georgia* (March 11, 1831) and *Worcester v. Georgia* (November 27, 1831). He ignored the first and announced of the second that he would "disregard all [such] unconstitutional requisitions" (category *e*, Table 3). The Georgia legislature declared that it would "resist and repel" any attempt by "outsiders" to interfere with the criminal processes of the state (category *f*, Table 3). In 1832 the Supreme Court decided *Worcester v. Georgia*, declaring the state law unconstitutional and ordering the release of prisoners being held under it. Governor Lumpkin called the decision "an attempt to prostrate the sovereignty of the State" (categorys *b*, Table 3) and pledged "determined resistance" to it (category *a*, Table 3). The Georgia legislature called for a national convention to reconsider the jurisdiction of the Supreme Court. In 1833, the governor pardoned the prisoners in exchange for their withdrawing their appeal from the Supreme Court.

As both this single narrative and the "subject matter" listing in Table 3 reveal, this seventy-year period of frequent and widespread (albeit intermittent) state defiance of federal authority across a wide range of issues focused particularly on federal authority as manifested in Supreme Court decisions voiding state laws or overruling state supreme courts; it also gave rise to a number of state-generated proposals to rein in Supreme Court power. These included proposed constitutional amendments to create an "impartial tribunal" to decide all state-federal conflicts, to give decision-making authority for such conflicts to the U.S. Senate where all states had equal influence, to render state supreme court decisions unreviewable by the federal courts, and/or to limit the terms of office of federal judges in order to render them more politically responsive (or, short of the latter, to render them removable from office at a request of both houses of Congress). Despite their frequency in the 1805–35 period, these proposals never won even the support of one house of Congress.[30]

On the other hand, state claims that various federal measures were illegitimate from time to time did bear fruit in the sense that the contested policy was sometimes reversed. The Alien and Sedition Acts, nullified in the Virginia and Kentucky Resolutions, were allowed to lapse by the Congress elected in 1800; the Embargo Act nullified by Massachusetts and Connecticut in 1808 was repealed by Congress in 1809; Congress voted down a bill in 1832 that would have stiffened sanctions for violations of Section 25 of the Judiciary Act of 1789 (giving Supreme Court jurisdiction over states); Congress altered the Tariff Law in 1833 in sympathetic response to South Carolina's nullification of the earlier version of it the year before; the federal army withdrew in the face of violent resistance by Alabamians armed to protect their own attacks on Indians in 1833; and the Wilmot Proviso, which had provoked a secession threat by Georgia in 1850, was voted down in the U.S. Senate.[31]

Despite this evidence of the fragility of federal sovereignty, support for its official legitimacy was also widespread and explicit. When Virginia and Kentucky issued the nullification resolutions of 1798–99, seven states issued condemnations of their actions. When Pennsylvania purported in the property dispute of 1803–09 to nullify federal court decrees, including that of the Supreme Court in *United States v. Peters,* ten states issued resolutions of disapproval. Nine states issued condemnations of the Hartford Convention's authorization of state interposition to block military recruitment for the War of 1812, authorization that had been endorsed by Massachusetts and Connecticut. Massachusetts, then, in response to actions by Ohio and Kentucky nullifying Section 25 of the Judiciary Act in 1819–22, specifically endorsed the legitimacy of this federal Supreme Court authority. South Carolina's ordinance purporting to nullify the federal tariff in 1830 provoked explicit condemnations not only from various northern states that benefited from the tariff, but also from North Carolina, Mississippi, and Alabama. And on two occasions, condemnations of state resistance to federal authority came from within the state itself: the South Carolina Supreme Court in 1834 ruled unconstitutional its own legislature's nullification of the 1832 federal tariff, and the California legislature (threatening impeachment of the judges) in 1855 ruled illegal its state's supreme court measure of the previous year that purported to nullify Section 25 of the Judiciary Act.[32]

Prior to the Civil War, in sum, federal authority, and specifically Supreme Court authority to declare void state law, was accepted as legitimate, in almost all the states, almost all the time, and on almost all issues. Nonetheless, this authority encountered a steady stream of intermittent but fierce resistance from states in all parts of the country on occasional issues, resistance so intense that federal authority in practice sometimes had to give way.

After the Civil War and one isolated incident in 1872,[33] the American states ceased official resistance to federal authority. The desegregation controversy of the 1950s and 1960s again produced some scattered official state resistance in the South, to the point that federal troops were deployed, but this waned quickly.

RESISTANCE BY EUROPEAN STATES TO EC AUTHORITY

As early as 1963 the ECJ declared that provisions of the Treaty of Rome have direct effect as immediately binding law within all member states and that such treaty provisions are laws that take precedence over member-state law to the contrary. In so declaring, the ECJ announced that member states had constrained their own sovereignty, "albeit within limited fields," when they signed the treaty.[34] This rule of Treaty of Rome supremacy was extended a year later to cover treaty supersession of national laws adopted subsequent (not merely prior) to the treaty;[35] and, in 1970, to cover even provisions in national constitutions. In the same 1970 case the ECJ gave precedence to all law adopted under proper treaty authority by European Community bodies over any member-state law or national constitutional provision to the contrary.[36]

The response to this massive alteration of the national legal order within the EC presents a number of contrasts to the pattern of American state defiance of federal authority. Defiance in Europe was not only more limited but also much more localized. Of the original EC member states, resistance has occurred not at all in Belgium, the Netherlands, and Luxembourg, and only in a narrowly limited way in Italy and Germany.

In the earliest years of the EC, the German Finance Ministry attempted to follow Germany's own courts' logic in preference to new doctrine from the ECJ that had been announced in *Lutticke v. Hauptzollamt Saarlois* (1966), but it was quickly brought into line by a scolding from the Bundestag (legislature). Then in one of the German high courts, the Supreme Tax Court, a couple of instances of overt defiance did occur, but the more direct of these was immediately overruled by the German Constitutional Court.

National Constitutional Courts both in Germany and in Italy have issued abstract judicial pronouncements reserving authority in principle for the judges on the national constitutional court to decide whether a European authority has attempted to exercise power in a way that transgresses the "fundamental rights" of their nationals. Still, it is not entirely clear that these should be viewed as resistance, since the ECJ claims that it upholds the "fundamental rights" of the traditions of the member states.

Only France has repeatedly, and over a period of considerable duration, defied the authority of the European Community, and particularly of its Court of Justice. Indeed, the more recent members of the EC/EU have also refrained from official overt rejection of ECJ authority.[37] The details of the limited instances of overt defiance that did occur within the original member states are as follows.

Both the German and Italian Constitutional Courts do acquiesce in the ECJ doctrine that EC law supersedes their own constitution. They nonetheless have insisted that certain fundamental rights are even more authoritative than the constitution per se, and they claim the authority to protect these rights. The difference between this situation and that of Virginia and Kentucky Resolutions in the American situation is that these American states claimed the highest authority to interpret the federal charter, whereas Italy and Germany seem to claim that, at least in principle, their own people's fundamental rights supersede the law of the federal union. Or, alternatively, their logic may amount to a claim that their own people's fundamental rights prevent its government from having validly signed a treaty that could abrogate these rights, and therefore neither the treaty nor any laws resulting from it may transgress these rights.

While these pronouncements have provoked some controversy, particularly since (after initial hesitation) the European Court judges have repeatedly acknowledged that they consider themselves bound to honor the fundamental rights that exist in the combined legal traditions of the member nations,[38] the practical import of the national pronouncements is more aptly characterized as warning than as defiance. They carry something of the tone of the Virginia and Kentucky Resolutions in that they announce a right to interpose state authority between the citizen and wrongful federal action, but they differ in not voiding any law. Contrary to the situation in the early United States, neither the Italian nor the German Constitutional Court has ever directly contravened an ECJ decision or declared void any European law. Indeed, the ECJ's pronouncements that it honors the shared fundamental rights traditions of the members have now been given official treaty sanction in the new Articles 6(2) and 46(1)(d) of the Treaty of the European Union, the Treaty of Amsterdam, signed in 1997 and put into effect in the spring of 1999.[39]

German officialdom produced two brief flare-ups of outright defiance of ECJ doctrine, both of which were quelled by higher government authority within a short time. In 1966, the Ministry of Finance publicly announced that it would defy a ruling of the ECJ (*Lutticke v. Hauptzollamt Saarlois*) that it regarded as erroneous, in contrast to the earlier German judicial doctrine. The ministry thus ordered customs officials to reject any claims brought under the ECJ *Lutticke* doctrine. Shortly thereafter, the finance minister was hauled before the Bundestag (one of the two legislative chambers), and scolded for undermining the rule of law. The finance minister then reversed himself and accepted the ECJ policy.[40]

In the 1980s, in two instances involving the European Value Added Tax Directive, the German Supreme Tax Court issued pronouncements that were at variance with the official doctrine of the ECJ. The disagreement rested on the nature of a directive, one of two kinds of legislation that could be adopted by the EC's Council of Ministers.[41] In contrast to a regulation, which sets forth a rule of behavior, as statutes do, a directive establishes instead a result to be achieved (sooner or later) by methods of the member states' choice. To the surprise of many observers, the ECJ ruled in 1970 that directives also may (depending on their contents) take "direct effect" in member states, creating legal rights on which individuals may rely in courts.[42] At the time of the first of these German tax cases (in 1981), the ECJ had not yet ruled whether the specific directive at issue in the case did or did not have direct effect. Thus, the disagreement between the two courts was theoretical rather than practical; the German Court engaged in doctrinal dispute (claiming directives in general did not have direct legal effect) as distinguished from actual refusal to carry out specific law.[43] Four years later, however, after the ECJ had applied the disputed doctrine (direct legal effect) to the European directive in question, the German Supreme Tax Court persisted (in *VAT II*) in its defiant course, refusing to give direct effect in Germany to the European VAT directive. This time the German Constitutional Court stepped in and overruled the Supreme Tax Court. Thus, while this can be viewed as an important instance of defiance by one of Germany's prominent courts, the incident as a whole, nonetheless, shows the German judiciary formally accepting the authority of European law in general and of the ECJ in particular, just as the 1966 case shows the legislative authority reining in ministers who attempted to defy European authority.

The massive exception to this overall picture of European acceptance of federal judicial authority is France. In France both the Conseil d'État (Council of State, the Supreme Administrative Court) and the French government as a whole have openly defied European judicial authority.[44] Although Article 177 of the Treaty of Rome requires that any member-state court of last resort refer to the ECJ any questions of European law that have been raised, in 1968 the Conseil d'État openly rejected this rule in the *Semoules* case, which dealt with grain imports from Algeria.[45] It did so guided by the advice of the Commissaire du Gouvernement (similar to the U.S. Solicitor General) that any such referral would conflict with the French institutions of government. (In what was probably a related political maneuver, that same year President DeGaulle attempted unsuccessfully to persuade the other EC members to adopt rules scaling back the ECJ's jurisdiction.)[46] The Conseil d'État toned down the flagrance of its defiance in 1978. Instead of rejecting all authority of the ECJ to establish rules that govern French courts, it retreated to its *"acte clair"* doctrine, which essentially stated that it would submit European law questions to the ECJ, as commanded by Article 177, but only when in its own judgment a genuine rather than frivolous question of legal interpretation was presented.

Karen Alter has argued (following Gerhard Bebr) that while the *"acte clair"* doctrine itself did not so much amount to resistance to the ECJ, still, particular courts, specifically courts of last resort who resented a loss of their power to the ECJ, abused the doctrine. She claims that these resistant courts in fact referred the obvious, easy technical decisions to the ECJ, reserving the important, controversial decisions to themselves.[47] One can note that since lower courts were still free, at their option, to refer the difficult cases to the ECJ, this passive resistance (if resistance it was) would have accomplished little.

Nonetheless, despite the less confrontational approach of the *"acte clair"* doctrine, the Conseil d'État did again directly defy treaty rules in the 1978 case, *Minister of the Interior v. Cohn-Bendit,* which dealt with a deportation order on a German citizen who was a former political agitator, Daniel ("Danny the Red") Cohn-Bendit. The Conseil d'État blocked a request from a lower French administrative court for an ECJ preliminary ruling, in direct defiance of the command in Article 177 of the Treaty of Rome that any lower court may at its discretion request from the ECJ an interpretation of European law needed for a pending case.

Meanwhile, in five cases between 1978 and 1985, the Conseil d'État insisted on specific interpretations of European directives, regulations, or treaty law, at odds with those given by the ECJ.[48] During the same period of time, the French legislature in 1980 enacted at least one law (concerning nuclear energy) that French legal scholar Buffet-Tchakaloff has depicted as directly contrary to the reigning ECJ interpretation of one of the three treaties forming the EC (the Euratom Treaty).[49] The Assemblée Nationale (one of the two legislative houses) showed itself willing to be even more directly confrontational—for example, by forbidding all French judges to follow ECJ doctrine—but cooler heads prevailed in the Senate. The French government as a whole was condemned by the ECJ on five occasions as a result of charges brought by the European Commission for failure to carry out its obligations under European law (three times in the Anglo-French conflict over mutton policy in 1978–80, twice in the controversy over tobacco prices in 1982–92).[50] However, by 1989 the Conseil d'État finally accepted (in the *Nicolo* case) the principle that the Community Treaties are supreme over French statutes, and in 1990 (in the *Boisdet* case) it extended this supremacy to EC regulations and in 1992 to EC directives.[51]

Table 4 presents a detailed chronology of instances of resistance by member states to the federal authority of the European Community and of later official abjurations of such resistance. The table includes even a legislative measure that garnered serious momentum but ended up tabled. Because it was tabled it was not get tallied in Table 2, but it is described here for purposes of drawing attention even to unsuccessful efforts at resistance to EC authority. In sum, the European member states, with the exception of France, have rather docilely accepted EC authority as espoused by the ECJ.[52] Germany's Supreme Tax Court and Finance Ministry produced relatively brief periods of defiant policy, but these deviant courses were corrected by the German Constitutional Court and by the Bundestag. Constitutional Courts in Germany and Italy have warned the ECJ that it must respect the fundamental rights of their citizenry. But France, and only France, directly defied European authority repeatedly: the French government provoked five different condemnations on charges by the European Commission, and the French Conseil d'État twice openly denied that it would honor its treaty obligation to refer cases to the ECJ, rejecting the legitimacy of such an obligation. The Conseil d'État, with the support of the French government, turned its back on this defiant course in 1989–92. In short, defiance of the central federal authority of the European Union has been much more geographically localized and far less frequent than in the early decades of the American union.[53] And it ended much sooner.

A second important contrast with the American pattern is that so far, at least, the European states have exhibited a steadiness in their approach to European authority that was lacking in the early American states. In Europe one does not see the issue-stimulated flip-flops in acceptance of federal authority that characterized the early American states. Once a European nation-state judiciary announced that it accepted the European

Table 4. Chronology of Member-State Resistance to European Community Authority, 1958–1994

KEY

a = action in defiance of ECJ interpretation of EC law

b = rejection of ECJ doctrine that EC law is supreme over national law

c = defiance of evident meaning of Treaty of Rome

e = governmental (legislative/executive) refusal to comply with ECJ decision

j = announcement that in theory national sovereignty sets limits to European law and claiming power to draw the line

*anti-[letter] = abjuration by member state government of that type of resistance

Year	Member State	Type of Resistance by Member State	Subject of Dispute/Case	Defiance Branch of Government
1966[1]	Germany	a	Taxes/Lütticke I[2]	Finance Ministry (countered by legislature)
1968[3]	France	c; b, c	Grain imports from Algeria, Article 177 obligation to refer to ECJ/Semoules	Conseil d'État; Commissaire du Gouvernement
1970[4]	France	*anti-b	Supremacy of EC regulations over French law/Ramel[5]	Cour de Cassation
1973[6]	Italy	*anti-b; j	Direct effect of EC regulations; dicta/Frontini[7]	Constitutional Court
1974[8]	Germany	j	Dicta on fundamental rights/"Solange I"[9]	Constitutional Court
1975[10]	France	*anti-b	Supremacy of ECJ doctrine over French law/Jacques Vabré[11]	Cour de Cassation
1975[12]	Belgium	½ b	Judicial power to void national laws that conflict with Eurolaw	Senate (failed in House of Representatives)
1978[13]	France	a[14]	ECJ interpretation of Euratom Treaty	Proposed but tabled in Assemblée Nationale
1978[15]	France	a; c	Lifting of deportation order of	Conseil d'État

(continued)

Year	Country		Ruling/issue and case	Institution
1979–80[18]	France	e, e, e	(German) former political agitator; ECJ rule that directives can have direct effect;[16] Art. 177 obligation to refer ro ECJ/Cohn-Bendit[17]	Legislative-executive
1980[20]	France	a	"Mutton War" with U.K.; 3 charges of noncompliance by European Commission/Mutton War cases[19]	Conseil d'État
1980[22]	France	½ b	ECJ interpretation of EC regulation/ONIC[21]	Assemblée Nationale but failed in Senate
1980[23]	France	a	Judicial power to void national laws that conflict with Eurolaws	Legislature
1980	France	a	ECJ interpretation of Euratom Treaty	Conseil d'État
1980	France	a	ECJ rule that EC directives can have direct effect/Société Sovincast	Conseil d'État
1981[24]	France	a	ECJ rule that EC directives can have direct effect/Dentaire	Conseil d'État
1981[25]	Germany	a	ECJ rule that EC directives can have direct legal effect/Value-Added Tax Directive (VAT I)	Supreme Tax Court
1983–88[26]	France	e, a, e	ECJ ruling that the tobacco pricing directive does have direct effect	Legislature/Executive and Conseil d'État
1984[27]	Italy	j	Dicta on fundamental rights/Granital	Constitutional Court

Table 4. (*continued*)

Year	Member State	Type of Resistance by Member State	Subject of Dispute/Case	Defiance Branch of Government
1985	Germany	a	ECJ ruling that the VAT directive does have direct effect/*VAT II*	Supreme Tax Court
1986[28]	Germany	*anti-j	fundamental rights limit on ECJ/*Solange II*	Constitutional Court
1986–87[29]	Germany	*anti-a	ECJ rules on the direct effect of directives/*VAT II*	Constitutional Court
1988[30]	Italy	j	dicta on fundamental rights/*Fragd*	Constitutional Court
1989	France	*anti-a *anti-b	Treaty of Rome supremacy over French law/*Nicolo*	Conseil d'État
1990	France	*anti-a *anti-b	EC Regulations' supremacy over French law/*Boisdet*	Conseil d'État
1992[31]	France	*anti-a *anti-b	EC Directives' supremacy over French law/tobacco pricing cases[32]	Conseil d'État
1993[33]	Germany	j	Sovereignty and fundamental rights restraint on ECJ/*Maastricht II*	Constitutional Court

Sources

1 Alter, "Court's Political Power," 475.

2 Lutticke v. Hauptzollamt Saarlois (1966).

3 Volcansek, *Judicial Politics*, 51–52; Plötner, "Report on France," 6.

4 Van Empel, Schermers et al., *Leading Cases*, 206–8.

5 *Administration des Contributions indirectes et Comité Interprofessionel des vins doux naturels v. P. Ramel* (1971) ("Ramel case").

6 Bibas, "Fundamental Rights," 263–64; Gaja, "Annotation," 764–72; Cartabia, "Italian Constitutional Court," 11–15.

7 *Frontini v. Ministero delle Finanze* [1974] (hereafter *Frontini*).

8 Bibas, 264–65; Frowein, "Solange," 201–6; Kokott, "Report on Germany," 10–20, 51–56; Rasmussen, *On Law*, 397–400, n. 54; 423; Volcansek, *Judicial Politics*, 107–9.

9 *Internationale Handelsgesellschaft v. Einfuhr-und Vorratsstelle* (1974); case is known as "Solange I."

10 Volcansek, *Judicial Politics*, 68–69.

11 *Administration des Douanes v. Société Café Jacques Vabré* (1975).

12 Bribosia, "Report on Belgium," 35.

13 Rasmussen, *On Law*, 347–55.

14 Because this bill was merely tabled, it is not counted as an act of governmental defiance in Table 2. However, its equivalent, which was enacted in 1980, was counted for Table 2.

15 Volcansek, *Judicial Politics*, 56–59; Rasmussen, *On Law*, 311–12; Plötner, "Report on France," 9–10; Bebr, "Rambling Ghost," 442–45.

16 The ECJ in *Van Duyn v. Home Office* (1974) (hereafter *Van Duyn*) had given direct effect to a particular directive, and the *Cohn-Bendit* court refused to honor that ECJ ruling.

17 *Minister of the Interior v. Cohn-Bendit* (1980).

18 Rasmussen, *On Law*, 338–46, 452–54.

19 *Commission v. France*, ECJ Case 239/78 [1979] European Court Reports 2729. Also, Cases 24/80 and 97/80 in 1980.

20 Rasmussen, *On Law*, 312–14, nn. at 367; Audeod, "Community Law in France," 300–301.

21 The decision in ONIC was contrary to the ECJ interpretation rendered in D.G.V. (Oct. 4, 1979).

22 Volcansek, *Judicial Politics*, 70; Plötner, "Report on France," 25.

23 Buffet-Tchakaloff, *France devant la Cour*, 366.

24 Bebr, "Rambling Ghost," 445; Audeod, "Community Law in France," 292.

25 Frowein, "Solange"; Volcansek, *Judicial Politics*, 116; Rasmussen, *On Law*, 319–21; Stein, "Case VR 123/84," 727–36.

26 Dutheil de la Rochère, "Société"; Plötner, "Report on France," 26–28.

27 See sources in note 6 above.

28 See sources in note 8 above.

29 Frowein, "Solange"; Rasmussen, *On Law*, 321–22; Stein, "Case VR 123/84,"; Kokott, "Report on Germany," 49–50.

30 See sources in note 6 above.

31 Dutheil de la Rochère; Kent, *European Community Law*, 47–48; Plötner, "Report on France," 7–9, 29.

32 *Rothman's and Phillipp Morris*.

33 Herdegen, "Maastricht," 235–49; Kokott, "Report on Germany," 21–45, 57–61.

higher law doctrine of the ECJ, that doctrine remained accepted within that national jurisdiction. (There are two qualifications to this point. In France the national civil jurisdiction of the Cour de Cassation accepted European authority from the start, while the national administrative jurisdiction of the Conseil d'État resisted it until 1989. In Germany the Constitutional Court did waver on its doctrine that fundamental rights within German law constrain the EC/EU and that the Constitutional Court itself, not the ECJ, must have ultimate power to decide whether a conflict exists. The German Court announced this doctrine in *Solange I* (1974), wavered away from it in *Solange II* (1986)—appearing to say that the ECJ could henceforth be relied on to guard these rights—and then reasserted the doctrine in *Maastricht II* (1993).[54] Because of this general pattern of national steadiness, the account in Table 4 describes not only the occasions of overt resistance to European authority, as represented primarily by the ECJ, but also those moments when national authorities declared their abjuration of such resistance to European higher law.

A related contrast between the two unions is that such judicial resistance to federal authority as did take place in Europe appears to have been more genuinely motivated by concerns about loss of sovereignty than about specific case issues; by contrast, on the American side, while the defiant government would talk of sovereignty, the intensity of interest in particular issues at the time seems to have been more often the driving force. (American state courts would routinely accept and cooperate with federal authority for years and then on some particularly intense controversy would declaim a paraphrase of the following: "The authority of the federal courts to tell us when our law clashes with federal law has never been established and we reject such authority." The cycle might repeat more than once in a given American state.)

If all such abjurations of resistance were removed from the chart and if the abstract warnings against hypothetical future violations of fundamental rights were also removed, there would remain the years when outright defiance of EC law took place. Such defiance occurred in 1966, 1968, and annually from 1978–81 and 1983–88. Both the limited duration of official defiance and its narrow geographic spread (three branches of government in France and one ministry and an overruled court in Germany) pose a sharp contrast with the American picture documented in Table 3.

State Resistance in the United States and the European Community: Unraveling the Puzzle

Chapter 1 has documented a striking contrast: the American federation combined clear-cut legal supremacy of central federal authority with many decades of active resistance to this authority by individual state governments, whereas the Treaty of Rome initiated the European federal union without any clear acknowledgment that it would function any differently from ordinary multilateral treaties. Despite this inauspicious beginning, the European Court of Justice quickly transformed the treaty into a higher law constitution, and it has been successfully exercising power in the name of that constitution for more than thirty years. At this point, the questions posed in Chapter 1 can be addressed: first, why were the American states so restive under central authority, and, second, why have the EC states been so relatively placid?

AMERICAN INSTITUTIONAL CRITIQUE AND EUROPEAN REMEDIES

An intriguing piece of the explanatory picture comes to light by direct comparison of the American institutional arrangement with that of the EC. It turns out that virtually every institutional reform advocated by rebellious voices during those antebellum decades of state protest against U.S. Supreme Court authority was implemented in one or another version on the European side. The only exceptions to this were the suggestions for state powers to nullify federal law (a power claimed but not acted upon by the Constitutional Court in Italy and Germany, and not institutionalized in the EU) and state power to secede from the union.[1]

From the mid-1960s until the late 1980s, the member states of Europe each had a veto power on the European Community's basic decision-making authority, the Council of Ministers.[2] Surely if America had structured its federal system along the state–veto power lines long advocated by John C. Calhoun, there would have been fewer national laws passed (if any), and therefore less occasion for discontented states to rebel against them.[3]

A somewhat parallel veto power suggestion came forth in the United States in unsuccessful proposals for legislation (in the Senate in 1823 and in the House of Representatives in 1867) that would have required a unanimous Supreme Court vote in order to declare unconstitutional state or federal legislation.[4] While the ECJ does not officially require unanimous voting, its practice of issuing unsigned opinions with no dissents or concurrences certainly creates an appearance of such unanimity. And this appearance in turn surely must have had a positive impact on maintaining public esteem for the judicial decisions.

Although bills to require judicial unanimity in the United States garnered little support, a more modest reform in the same direction appeared to have more staying power: on several occasions bills were proposed in the House and Senate (both on the floor and in the Judiciary Committee) during the 1820s, to require a two-third's majority on the Supreme Court in order to overturn any state law.[5] While the parallel is not exact, this reform proposal does have a certain echo in the post-1987 system of weighted voting that has been adopted for the European Council of Ministers (the sole legislative body of the EC prior to 1994).[6] Both reforms (the actual one in Europe and the one proposed in the United States) implement supermajority requirements, presumably out of a concern that transstate policies reflect at least a broad consensus among members of the union.

It is no doubt true that the Council of Ministers' veto power (while it lasted) produced a notorious political "*lourdeur*" (sluggishness). This in turn (as is commonly remarked) made the EC safe for judicial attribution of power to EC law (since virtually none was being passed). But this common explanation of the European state acceptance of judicial policy-making by the ECJ can account for only part of the picture. For the ECJ did not accord power only to council-adopted regulations; it also took goal-pronouncing sections of the treaty itself and turned them into judicially constructed and judicially enforceable policy rules—rules which, again, "took precedence over" both legislation and constitutional provisions of the member states. For instance, without any implementing legislation by either the Council of Ministers or relevant national legislatures, the ECJ adopted its own rules for implementing the treaty's Article 119 mandate of equal pay for men and women in the 1971 *Defrenne I* case.[7] Even more controversially, the ECJ ruled that the treaty frees Irish women to travel out of Ireland to obtain abortions despite the ban on abortions in that country's constitution.[8] Member states accepted these and many similar moves,[9] in stark contrast to the early-nineteenth-century U.S. picture.

Incidentally, the pattern of an active centralizing judiciary in the EC during the initiating period, while the legislative authority was more or less quiescent, parallels the pattern in the antebellum United States.[10] According to legal theorist Hans Kelsen, this is the typical pattern in the early stages of evolution from pre-state communities into states—first an active judiciary, later an active legislative role.[11]

Another of the prominent reform suggestions from the American states that has echoes in the EC was to give authority for judging the line between state and federal power to a new institution that would have one representative from each state, or to give it to the federal Senate, which had two representatives from each state (the suggestions were in 1822 and 1867).[12] The ECJ does have one judge from each member state, and thus no state can legitimately claim that it lacks input into the decision-making process.[13] In addition to providing each state representation on the court, as Joseph Weiler points out, because the judges appointed to it all rank among the most prestigious jurists in their home country, this system assures a certain degree of prestige for the ECJ and for its jurisprudence in each member state.[14]

Another of the reform suggestions that emerged from state resistance in the United States (in the form of a constitutional amendment repeatedly proposed in the Senate—in 1808, 1831, and 1832), and which parallels arrangements in Europe, was to change the federal judges' term of office from life to a fixed number of years.[15] The Eurojudges serve fixed six-year terms that are renewable, so they are likely to reflect current "establishment" sentiment in their home countries. The role of fixed terms has had an additional important effect in fostering member-state acceptance of European jurisprudence. Both ECJ judges and advocates-general (somewhat similar to the American solicitor general, but more prominent and perhaps more influential in the decision-making process) return to their home countries when their terms end. There, newly socialized by service on the European court to be pro-Euro law, they serve as eminent jurists, serving on supreme courts, in important governmental posts, or teaching in prestigious law schools.[16]

Finally, the European judicial decision-making structure provides a number of face-saving procedures to the member-state judiciaries—procedures that were sought by some of the American states but without success. First, in principle the European Union leaves it to the nation-state judges to adjust their national legal orders to the European supreme law requirements. The official job of the ECJ ends with articulating the meaning of European law (whether of treaty, regulation, or directive). Technically speaking, it is left to the national judges to decide whether national law alleged to be in conflict with European law can be "reinterpreted" to fit the ECJ's ruling or must be declared void instead. Anne-Marie Burley and Walter Mattli, in attempting to account for the alacrity with which national courts accepted ECJ authority, have termed this arrangement an "all-important fiction."[17] It is fictional in the sense that member-state judges appear autonomous, whereas the level of specificity of the ECJ ruling may well, for practical purposes, dictate the state-level outcome.

This face-saving technicality parallels demands put forth by the Virginia Supreme Court in the litigation that culminated in *Martin v. Hunter's Lessee* (1816), the most famous instance of early state resistance to the U.S. Supreme Court. In this decision, where the Virginia Supreme Court insisted on its right to overrule the U.S. Supreme Court in all cases that originated in the state courts, the Virginia Supreme Court suggested that the federal government route all questions involving interpretation of federal law through federal courts from start to finish. Thus, each "sovereign" system, federal and state, would have its own judiciary to interpret its own laws, but (notwithstanding the supremacy clause) the surface appearance would be that of coequal sovereignties (*Hunter's Lessee v. Martin*, 1815).[18] Precisely such a surface appearance has been preserved in the European arrangement.

Had the views of the Virginia Supreme Court in the *Martin* litigation prevailed, state courts would have been immune (as they formally are in Europe) from federal judicial process, but other state officials might still have been subject to federal court orders. A partial (but only partial) shield from such liability was erected by the Eleventh Amendment, adopted specifically to override the American Supreme Court's intensely unpopular and flagrantly disobeyed first decision, *Chisholm v. Georgia* (1793). According to the Eleventh Amendment, no lawsuit against a state can be "commenced" in federal court "by citizens of another state" or by foreigners. (The laws within a state, people assumed, would control suits by its own citizens.)[19] This amendment shielded state officials from citizens' lawsuits in federal courts throughout the turbulent nineteenth century, except for appeals on federal grounds that challenged resolutions of cases originally commenced by state authorities.[20] In *Cohens v. Virginia* (1824), the U.S. Supreme Court established this massive jurisdictional exception, and it did so (as in *Martin*) in the face of contrary arguments by Virginia's attorneys, but this time without opposing state authorities on the merits (thus leaving no occasion for state defiance). As a result, American state officials found themselves routinely brought into federal court by private citizens who appealed state decisions on grounds of conflict with federal law.

Private citizens do not have this power in the EC system. Only other government officials—in-state judges seeking guidance (Article 177 of the Treaty of Rome), or the European Commission (Article 169) or another member-state government (Article 170) charging violations of European law—can take a national government before the bar of the ECJ. That this is a considered, not an accidental, feature of ECJ jurisdiction is evidenced by the fact that a proposal to alter it to allow private citizens' actions against member states (or their agents) at the ECJ was rejected in the course of negotiations over the Single European Act.[21]

Private citizens are free to challenge a law of their own nation-state in European member-state courts on grounds that it conflicts with European law, but referral to the ECJ for an interpretation to resolve the challenge can occur only by action of the member-state judges under Article 177 of the treaty. The vast majority of ECJ cases arise under this procedure.[22] Judges of low-level courts, in the treaty's words, "may" refer at their option; judges on courts of last resort (as to the issues of a particular case) "must," in principle, refer to the ECJ. Of course, even judges on courts of last resort end up exercising judgment as to whether a bona fide "question of interpretation" has in fact been "raised."[23]

Joseph Weiler has argued that this requirement of member-state judicial initiative for taking cases to the ECJ has had enormous impact in garnering, first, member-state judicial acceptance of ECJ doctrine, and then, consequently, parallel acceptance by nonjudicial branches of member-state governments and by member-state citizenries. By virtue of this procedure the member-state court comes, as it were, to own the outcome: its judges requested an interpretation by the ECJ; these judges are the ones who must subsequently interpret the relationship between national law and the doctrine set forth by the ECJ; in the interpretation of these judges, the ECJ doctrine becomes, for practical purposes, part and parcel of national law, difficult for other governmental officials to disobey, precisely because their own judges have announced it as the law of the land.[24]

Had states like Virginia prevailed in the early nineteenth century, the American union too would have allowed only state courts to interpret state law (Virginia's Supreme Court in *Hunter's Lessee v. Martin*, 1815, insisted in vain that federal courts should be limited to matters "of federal cognizance," which could never include the issuance of orders to a state court). And in the American union, too (per Virginia's arguments in *Cohens v. Virginia*, 1824), any lawsuits involving a state that went to federal court would have been permitted there only at the initiative of state officials. Virginia failed in her jurisprudential bid for these goals, goals Virginia claimed were needed to honor the "sovereign" nature of each American state, but in the European Community they were implemented from the start.

Comparative analysis to this point indicates the conclusion that formerly sovereign states may well have characteristic desires upon relinquishing sovereignty to join a federal union. To the extent that the European Community honored those desires that were revealed in the early history of federal-state conflict in the United States, the European Community managed to avoid the kind of centrifugal rebellion so endemic among the nineteenth-century American states. One cannot prove that the designers of the European Community consciously took into account this American history, but it is a commonplace among American legal and political scholars that their European counterparts are strikingly well informed about the history of the U.S. Supreme Court. Moreover, there is evidence that Jean Monnet, one of the most influential founders of the EC, strongly admired the arguments of James Madison, Alexander Hamilton, and John Jay in defense of the American federal union. Reportedly, he always kept a copy of *The Federalist Papers* on his desk.[25]

VARIABLES PRESENT IN ONLY ONE OF THE TWO UNIONS

One can also identify institutional features present in one of the two unions but absent from the other that seem plausibly to have contributed to the success of European federal organs or to the difficulties faced by the American federal government in establishing the legitimacy of their authority. Because this type of analysis is essentially examining only a single case, one cannot be sure whether what seems a plausible insight will hold true once applied to additional test cases. Nonetheless, an explanation may be truly insightful even if unprovable, and this section explores explanations that seem to meet this description.

America-Focused Explanations
The Routinization of Authority

Part of the American explanation appears attributable to the fact that America of the late eighteenth and early nineteenth century was simply a more "wild and woolly" society, one where—as compared to late twentieth century Euro-America—bureaucracy was less routinized and the populace was less respectful of authority in general. Even that cornerstone of the rule of law, the norm that judges should be independent of the pressures of public opinion, was treated as legitimately debatable both in the press and among politicians in early-nineteenth-century America. Jeffersonian members of Congress in the 1802–4 period unabashedly condemned the idea of judicial independence as contrary to rule by the people.[26] Proposals cropped up in 1808, 1822, and 1830 for making individual justices removable from office when their decisions displeased large numbers of elected legislators.[27] Institutional resources needed for the rule of law, as basic as published reports of appellate court opinions, were not yet readily available during this period in the United States.[28] At one point in 1820s Kentucky, the legislature, unhappy that the state appeals court had invalidated certain debtor-relief laws, simply created a new appeals court to take the cases. The sympathetic governor then packed the court to obtain the politically desired results.[29] Moreover, before 1850, if juries wished to contravene a judge's instructions as to how the law applied to a given defendant, they were officially permitted to do so.[30]

An absence of routinization of the rule of law is discernible not only with respect to the court system; the electoral system too exhibited symptoms of lawlessness. For instance, in the 1787 Delaware election for delegates to the U.S. Constitutional Convention, supporters of one faction kept political opponents away from the polls at gunpoint. On this ground, the legislature revoked the election results and held a second election. The same thing happened the second time. The legislature gave up; despite substantiated complaints that violence had skewed the outcome, legislators let the election stand.

Even the president of the United States experienced difficulty executing federal law against intransigent state sentiment on a number of occasions. President Andrew Jackson wrote one of his generals regarding the *Worcester v. Georgia* decision: "If orders were issued tomorrow one regiment of militia could not be got to march to save [the Cherokee] from destruction and this the opposition know, and if a collision was to take place between them and the Georgians, the arm of the government is not sufficiently strong to preserve them from destruction."[31] The next year federal troops did intervene to stop armed attacks by Alabamians against Indians, and had to withdraw in the face of massive force from Alabamians.

In a situation lacking powerful norms of respect for hierarchies of authority, where state judges were elected to limited terms or appointed to them by elected officials, it is, then, not terribly surprising that not only state politicians but even state judges frequently resisted federal authorities on those issues where political passions ran high.

While this thesis amply fits the evidence, one should concede that there is no evidence to support what might be thought of as a possible corollary. As one moves later into the nineteenth century one does not find any discernible difference in the defiance pattern of the eastern, more settled states as compared to the western, less settled ones. Massachusetts, Connecticut, Rhode Island, and Georgia continued to defy federal authority well into the 1850s, even as western states like Ohio, Michigan, Wisconsin, Kansas, and California joined them on the defiance bandwagon. Thus, this explanatory proposition is not a "frontier thesis"; it is, rather, a statement about epochal differences in level of routinization of obedience to lawfully constituted authority.

This routinization-of-authority thesis facilitates an understanding of why some phenomena alleged to have helped secure European member-state acceptance of federal, EC authority failed to garner the same outcome in the early United States. Karen Alter (adapting an argument from Paul Pierson) argues, for instance, "Following a well-known judicial practice, the ECJ expanded its jurisdictional authority by establishing legal principles, but not applying the principles to the cases at hand" in such a way that they would alter the status quo ante. Then, having stood by during the gradual evolution of Euro-friendly legal doctrine, "politicians [in the member states] had to follow the legal rules of the game."[32] She neglects to add that this practice is well known precisely as having been pioneered by John Marshall in *Marbury v. Madison* (1803) against Congress, and then reutilized in *Cohens v. Virginia* (1824) to establish U.S. Supreme Court authority over appeals of criminal convictions in state cases. It is true that there was no state resistance to the *Cohens v. Virginia* decision, precisely because although doctrinally Marshall ruled against the state government's long-term preference (that there be no federal jurisdiction in this category of case), for the specific outcome in the case he agreed with the decision of the Virginia authorities (that the Cohens were punishable)—the state's short-term preference. In the United States, however, Marshall's strategy did not suffice for preventing states from later resisting U.S. Supreme Court authority in similar cases when the Court decided contrary to the short-term preferences of particular states. (Nor did it suffice even to stave off harsh contemporaneous criticism of the *Cohens* decision as usurping state authority. No fewer than seven issues of one newspaper ran thunderous criticism of the decision.[33] The ECJ decisions, as a general matter, have not attracted much news media attention.)

The reason this strategy was not as effectual in the early United States is precisely that the norm that governmental authorities must follow lawfully constituted authority had not yet been deeply and widely internalized. It was not yet the case that politicians felt they had to follow the legal rules of the game.

A similar critique would apply to Mark Pollack's suggestion that the absence of government resistance to the ECJ stemmed from reputational concerns: "Unilateral noncompliance has significant costs in terms of member state's reputation among its partners."[34] Such concerns would matter only if a favorable reputation for heeding lawfully constituted authority were a widely and deeply internalized norm. Such appears not to have been the case in the early United States.

In fact, in the mid-1990s, a number of scholars, including Karen Alter in a different article, have identified the societal commitment to the rule of law itself as an important causal variable to explain European states' acceptance of legal integration of the EC.[35] Perhaps the recent alertness to its importance is related to the fact that the chaos in the former Yugoslavia of the early 1990s reminded people that this commitment can be absent even in Europe. Indeed, an appreciation of the role of societal commitment to the rule of law has spread to other aspects of international relations literature, too. Andrew Moravcsik has argued that the willingness of "sovereign" authorities to accept the jurisdiction of transnational human rights courts is attributable to the prevalence of a civic and institutional domestic member-state culture that is hospitable to human rights, just as the thesis here is that EC countries' civic and institutional culture was already primed to accept the legitimacy of pronouncements of established judicial authorities—unlike the more rambunctious, barely settled United States of the early nineteenth century.[36]

Recent History of Rebellion from Empire

Apart from this difference, early-nineteenth-century America also was distinguished by a fresh recent history of successful colonial rebellion against a distant central authority. The annual Fourth of July encomia for that rebellion, and related patriotic rituals honoring the American Revolution, must have played some role in stiffening state resistance to distant federal authority when that authority bore down heavily against pressing state interests. Resisting distant central authority must have felt, to some degree, like a reaffirmation of values central to the American political tradition. Indeed, the 1860s secession effort in the South self-consciously affirmed this sentiment by modeling its constitution on the Articles of Confederation—the framework of the league adopted by the "independent" American states during the Revolutionary War, which had prevailed during their quasi-sovereign (1781–87) period before they strengthened central authority with the Constitution in 1787–90.

Europe-Focused Explanations
Judicial Empowerment

Scholars who have looked specifically at the European side of this picture to explain the remarkable success of the ECJ have drawn attention to a number of important elements unique to the European scene. Joseph Weiler has noted that the major force for acceptance of ECJ doctrine has been the alacrity of home state judges to apply it. Why should they do so rather than remaining loyal to their parochial legal regimes? He posited the insightful answer: judicial empowerment. Applying European law as "supreme law of the land" gives lower-court judges a power of judicial review over enacted legislation that none had before. It empowers them generally vis-à-vis the political branches of government, and in Italy, Germany, France, and Belgium, vis-à-vis the highest court of the land, to whom judicial review had previously been reserved.[37] Weiler's empowerment thesis has been seconded by Burley and Mattli, who have identified specific rhetorical ploys in ECJ opinions that appear calculated to appeal to the member-state "judicial ego."[38] This incentive would not have played a role in the early United States because judges within every state already exercised judicial review on the basis of the home state constitutions as well as the national one; from their perspective, the U.S. Supreme Court's claim to supremacy over them in cases like *Martin v. Hunter's Lessee* reduced rather than enhanced their power.[39] Also, judicial empowerment meant more in Europe than it could have meant in the United States because low-level member-state judges in Europe have civil service protection; in contrast to the American states, they are not political appointees or elected officials subject to state-level electoral pressures.

Well-Financed Indoctrination Campaign

Second, with respect to the European Union, Burley and Mattli have also documented in the European Community an elaborate, deliberate, and well-financed pro-ECJ socialization campaign that included "seminars, dinners, regular invitations to Luxembourg" (for judges and legal scholars of member nations), "visits around the European community" (by ECJ judges), and a program by the European Commission that created fifty-seven new full-time teaching posts in community law as part of an even broader pro-European integration educational program.[40] To be sure, in the nascent United States, patriotic, pro-federal education or socialization in various formats also took place. It included the stuff of daily life, such as teachings in primary schools that consciously aimed to build a shared sense of national identity, as exemplified in Noah Webster's efforts to spread knowledge of a standardized language and geography;[41] the development of public architecture and iconography;[42] works of historical and patriotic popular literature, such as those by Mercy Warren; and national celebrations like those for the Fourth of July. (Celebrations specifically of the American Revolution, however, as noted earlier, would have functioned as a two-edged sword. Although on the surface it would have been pro-federal, nonetheless, because the American federation began as a colonial rebellion against distant central authority, any celebration of this rebellion carried the subversive undercurrent of an antifederal subtext.)

Pro-federal American socialization also included self-conscious efforts by the national leadership, such as creating the government-financed post of Supreme Court reporter in 1817, so that U.S. Supreme Court decisions would be reliably reported and disseminated among America's attorneys.[43] And in an important sense it included repeated participation in specific federal political institutions, such as using federally coined money and voting every two years for federal-level officials in which federation-wide parties competed against each other for the popular vote. The European Union has yet to develop such parties to compete for seats in the European Parliament, although it is in the early stages of using federally minted money. Evidently the fact that the American union had a federation-wide elective presidency, whose election was expected to be settled in the federal House of Representatives, promoted the formation of federation-wide parties rather than the merely state-based ones that exist in Europe. The United States had such parties by the end of the eighteenth century, and voting in them no doubt shaped the federal sense of identity.[44] Nonetheless, nothing on the U.S. side approached the massive, concerted, federally financed effort to indoctrinate member-state legal elites that went on in Europe.

Elite-Mass Opinion Gap and Non-Elected, Anonymous Judges

Third, several authors have pointed to the interaction between specific political and judicial processes in the EC to explain the acceptance of dramatic judicial policy-making by the ECJ. Just as in contemporary America it is a political science commonplace that electorally vulnerable political branches often rely on the life-tenured federal judges to effectuate unpopular but necessary policies, something of this sort apparently went on in Europe.[45] Rasmussen, for instance, notes that particular member-state governments may have seen the necessity for certain transparochial policies but felt electoral pressure to exercise their council veto against those very policies.[46] Membership on the Council of Ministers, which was the legislative authority of the EC, at least before 1994 (when the powers of the European Parliament were somewhat enhanced), is comprised of ministers who simultaneously hold office in the cabinet of the member-state government. In other words, everyone on the Council of Ministers is subject to electoral pressures in the member state. Thus the ministers would sometimes "tacitly welcome integration by judicial fiat."[47] The Eurojudges, although on fixed terms, were nonetheless freer to act, because they are protected by the invisibility of unsigned, unanimous opinions and by not being subject to recall from votes of no-confidence. Moreover, compared to other Euro-institutions (and even compared to national judges), they receive relatively little news coverage, and this relative obscurity arguably adds to their freedom from political constraints.[48] Burley and Mattli note that while "states do often strongly object to proposed [interpretations of Euro-law] *prior* to a particular decision," once an ECJ decision has been handed down they never have argued at the Court that a prior ECJ decision (even one they had earlier opposed) be overturned.[49]

(Fritz Scharpf offers a similar explanation for the formal replacement of the voting system of nation-state veto powers with the system of qualified majority voting. He posits a gap between elite- and mass-level support for EC institutions: ministers like the opportunity to say they voted against measures unpopular at home, and the weighted majority system offers more likelihood that when such measures are sorely needed, they will be adopted anyway.)[50]

While this hypothesized disjunction in Europe separating the views of member-state elites, both political and judicial, from member-state voters as to the desirability of stronger federal-level policies is not entirely uncontroversial in the EC literature,[51] it evidently did not arise in those American states whose government officials rebelled against central federal authority. The absence of social distance between state government officials and state voters in late-eighteenth-century America has been identified by Gordon Wood as a major reason that the federalists during the Constitution-forming era sought a stronger federal union, which would be led by more distinguished elites than were gaining power at the state level.[52] Its political significance may well extend to these nineteenth-century rejections by American state elites of the authority of federal elites. State elections were typically more frequent than national elections, which frequency was designed to keep state elected officials close to popular sentiment, and American state judges, not appointed for life, do not have the independence from politics that characterizes federal judges. In European member states, judges have civil service protection; in American states, they can be voted out of office, or fail to be reappointed by the governor when their term expires.

It is highly unlikely that elected state legislators and governors would trouble themselves to challenge the legitimacy of national-level authority on behalf of causes that were not hugely popular in the home state. Indeed, as listed in Table 3, defiant state legislatures—whose members typically had to face voters more often than did holders of executive or judicial office—(who took action fifty-one times) far outnumber both state courts (sixteen instances of defiance) and state executive branches (nineteen incidents of resistance) as organs protesting the legitimacy of federal-level authority. Thus, it is safe to infer that these frequently elected legislators from small districts were expressing the dominant political sentiment in their home state.

Moreover, it is probably the case that in America, pro-federal elites were drawn out of the states by the attraction of the prestige and authority of federal politics to a much greater degree than goes on in Europe. In the EC/EU one wields powerful decision-making authority both in the member state and in the European Council of Ministers by holding office in the Cabinet of the member state. In the EC/EU before 1994 it is as though a European approximation of what in America is the National Council of Governors were the lawmaking body for the federal union. In the European Community there was no federal legislature to be the target of aspiration of a capable statesperson who wanted to foster a strong federal union; such a person had to stay in member-state politics. Membership—outside of national member-state government—in the EC's parliament (a merely consultative body prior to 1994) or its commission (the administrative arm) would carry much less authority and prestige. Because of this difference of incentive structure, a greater portion of the political corps who remained active in home state politics in nineteenth-century United States were likely to be antifederal than is the case in Europe; the reason is that the pro-federal ones in the United States could be siphoned off to the federal capital, a source of power and prestige. To would-be leaders of Europe, there is no real incentive to leave the member-state government for "higher" elective office. In the nineteenth-century American states, by contrast, the lure to federal office was so great that even those political leaders who opposed the strong dominance of the federal government were caught up in the vortex of national-level politics because that was the only reliable way to shape the course of the federation. Thus, even political parties that stood in principle for devolution of power to the state governments, such as those led by men like Thomas Jefferson and Andrew Jackson, had to run candidates for the federal offices of president and Congress, which offices in turn shaped both federal policy and the U.S. Supreme Court.

In sum, in nineteenth-century America, state elites in defying federal authority were doing what voters wanted because those elites evidently wanted it too; by contrast, European member-state elites, on a significant number of occasions, wanted more federal integration but were not free because of their electoral accountability (and voter opposition) to pursue it directly, so they pursued it by handing power over to the non-electorally accountable judges on the ECJ and to the civil service–protected home state judges. That is, the nonjudicial member-state political elites, because they in fact liked the policy results, on at least some occasions went along with accrual of power in the hands of ECJ judges and of their own national judges who were implementing ECJ rulings, even as the nonjudicial officials (in order to maintain electoral support) publicly opposed these results both via arguments before the ECJ and vetoes on the Council of Ministers.

The argument here has been that the Council of Ministers system, by keeping EC rule-making power in the hands of national (member-state) officials, ended up (at least in comparison with the alternative U.S. system) creating a larger balance of pro-Europe sentiment in member-state level officialdom, since politicians with such sentiment, in effect, had nowhere to go, except into member-state government. (Indeed, even ECJ judges are member-state judges first, are selected by member-state officials, and return after their ECJ term, to serve in member-state positions.) Fritz Scharpf has argued exactly the contrary, claiming that the fact that elected leaders of member-state governments make EC/EU policy creates "less reason to expect a transfer of the loyalties of political elites from the national to the European level," in his eyes weakening the latter.[53] His frame of reference is the modern German "Bundesrat," a legislative house structured somewhat similarly to the Council of Ministers, in that its members are chosen expressly to represent their home state. One weakness of his comparison is that in Germany, pro-federation officials can seek federation-level office via the "Bundestag," the other legislative house, so unlike the EC situation they are not kept in home-state level office. While he has a certain point, in that serving in an office normally would build loyalty to it, it is also true that a person does not seek an office for a level of government in which that person is not already interested. If my argument is correct, and if the European Parliament, which does have members elected directly to it, is ever made a truly coequal governing branch, then one could expect, other things being equal, to see more open opposition to EU policies in member-state level legislatures after that time.

America as a Test Case for Propositions about the EC/EU

The scholars of the ECJ who have puzzled over its remarkable success in winning the adherence of purportedly sovereign nation-state governments to doctrines that established the supremacy and efficacy of European law have proffered a number of explanations in addition to the ones endorsed above. These turn out to be unpersuasive for the following reason: they attribute a formative centripetal influence in the European Union to an institutional feature of the EC system even though the same feature in the American union failed to bring about the centripetal outcome. Thus the Euro-American comparison can be helpful in directing attention to these hypotheses that may be of limited explanatory scope.

One such hypothesis is Joseph Weiler's attribution of influence to something he calls "transnational incrementalism" or "transnational judicial cross-fertilization": the impact of an accumulation of Europe-accepting precedents in other member states, which then has a kind of persuasive force in the not-yet-obeisant states.[54] Indeed, high courts in Europe are aware of each other's prominent decisions, citing them as respected, if not binding, authority not unlike the way the various coequal U.S. Circuit Courts of Appeal cite one another.

Such interstate citations occurred in America also. According to a London law journal in 1834, the courts of South Carolina cited the decisions of the New York Supreme Court more frequently than those of any British Court.[55] In addition, American states consciously attempted to influence each other to accept federal authority. When one or two states purported to nullify federal law, they were condemned by numerous other states. But what one can conclude from the American case is that such interstate influence is not fatefully determinative. During the turbulent antebellum period in America, states freely violated not only other states' but even their own earlier precedents acknowledging acceptance of Supreme Court legitimacy.

To put it another way, cross-state influence can operate in either direction: in 1815–22, Virginia chose to imitate Pennsylvania's (1809) example of rejecting federal authority, the very rejection that Virginia had once openly condemned. Georgia's rejection of *Chisholm v. Georgia* (1793) stimulated enough support from other states that the Constitution was amended to undo the decision. The Massachusetts Supreme Court in 1817 reiterated the position of the Virginia Supreme Court from *Martin v. Hunter's Lessee*. The doctrine justifying state nullification of federal law put forth in the Virginia and Kentucky Resolutions of 1798–99 was reiterated (to justify nullification of different federal laws) by Massachusetts and Connecticut in 1808 and again in 1814, by Ohio in 1819–20 (which action stimulated Kentucky to reendorse it), and by South Carolina in 1830 and 1833.[56] In striking contrast, no other European court of last resort imitated the blanket rejection by the Conseil d'État of the authority of the ECJ and European law over French law.

Thirty-seven years into the American union—the age of the EC in 1995—the country was still experiencing not only rejections of federal authority by individual state governments including, prominently, their judicial branches, but even periodic violent outbreaks of resistance to federal authority. This was in spite of the fact that virtually every American state had in one case or another accepted the supreme authority of the U.S. Supreme Court. Thus cross-state imitative influence has not always operated to cement federal union, even with a founding document as strongly pro-integration as the U.S. Constitution.

A similar objection can be raised to four other suggestions, two that have been endorsed both by Weiler and by the Burley-Mattli team, one suggested by Barry Weingast and Geoffrey Garrett, and one proffered recently by Karen Alter in an adaptation of an argument of Fritz Scharpf. The first of these is Weiler's proposal that legal formalism "has considerable force" in explaining the success of the integration of the EC by judicial means.[57] He refers to the image of law as being above politics, nonpartisan, neutral, motivated by a supposed intrinsic logic, theoretically set in motion by the goals implicit in the Treaty of Rome. This image, the argument goes, helped to convince governments in the member state that tighter union was in everyone's interest. Similarly, Burley and Mattli point to "the logic of law" and the image of a separation of law from politics as having been crucial integrative forces.[58] These things may indeed have been helpful in the EC, where the political forces stagnated for years while the judiciary transformed the treaty into an effective, unifying, legal structure.

However, the early-nineteenth-century American Congress, was also relatively inactive; much of the integration in the United States also took place on judicial terrain, and the U.S. Supreme Court similarly relied on formal legal reasoning grounded in the written Constitution, the understanding of its framers and ratifiers, and the common interests to be served in federal union. Moreover, words like "veneration" and "reverence" were commonly employed to describe American attitudes in 1820–50 toward the Supreme Court, as were terms like "unimpeachable" and "purity" for the Court itself.[59] Nonetheless, in the United States—in contrast to modern Europe—the then-prevalent belief that conscientious judges can, should, and do interpret law without simultaneously acting as agents of merely political will failed to prevent resistance at the state level to law as expounded by federal judges.

The same problem arises with respect to Burley and Mattli's argument, endorsed by Weiler (and first explored by Stuart Scheingold) that credits the attainment of legitimacy for EC law with development of a large, transnational interest group who had a personal and professional stake in that legitimacy.[60] This group includes private economic actors for whom the European legal regime is more profitable than individual member-state regimes; law professors who teach EC law; scholars who write for or work in the production of books and journals focused on European law; and attorneys who specialize in EC law (not to mention the aforementioned member-state judges, who as a group are empowered by the exercise of Article 177 judicial review). Except for these judges, the other members of the EC-law-related professional and corporate interest groups would have had analogues (albeit perhaps in more embryonic versions) in the early-nineteenth-century United States. The antebellum United States did have some law professors and legal-treatise writers (such as Joseph Story and James Kent, and Lemuel Shaw), who specialized in national law. More significantly, it had cross-state business interests who preferred the uniformity of federal law to coping with twenty or thirty differing sets of state rules.[61]

One such business interest, for instance took to the U.S. Supreme Court the appeal that led to the famous decision in *Gibbons v. Ogden* (1824). *Gibbons*, on the grounds of a federally granted coasting license possessed by the appellant, struck down a New York–granted steamboat monopoly, thereby opening waterways to competition from other states. Indeed, the set of interests favoring a strong and authoritative federal government in the United States was numerous and powerful enough that it set the tone of one of the two major national political parties, first called National Republicans (in the 1820s) and then Whigs (until 1856). One of the major lines of cleavage separating the two parties in the United States was precisely the question of strong national government versus the retention of power at the state level. These pro-national forces, however, were not sufficient in the American context to prevent periodic resistance to national legal authority by state governments. Once again, while this proposition undoubtedly has a certain validity in identifying social elements supportive of integration of the European Union, the fact that such support was not decisive in the American situation undermines its usefulness as a generalizable explanation of the relative absence of official state resistance to federal integration.

This same criticism would apply to the suggestion of Geoffrey Garrett and Barry Weingast that there is an explanation of rational-choice theory for the acceptance of the authority of the ECJ by member states: namely, it is in the overall self-interest of each state to accept the Court's interpretive and enforcement authority, even if it might go against the interest of the state in an occasional instance, because this authority prompts other states to obey the rules of the union.[62] Such a theory should certainly have applied to the American union as well, and, like the other suggestions being critiqued here, it may have indeed somewhat facilitated the acceptance of union authority in both settings. Nonetheless, in the United States at least, it failed to prevent chronic outbreaks of state resistance.

Thus, its explanatory power for the formative stages of unions as a general matter is open to question.

Finally, Karen Alter, adapting an insight of Fritz Scharpf, has pointed to the importance of the supermajority voting rules in the EC, which for all practical purposes amounted to a unanimity requirement for a long time.[63] This insight applies to all supermajority voting systems, including the requirement of ratification by three-fourths of the states to amend the U.S. Constitution. Alter has argued that the ECJ was able to have powerful member states do its bidding because of the extreme difficulty of overturning any specific ECJ decision or of altering its jurisdiction. Although a particular state may have been quite antagonistic to a given decision, and a majority of member states may oppose a decision, there is rarely the roughly 70 percent of support needed for the weighted majority system to alter regulations from the Council or the unanimity needed to amend the EC Treaties.

A poignant illustration of this difficulty was illustrated in recent discussions in the British Parliament, where (given current public antagonism to joining the euro) it is fashionable for members to make speeches attacking EU institutions in general and the ECJ in particular. Prior to the intergovernmental conference that produced the Amsterdam Treaty, Attorney General Nicholas Lyell was interrogated by MP Denzil Davis: "Will you [propose] . . . that *national democratic assemblies* should have the ability to overrule the ECJ when its decisions involve public expenditure?" Lyell's reply left a loud silence. Instead of addressing Davis's point on national member-state power to assert itself against the ECJ, he referred to a previous court decision, the "Barber judgment," which had been much criticized because of its potential $80 billion cost. The decision had been checked in principle by unanimous member-state agreement at Maastricht, but the ECJ itself had then "clarified" it to comply with the Maastricht outcome before that outcome technically took effect. Lyell said, "The way to overcome such problems is for *the member states to act collectively through the intergovernmental conference.*"[64] His reply did not at all address the question of ECJ power over individual member states.

In sum, any system that requires supermajority support for changing the rules thereby firmly entrenches the decisions of whichever authority has the power to interpret the rules—at least in an environment where norms of obeying lawfully constituted authority are powerful. It is precisely this institutional structure that makes the U.S. Supreme Court so powerful in the contemporary United States. However, in the early nineteenth century, where the routinization of obedience to legally constituted authority was apparently much weaker than in late-twentieth-century Western Europe, state officials frequently displayed a willingness to flout the authority of the U.S. Supreme Court. In that setting, the Alter-Scharpf argument does not succeed in explaining the outcome.

TENTATIVE CONCLUSIONS

There are several institutional features that have promoted integration of the European Union and that were also demanded by resistant states in nineteenth-century America. This category as a whole suggests that formerly sovereign states entering federal unions have characteristic desires, the satisfaction of which prevents or tends to prevent state resistance to federal authority. The propositions in this category, considered as a group, might appear to yield the conclusion that the more Calhounesque the federation—the closer the union comes to allowing a member-state veto of all union decisions—the less there will be state resistance to the center. However, as a federation institutionalizes the kinds of member-veto capacity recommended by John C. Calhoun, what it gains in the absence of centrifugal member-state resistance is likely counterbalanced by what it has sacrificed in centripetal power to act frequently and effectively on behalf of the whole federation. This two-union comparison has revealed that the cost of such effective power at the center may be a certain amount of member-state resistance. The unhappy experience with the Articles of Confederation in the first United States, which confederation lacked both an executive and a judicial arm, shows that there are probably outer limits to the degree to which any union of states can successfully institutionalize Calhounesque features.

Thus the conclusion on this point should be that when sovereign states join together into a federal union to which they are transferring some of their sovereignty, they can minimize member-state resistance to federal authority if they adopt institutions that create the appearance or reality of limiting federal action to measures that reflect the sentiment of a substantial majority—that is, a consensus, if not unanimity—of the member states, and that foster the appearance that member-state governments are not directly taking orders from the center. Such features of the European Community included the following:

1. Supermajority decision-making (Council of Ministers), or the appearance of it (ECJ) at the center, such that federal rules appear to be the product of consensus.

2. Equal representation of member states on federal decision-making bodies (ECJ).

3. Limited terms of office for federal-level legislative (Council) and judicial (ECJ) officials. The former remain directly accountable to member-state voters.

4. An appearance of honoring member-state sovereignty in decision-making structures of the judiciary (i.e., federal judges cannot give direct orders to state judges as though they were all part of the same system).

Some propositions suggested by other scholars to explain the relative absence of state resistance in the EC failed to so function in the early-nineteenth-century United States, and thus have been judged of limited utility as explanatory variables. These included the following:

1. Locating pro-federal decision-making in the judiciary, such that integrative decisions appear to be "legal" rather than "political."

2. Growth of pro-federal transstate interest groups (e.g., lawyers, law professors, or corporate or commercial interests).

3. Cross-state imitative influence.

4. Member states' rational perception that in the long run they benefit from accepting federal authority as a third-party enforcer and interpreter of the norms of the union compact.

5. The institutional difficulty of overturning judicial interpretations of federal-level rules because of supermajority voting rules for doing so.

Some explanatory propositions can be derived from differences between the two cases. While plausible, they are tentative because they apply to only one of the cases in the study. These explanations of differences between the two unions include the following:

1. A system founded by way of colonial rebellion against distant federal authority will face a barrier in the way of pro-federal socialization (a barrier present in the early United States but not in the EC).

2. Federated unions of societies where obedience to established governmental authority is more routinized will be more likely to sustain only minimal state resistance than unions of societies where obedience to lawfully constituted authority is less fully routinized.

3. If decision-making is structured to provide personal power/status

incentives to member-state officials for fostering tighter federal integration, such integration will proceed more smoothly. Giving higher law status to European law has empowered member-state judges, and this fact provided a personal incentive for (those) member-state officials to promote federal integration in Europe. This institutional feature was absent in the United States; in fact, the state judges had parallel personal incentives to resist federal judicial authority, since it disempowered them.

4. A coordinated, well-financed indoctrination/education campaign (such as the one in the EC) that targets legal and judicial elites within all member states appears to minimize official state-level resistance to federal integration.

5. If there exists a preference gap, such that (elite) elected member-state government officials on some occasions want pro–federal integration policies in the face of voter (mass-level) resistance, a mechanism for handing the decision-making to nonaccountable (elite) pro-federal member-state officials will minimize state resistance.

This last proposition presupposes the presence of nonaccountable, pro-federal state officials, such as were brought about in the EC by the judicial power incentive described above. It also presupposes at the state level an elite/mass gap as to preferences for federation, a gap that was evidently lacking in some early American states some of the time, perhaps because pro-federal elites had stronger incentive than in Europe to leave state-level politics and move into federal-level politics. This proposition may imply a certain pro-integration (or at least anticentrifugal resistance) payoff in structuring political incentives such that pro-federal elites remain in powerful offices at the state level. Members of the powerful European Council of Ministers hold office simultaneously in their home governments; there is no other way to serve in the Council of Ministers, which was the sole legislative body of the EC until 1994.

The late twentieth century appears to be an era of increased interest in transnational associations and transnational courts. The ECJ has been the focus here, but the North American Free Trade Agreement is supposed to produce an enforcing judiciary; the European Convention on Human Rights and the Strasbourg court that enforces it have recently acquired increased rigor and vigor of enforcement; and other examples could be cited. This expanded presence of multiple, nonexclusive sovereignties in the world

creates a need for a reexamination of the prevailing version of the concept
of nation-state sovereignty (rooted in the sixteenth- and seventeenth-
century doctrines of Bodin, Hobbes, and Locke). In this version only one
set of authorities has a legitimate monopoly on the use of force, and sovereignty is not a transferable commodity. Although this has been the
prevalent paradigm in sovereignty theory, there have been numerous
others stretching from Johannes Althusius in 1603, through Samuel
Pufendorf and the Federalist Papers in the eighteenth century, through a
variety of nineteenth- and early-twentieth-century thinkers in the United
States, France, Switzerland, and Germany[65] who attempted to describe
how sovereignty is allocated within federated states as a juridical phenomenon. The effort here has been not to explicate with further precision
the bounds and nature of legitimate authority within federal unions as
much as to explore the phenomenology of the voluntary transition from
sovereign, independent state to merely partially sovereign member of federated union. What elements of the phenomenon render the transition
smooth and nonconflictual? What elements make likely official and open
resistance to the sovereignty transfer?

The first several decades of the United States and the first four decades
of the EC/EU provide illustrative contrasting examples of instances in
which previously sovereign states in a voluntary process, rather than as
an outcome of military conquest, hand over significant portions of sovereign authority to federating governmental organs. But these respective histories also exhibit partial transfers of sovereignty as, in a sense, long-term
processes of negotiation, where the format of negotiation can be official
acts of defiance at the member-state level. Moreover, the absence or min-
imization of member-state resistance to this transfer of sovereign authority (contrary to common-sense expectation) is not directly correlated with
the shortness of time during which the member states have previously enjoyed the status of fully sovereign independent states. In other words, this
two-case study has started with the observation that, strangely enough,
long-time independent sovereign states that have entered a federal union
can actually offer less resistance to the transfer of meaningful portions of
their sovereignty than states forming a union after independent sovereignty of only a few years.

What this study seems to have uncovered is that neither length of time
of previous sovereignty, nor clarity of union document as to the transfer
of sovereignty, nor degree of cultural-ethnic heterogeneity across member-
state lines is decisive as to whether member states will later exhibit resistance to federal authority and official protestations that its exercise has il-

legitimately transgressed their sovereignty. One thing that does seem to be decisive is the institutional arrangement of the federal union in question, especially the degree to which it manages to honor in image or reality the continuing retention of "sovereignty" in the member state.

These propositions should now be tested against other cases. Just as a comparison with the early American union illustrated the nongeneralizability of certain causal assertions that scholars have proffered about state behavior within the EC, a comparison with additional examples of voluntary unions may prove a useful check on assertions that have been developed here to explain the American situation. We turn to the case of the seventeenth-century Dutch republic.

CHAPTER 3

The Seventeenth-Century Dutch Republic
and the European Union

One cannot assume that the propositions developed in the preceding chapters about the behavior of states in federal unions are generalizable without testing them against additional cases. Toward that end, this chapter and the next examine two additional examples of voluntary federal unions in the modern Euro-American cultural context: the seventeenth-century Dutch Republic and (in Chapter 4) the nineteenth-century Swiss federation.

Certain scholars have pointed to the federation that was known as the Dutch Republic, or the United Provinces of the Netherlands, for instructive parallels to the European Union.[1] This union, in some respects a confederation and in others a federation, formally dates from the Union of Utrecht in 1579, and endured until its conquest by France in 1795 when it was given and then chose to retain a centralized national government.[2] During those years of the federated Dutch Republic, sovereignty—in the sense of final governmental authority—was a continually contested matter between the member states and the Generality, as the central government of the union was known. This has caused some scholars to look to the Dutch precedent for understanding the locus, or nonlocus, of sovereignty in the European Union.

This chapter provides a brief description of the structure of the Dutch Republic as a preface to the analysis of member-state behavior within the Dutch union. Then it traces the most dominant lines of state resistance to federal authority within that seventeenth-century union, and examines the Dutch picture in light of the postulates developed in the preceding comparison of the American and European Unions. The Dutch case proves helpful in showing the need to qualify certain propositions developed in Chapter 2 even as it confirms others.

This chapter argues that the most reliable guide for discerning who had governmental authority in the Dutch union is actual practice, for neither the literal terminology of the constitutive document, the Union of Utrecht, nor the slogan of "provincial sovereignty" common to seventeenth-century Dutch political discourse was in fact followed. What actual practice reveals is that the central authority in the seventeenth-century Dutch Republic was the will of the broadest, feasibly attainable consensus in the States General (the central legislature). This is a controversial assertion precisely because political discourse in the Dutch union commonly asserted that in the States General each province could on important questions exercise veto power, thereby preserving the sovereignty of each province. But in fact the States General did act on the basis of the widest feasible consensus, not on the basis of unanimous consent of all seven provinces, and yet the provincial-level governments and various province-friendly commentators, nonetheless, continued to assert throughout the century that each province retained its legitimate authority to veto Generality actions. This combination means that in the seventeenth-century Dutch union official resistance to central authority by provincial level governments was endemic, chronic, and virtually continual.

THE STRUCTURE OF THE DUTCH REPUBLIC

The Dutch Republic began with the revolt of parts of the Netherlands against the Spanish Hapsburg emperor during the 1560s, for a combination of reasons including desire for religious autonomy (the Dutch Reformed Church versus the Catholicism of Spain) and resentment at heavy taxes. The republic was formalized in the Union of Utrecht of 1579, although the republic did not officially cast off King Philip II of Spain until the Act of Abjuration of 1581. The Dutch union's membership varied over the course of the war with Spain, with the Belgium section eventually going back to Spain, which imposed Catholicism on that area. The institutions of the Dutch Republic evolved rapidly over the last forty years of the sixteenth century. By the 1590s it included seven voting provinces: Holland, Zeeland, Utrecht, Gelderland, Groningen, Friesland, and Overijssel, the last of which never officially signed the Union of Utrecht (because of ongoing warfare) but agreed to pay its requisite share of taxes at the end of 1585, and which began regular participation in the union's States General by the early 1590s.[3] (The republic also included two non-voting sections: the province of Drenthe, deemed too small and poor to be accorded voting rights, and, after their capture in 1629–37, the conquered Generality Lands near the Belgium border, containing substantial numbers of Catholics.)[4]

As its membership evolved during these decades, so did its sense of an appropriate governmental form; the States General of the United Provinces offered "sovereignty" (in the sense of suzerainty) to the Duke of Anjou in 1580; after the Duke's failed military coup and consequent departure in 1583, first Henry III of France and then Elizabeth of England received the offer of sovereignty, both in 1585. Meanwhile, Holland and Zeeland, the two largest provinces, had been resisting the rule of (Catholic) Anjou by trying to persuade the military leader of the revolt, William the Silent, Prince of Orange, to accept the title of Count of Holland and Zeeland. Before that could happen, he was assassinated in 1584. According to the terms of the 1585 Treaty of Nonsuch, Queen Elizabeth, in return for military help, was allowed to name the political and military head of state (the governor-general) and two additional members to the ruling executive body, the Council of State. The council, headed by the governor-general, would appoint the stadholders—the provincial governors—for each province. Her appointee as the ruler of the United Provinces, Robert Dudley, Earl of Leicester, lasted for only two years, after which he too departed, unsuccessful both politically and militarily. After these failed experiences with a "governor-general," the Dutch Republic chose to continue without a unitary chief executive until 1747.[5]

Over time the Council of State was transformed into a body that lacked policy-making authority but that served in an administrative capacity over the army, admiralty, and taxation. In it, Holland had three votes; Zeeland, Friesland, and Gelderland, two each; and Utrecht, Overijssel, Groningen, and the stadholders, one each.

The policy-making body for the Generality, at a formal level, became the States General, for which the presiding officer rotated on a weekly basis among the seven voting provinces there. The delegation from each of these provinces was accorded one (collective) vote. In principle, votes were cast in compliance with instructions from the provincial states. (As a matter of practice, there was much back-and-forth travel to obtain such instruction, but sometimes conditions of geography or of military or political turmoil made actual instruction impossible.) Each provincial states (legislature) in turn had delegates from particular towns, as well as certain nobles to represent rural areas. The town delegates similarly voted in accord with instructions from their respective town councils. Each town government was run by a closed, self-perpetuating group of oligarchs of commercial wealth (known as regents).

At an informal level, actual leadership of the Generality was provided in alternating time periods by one or another of the two leaders of Holland, by far the largest, wealthiest, and most powerful of the seven provinces. Holland contained 48.2 percent of the republic's population in 1650, and officially provided 58 percent of the tax revenue, though in practice it was an even larger fraction because the smaller provinces chronically failed to pay what they owed and the financiers of the consequent public debt almost all resided in Holland.[6] These two alternating leaders were (1) Holland's "advocate" (later called "pensionary"), the man who chaired the meetings, set the agenda, and formulated resolutions for the Holland States (legislature), and served as spokesman for Holland's delegation at the States General; and (2) Holland's "stadholder," an office generally held by the Prince of Orange. (The title of office derived from the provincial governor appointed by the Hapsburg emperor, and the officeholder typically served as governor of more than one of the provinces of the Netherlands.)

Holland, Zeeland, and Utrecht at the time of the rebellion from Spain shared the stadholder William the Silent, Prince of Orange. After his assassination (by which time he was serving as stadholder of six of the seven provinces), the Dutch Republic for five years resumed the pre-Revolt tradition of parceling the seven provinces among three stadholders. In 1589, when the stadholder (von Neuenahr) of Overijssel, Utrecht, and Gelderland died, those provinces went to the then-stadholder of Holland and Zeeland, Prince Maurits of Orange (which assignment again reduced the number of stadholders to two).[7] Friesland, most of the time with Groningen, continued to have a separate stadholder (from the Nassau branch of the Orange family) until 1747, when for the first time all seven provinces shared a single stadholder.

Technically, Maurits did not become a prince until 1618 when his Catholic older brother, Philips William, died.[8] Except for this technicality, Holland's stadholder after the Revolt (when it had one) was always the Prince of Orange. Thus the pro-stadholder forces were known as Orangists. The pro-pensionary faction thought of themselves as "republicans," although this is a misnomer by modern terminology. When the prince and his political patrons were not dominant, the provinces were ruled by a combination of landed nobility in rural areas and, in the increasingly powerful cities, a small group of men from very wealthy merchant families who decided among themselves whom to admit as a newcomer when someone died. In short, each province (except for Friesland, which alone gave some influence to elections in which 10 percent of the population could participate), when the prince was not dominant, was ruled by a self-perpetuating oligarchy, which thought of itself as republican, evidently because it was of nonroyal and non-noble lineage and in that sense of the people. For much of the history of the Dutch Republic, 1650–72 and 1702–47, Holland did without either a stadholder or governor-general.[9]

In the nonstadholder periods, and also in the formative decades of 1588–1618—during the first two decades of which the stadholder Prince Maurits of Orange was preoccupied with leading the war effort against Spain—leadership of the Generality was taken up by Holland's advocate/pensionary. (More precisely, this was the pattern except for the interlude of 1609–18, an era of power struggle between the advocate and the stadholder, during which the republic was in a chaotic state, racked by a religious schism so intense as to produce widespread rioting and urban-level coups across the country. In a sense there was no single national leader during this power struggle.) Scholars characterize the eras of pensionary dominance (1588–1618, 1650–72, 1702–47) as periods in which Holland dominated the Dutch Republic, and the others as times of dominance by interests of the Generality as a whole—or at least a less Hollandocentric vision of those interests—even though technically the stadholder, too, was an official of the province of Holland.[10]

This perspective prevailed in part because Prince William the Silent (like George Washington in the United States) was remembered with gratitude as father of his country for his leadership role during the Revolt; thus his descendants, in the House of Orange, came to be viewed as belonging to the whole country, not just to Holland. Moreover, from the time of the Revolt, the job of stadholder of Holland included that of commanding officer (usually but not always called captain-general) of the union army (which he occasionally used against other officials or cities of Holland). Unlike the advocate/pensionary, he was an official of the whole union by virtue of his army post. Finally, his military command provided him with a good deal of patronage influence over the nobility in rural parts of the union who sought military careers. This nobility had considerable clout in the provincial "states" (legislatures) of the more rural provinces (and noble titles of the prince himself gave him a vote as First Noble in the Zeeland States). Therefore, while the Holland stadholder did not have an official vote in the States General, he did control the votes of a number of the provinces there during a substantial portion of the century. And because the geographic position of these provinces gave them reason to fear imminent harm from a foreign invasion, they shared the stadholder's policy preference for a strong military and willingness to wage war (whereas Holland, which prospered when commercial shipping flowed freely, tended to prefer avoiding war and reducing military spending).

Some scholars insist that despite the complicated machinery of government, the Dutch Republic's political system "worked remarkably well."[11] Whatever may be meant by that insistence, the transitions between periods of advocate/pensionary leadership and leadership by the Prince of Orange/stadholder of Holland (which during the seventeenth century took place in 1618–20, 1648–50, and 1672) were not smooth; instead they were characterized by such events as the imprisonment or execution of political enemies, purges of opponents from office, and—in the most egregious case—the murder of pensionary Johan De Witt and his brother Cornelis, in which a mob beat, stabbed, and shot the men and hung the corpses by their feet, after which, according to highly reliable historian Jonathan Israel, their bodies were cut into pieces, roasted, and eaten.[12] These convulsive transitions between pensionary and Prince of Orange leadership occurred approximately every thirty years during the 1588–1702 heyday of the Dutch Republic. And the first two of these convulsions (1618–1620 and 1648–1650) were inextricably bound up with the contested issue of provincial versus Generality sovereignty.

Even the third of these crises, in 1672, did not lack for arguments about the locus of sovereignty, in this instance a debate over whether it lay in the town governments directly or in the Holland States. However, the upheaval at this time was not a matter of government against government, but rather people against government; riots in towns all across the not-yet-conquered provinces of Holland and Zeeland pushed the States General away from its willingness to negotiate for peace terms with France and England, the former of which had taken Dutch territory up to the flooded buffer areas around Holland and Zeeland. The riots produced the murder of the pensionary, the reappointment of a stadholder (which the Holland States and the States General had in 1667–68 "perpetually" banned), widespread political purges with pro-Orange replacements, and an eventual turnaround in the war.[13]

THE SOVEREIGNTY DEBATE

The seventeenth-century Dutch federation endured a chronic and continual dispute over the locus of sovereignty between the provincial members of the union and its central authority, the States General. This dispute took place both at the official governmental level and in periodic eruptions of pamphlet wars arguing one or another side for the highly literate Dutch population. The debate was rooted in a lack of clarity in the federation's founding document, and it focused on several specific topics.

Sovereignty and the Union of Utrecht

The Union of Utrecht, the formal constitutive document, contained a number of ambiguities as to the locus of final authority on various matters; these ambiguities remained unresolved because they were nurtured by the Dutch mindset of the era, which viewed the provinces as having retained sovereign authority even though in a practical sense they had banded together into a unified, albeit highly decentralized, new state. Thus, a tripartite mixture—ambiguous founding document, strong belief in provincial sovereignty, and practical necessity to act as a unified federation—produced several topics over which sovereignty was contested for extended periods.

In its first article the union document bills itself as an "eternal alliance and confederation" by which these provinces "unite . . . as if they were but one province, and [pledge that they] shall not separate themselves from each other nor have themselves separated." They pledged further to respect the "traditional . . . rights of each province, town, member, and inhabitant" and to give mutual assistance of their lives and property for securing these rights.[14] Even by the end of the first article, the union appears to be a hybrid—in part merely a mutual defense pact but in part an eternal union from which each has perpetually abjured the option of secession.

Moreover, the pledge to protect traditional provincial rights appears to be undercut at various other sections: Article 10 forbids any outside alliance without the consent of all the provinces. Far from preserving traditional rights, this article seems to give each province veto power over the foreign policy of each other province and over the collectivity. Article 12 sets forth the agreement to abide by a common currency exchange rate (for the different mints in each province). This was done in 1606;[15] previously each had set its own exchange rate. Article 18 forbids any one province from imposing imposts or convoy duties burdening other provinces "without general consent." If general consent is understood as concurrence of all seven provincial delegations, again this created new veto rights against traditional powers.[16]

An additional constitutional ambiguity later arose because of the history of Article 13. Article 13 assigns the regulation of religion to each province, with special wording for Holland and Zeeland, which had joined their ecclesiastical administrations in their Particular Union of 1576,[17] and adds the proviso that liberty of individual conscience is protected. During the political and church purges of 1618–20—the peak of a religious schism that produced rioting from 1608 into the 1620s in cities all across the republic, to a degree that bordered on civil war—the States General called a National Synod to develop the regulations for the national Dutch Reformed Church.[18] After the 1619 National Synod of Dordrecht, as a matter of precedent, religion was a Generality matter, but Article 13 provided a continuing, formal legal foundation for the advocates of provincial sovereignty over religious issues.

The article that gave rise to decades of dispute over whether a particular province was or was not obliged to accept the central Generality authority was Article 9:

> No armistice or peace treaty shall be concluded nor any war started nor any duties or contributions pertaining to the Generality of the United Provinces demanded but by the unanimous consent of the aforementioned provinces. But in other matters concerning the conduct of this confederation . . . all decisions shall be taken in accordance with the advice and opinion of the majority of the provinces of this alliance. . . . But *if it happens that the provinces cannot reach an agreement on matters of armistice, peace, war or contributions,* their differences must provisionally be referred and submitted to the present stadholders of the provinces who will bring about a settlement or at their own discretion give the judgment on the differences. If, however, the stadholders cannot agree among themselves they will select and ask such impartial assessors and assistants they themselves choose to consult. *And the parties shall be bound to accept the decisions taken by the stadholders in the aforesaid manner.* (emphasis added)

In its totality, Article 9 does not mandate a veto power to each province, even on war, peace-making, and taxes. It ultimately says that in the absence of unanimity, the stadholders shall provisionally pursue unanimous consensus ("bring about a settlement") but, failing that, will simply judge what course of action to take, which decision the provinces are "bound to accept." However, the political ethos of the day was characterized by talk of each province as "sovereign" and as having a real veto power on these issues.[19] Similarly, the provinces spoke of themselves as "allies" rather than as co-members of a single federated state.[20]

As a matter of practice, the effectively governing system seems to have been the following: the provincial governments generally accepted (eventually) the majority will of the States General. The talk of provincial sovereignty translated into an operative norm of seeking unanimous consensus to the degree feasible before acting, rather than simply counting votes and then acting as soon as there was a bare majority. Thus, consensus to the degree feasible was the operative norm, not a provincial veto power.[21] This was so despite the misleading appearance to the contrary in the first sentence of Article 9 of the Union of Utrecht, which sentence perhaps fueled the common pattern of provincial insistence that provinces did have such a veto power. Indeed, Jonathan Israel quotes Zeeland and Gelderland delegates making precisely this Article 9 argument in an attempt to wield a minority veto against the Peace Treaty with Portugal of 1661.[22] The reply that defeated them was a listing of the past treaties made without unanimous consent.

Nor was it true that the stadholders were "at their discretion" in choosing to abide by majority will on the subjects of war, armistice, and tax assessment, as specified in Article 9. An examination of some of the prominent non-unanimous decisions reveals that it was the majority (of the number of voting provinces) itself that repeatedly carried the day, for the Dutch federation followed the will of the majority of provinces, even when the stadholder sided with the minority of provinces. Several prominent examples of non-unanimous decisions can be identified, including several where not even the will of the stadholder fortified with dissenting provinces managed to block Generality action: Overijssel never signed the 1585 Treaty of Nonsuch; the States General deprived the Council of State of its authority to shape foreign policy in 1588 against the vote of Utrecht; the truce with Spain of 1609 was signed in the face of intense opposition by Zeeland and the stadholder Prince Maurits of Orange; the States General altered the provincial tax quota amounts in 1616 by majority rather than unanimous vote, raising the level owed by two provinces; the number of army troops was cut in 1642 despite opposition by Zeeland, Utrecht, and the stadholder Prince Frederick Henry; the Treaty of Munster ending the eighty-year war with Spain in 1648 was accepted by the States General despite Utrecht's refusal to sign it, Zeeland's refusal to ratify it, and the determined opposition of stadholder Prince William II; the declaration of war against Portugal in 1657 lacked unanimous support, and the treaty ending this war in 1661 was signed contrary to the votes of Zeeland and Gelderland; and the twenty-year truce treaty with Louis XIV was ratified in 1684 by a 4–3 vote, in the face of opposition by Zeeland, Gelderland, Utrecht, and stadholder Prince William III.[23]

In fact, for lengthy periods when Holland and three or four other provinces were refusing to have a stadholder,[24] it was inconceivable that the absence of unanimous consent would actually cause Generality decisions on war, peace, and taxes to be turned over to the lone stadholder, who reigned in only two or three small provinces, as a literal reading of Article 9 would mandate. Instead the States General, as before, pursued consensus but then ultimately followed the majority vote.

A number of recent scholars have attempted to reconcile the combination of repeated claims of a provincial veto power with the evident reality that numerous policies prevailed even in the face of dissents from certain provinces, by suggesting that provincial veto (or provincial sovereignty) was the theory but that dominance by only one province, Holland (with its 60 percent of the finances and half the population), was the practice.[25] That suggestion cannot account for the instances in 1618–20 and 1648–50, when Holland was outvoted at the States General, and then the will of the majority of the provinces was implemented by the army leader, the Prince of Orange (who was also stadholder of most of the provinces, including Holland). Nor can the suggestion account for the January 1672 vote in the States General when the pressure of opposition by six of the seven provinces moved Holland to change its vote and agree to a lifetime appointment of the Prince of Orange as captain-general of the Generality army.[26] The will of the considered majority—understood as the majority of provinces in the States General after efforts to maximize consensus to the extent feasible—was the reigning central authority in the Dutch Republic of the seventeenth century.

I have uncovered only one apparent exception to the argument that the will of the considered majority in the States General was really the central authority of the Dutch union. In 1654 four of the provinces condemned Holland's Act of Exclusion, which barred the House of Orange from Holland's stadholderate forever. This latter act was adopted in subservience to England's condition for peace terms at the time, and a bare majority of the provinces censured it as violating the Union of Utrecht's ban on separate, nonconfederation alliances by single provinces. However, the appearance of exceptionality in this example is altered, or perhaps even negated, by the fact that Holland's pensionary De Witt continued to negotiate on the subject within the States General, until by 1657 he had persuaded enough provinces that Holland eked out a bare majority in its favor. Then by September 1660, Holland itself gave in to a later, second reversal of majority-of-the-provinces sentiment, revoking its Act of Exclusion.[27]

Overview of Sovereignty in the Dutch Republic

The next section in this chapter contains a detailed narrative chronicling the more prominent topics that occasioned extended disputes over sovereignty in the seventeenth-century Dutch Republic. These included, in brief, (1) the question of which level of the government, Generality or Province, acceded to King Philip II's erstwhile power to appoint a stadholder for each province; (2) the issue of who decided upon the level of taxes to be paid by each province to the Generality; (3) the issue of whether the province or the Generality had authority over which religion prevailed in each province; (4) which level of government—town, province, or Generality—was to be the primary object of loyalty of the armed forces (provinces funded the regiments and appointed mid-level officers; provincial and city governments recruited the troops; and the Generality appointed the commanding officer, set military policy, and provided for military discipline; (5) which level of government should be specified as sovereign within the official prayers of the state-established Dutch Reformed Church; and (6) which level of government controlled the size of army units to be paid by each province. As documented below, the de facto sovereign in the Dutch Republic was the broadest consensus attainable after extensive negotiations among the seven provincial delegations at the States General. A contemporaneous description of this process of negotiating toward consensus sheds some light on how the process worked. Philip Dormer Stanhope, Fourth Earl of Chesterfield, described it in a letter to his son in 1745 as follows:

> However, should one, or even two of the lesser provinces . . . obstinately and frivolously, or perhaps corruptly, persist in opposing a measure which Holland and the other more considerable provinces thought necessary, and had agreed to, they would send a deputation to those opposing provinces, to reason with, and persuade them to concur; but if this would not do, they would as they have done in many instances conclude without them. . . . But as this is absolutely unconstitutional [sic], it is avoided as much as possible.[28]

If the central authority in the seventeenth-century Dutch Republic thus is understood as the will of the considered majority in the States General—as the will of the broadest consensus that could be reached after ne-gotiations to the maximum extent feasible—then official resistance to central authority by provincial level governments in the republic can fairly be described as endemic, chronic, and virtually continual. The initial dis-pute over the locus of sovereignty in the Republic was occasioned by the question of whether provincial level or Generality level authority had power to appoint the stadholder; the provincial level actually won out, despite a formal treaty statement to the contrary signed by six of the seven provinces. On later major controversies concerning the power to refuse to pay taxes, provincial control of religion, and the power to reduce the size of the military, the Generality did prevail but had to do so in the face of repeated insistence that its authority was illegitimately trampling upon spheres of provincial sovereignty. These claims of provincial sovereignty reached such an intense level that the Generality army, purges of local gov-ernments from the center, and politically motivated arrests, imprison-ments, and even execution, were all deployed to quiet them down.

Indeed, claims of provincial sovereignty were so chronic that most his-torians of the period describe that sovereignty—at least as to "the most important decisions"—as the formal legal reality.[29] A couple of histori-ans are more measured, describing such sovereignty as "supposed" or "in theory," while the practical reality was one of a unitary (albeit decentral-ized) state.[30] Among the English-language sources I have found, only Jonathan Israel, whose recent 1,200 page tome is likely to be viewed as the definitive source on the seventeenth-century Netherlands for some time to come, states baldly that the claim of provincial sovereignty not only was a fiction, but also was one that all parties concerned recognized as a fiction.[31] This statement may go too far; statesmen or legal theorists may argue a rule's propriety even in the knowledge that the rule is con-trary to repeated precedent. In any event, as a matter of practice, it is clear that in the Dutch union of the seventeenth century, no single province (not even Holland) could exercise a veto power if six other provinces were firmly united in opposition. And nonetheless, the various provincial gov-ernments individually insisted on frequent occasions stretching through-out the century that, as a matter of rightful authority, they did have such a veto power.

CHRONICLE OF SOVEREIGNTY DISPUTES

For the reader interested in a greater degree of historical detail on the specific sovereignty disputes, this section is included. Those readers who would like to pursue more directly the comparative analysis of the Dutch Republic as an instance of a federated union may wish to move ahead to the section on Dutch provincial resistance.

Sovereignty and Stadholder Appointments

The first concrete subject over which a sovereignty dispute for the Netherlands arose took the form of a years-long debate over which governing body had succeeded to the former power of King Philip II (and his predecessors) to appoint a stadholder for each province. Had the king's authority been appropriated by each rebellious province, or did it belong to the Generality, and therefore reside in a union authority such as the States General or Council of State?

As an act of revolt, the provincial states of Holland, Zeeland, and Utrecht had each appointed the Prince of Orange, William the Silent, as their stadholder in 1572. After the 1579 Union of Utrecht, the States General appointed stadholders for the other provinces, and when these lost their stadholders through death or defection, the States General named the replacements—except for those of Holland and Zeeland. A month after William's assassination in 1584, the legislatures of Holland and Zeeland named Maurits of Orange as the head of the Council of State and as their future stadholder, to take office as of his maturity. The Treaty of Nonsuch in 1585 gave the Council of State, to be headed by the Earl of Leicester, authority to appoint all stadholders. But Holland and Zeeland moved quickly to name Maurits (age seventeen) their stadholder in November 1585, prior to Leicester's arrival, evidently motivated by concern over the potential hegemony of Queen Elizabeth via her governor-general Leicester and her two additional appointees to the Council of State. In January 1586, in response to the predictable protests from Leicester on behalf of the Council of State, Holland and Zeeland insisted that the power of appointing stadholders was within provincial rather than Generality jurisdiction, that each province had inherited from the formerly sovereign king this piece of his sovereignty. Agreeing with Holland's arguments, the States of Friesland insisted on reappointing, in their own name, the stadholder already appointed for their province by the States General.[32]

Despite Leicester's departure in 1587, the issue of English influence seems to have continued to lurk in the background of the dispute, for England retained its presence on the Council of State. When vacancies arose in 1589, the States in Overijssel and Utrecht each appointed a stadholder, and the States General (evidently with the approval of the Council of State, its executive body) formally enacted the appointment thereafter. Gelderland, however, pointedly refused to go through the motions of nominating two candidates so that one could be officially selected by the Council of State and approved by the States General. This led to diplomatic protests by the English Council members, an admission by Maurits himself, the appointee, that this violated the treaty, months of delay, eventual compliance with the prescribed formality by Gelderland, and then official appointment by the Council of State. In 1595, stadholder vacancies in both Groningen and Drenthe were filled by proclamation of the States General, not the provinces.[33]

After that no vacancies arose until 1620. Then, for the first time since 1572, provincial states—those of Friesland, Groningen, and Drenthe—managed to appoint stadholders without intervention by a Generality institution, either Council of State or States General. In the years preceding, 1618–20, the republic had undergone a massive upheaval that had culminated in a "*wetsverzetting,*" or purge. Under a claim of inherent emergency authority, Stadholder Prince Maurits of Orange removed his opponents in Holland, Utrecht, Overijssel, and Gelderland from the local governing bodies that chose the tightly controlled delegates to Provincial States, who in turn chose delegates to the States General. As a result of the purges and consequent replacements, the States General became totally dominated by Orangists; they had no substantive objections to Friesland's choice, Ernst Casimir, who had assisted in the purging of Holland's town councils. And they certainly were not about to object to Groningen's and Drenthe's choice of Prince Maurits of Orange. Seven years later England's practice of appointing members to the Council of State ended, eliminating one remaining source of Generality desire to control stadholder appointments. After this the custom of permitting each province to name its own stadholder took hold.[34]

However, the related sovereignty question did not disappear; it simply took on new shape when Holland and Zeeland announced their intent to remain stadholderless upon the death of Prince William II in 1650, whose sole surviving progeny was an infant son. This provoked Friesland and Groningen to accuse Holland and Zeeland of violating the Union of Utrecht, which had rendered the stadholderate a Generality institution by its stipulation in Article 9 and elsewhere that disputes between provinces would be settled by the stadholders. Gelderland and Overijssel (with Utrecht too divided to act), like Holland and Zeeland, chose to remain for the time being without a stadholder.[35]

At this point another of the sovereignty riddles created by the Union of Utrecht becomes apparent. The document stipulated in Article 21 that its interpretation "shall be determined by the allies [provinces] who shall with general advice and consent decree what they consider proper. If they cannot agree among themselves they shall ask for the intervention of the stadholders of the provinces," after which the article referred back to Article 9 for the method of procedure for the stadholders.[36] (There was no one Generality court to interpret the law of the land; each province had its own high court, except for Holland and Zeeland, who shared one.) In a situation of interprovincial disagreement on the meaning of the document, where five of the seven provinces chose not even to have a stadholder, let alone submit to him interpretive disputes (including the question whether they were free under the union document to refrain from having a stadholder), it becomes clear that Article 21, creating stadholder supremacy for such interpretation in the absence of unanimous accord by the provinces, was rendered a dead letter. Instead, the States General would constitute itself or a subcommittee to act as a high court of appeal. Unanimity does not appear to have been the decision rule for these courts.[37]

Sovereignty and Taxes

Marjolein 't Hart, author of a specialized study of the development of the fiscal apparatus of the Dutch state, posits flatly that "the provinces . . . were sovereign in fiscal matters."[38] Historian Jonathan Israel argues, to the contrary, that the autonomy enjoyed by each province as to the form of its taxation was not as significant as the fact that the overall expenditure level and percentage owed by each province (its quota) were centrally set by the States General with the guidance of the Council of State. Thus, provincial autonomy as to taxation "was more apparent than real."[39]

'T Hart's conclusion evidently stems from her observation that the Council of State's proposed list of annual requisitions (*staat van oorlog*) was presented formally as a petition to which each province was free to consent or not. Frequently, lower sums were consented to than were requested. These lower consent levels were honored, with the deficits eventually made up by borrowing.[40] At the very least, this practice indicates a widespread belief in the prudence of gaining a member-state government's consent to the taxes assessed from its residents. Prior to 1615, there is some evidence that this formal requirement of consent was treated as binding; in the 1605–15 period the requirement that consensus be negotiated was powerful enough that mediators from France and England were brought in to attain it.[41] Negotiations to attain consent to the lowering of Zeeland's quota because of economic hardship induced by the Truce of 1609 lasted from that year until 1613, when Friesland was finally brought on board.[42] And the provincial delegates did talk as though the power to refuse taxation was retained as one of their sovereign prerogatives. Also, 't Hart seems swayed by the fact that the central government employed force to extract taxes from provinces only when the province failed to pay taxes to which it had consented.[43] This use of force against the provinces occurred with some frequency; the Generality for this purpose sent troops to Groningen in 1599, Drenthe and Groningen in 1604–5, and Friesland in 1626 and 1635–37.[44] The Generality also used the technique of seizing provincial officials and holding them as hostages until the taxes were delivered; this happened to Drenthe in 1622 and Gelderland in 1625 and 1640.[45] Moreover, the Generality sent troops on numerous occasions to Groningen (in 1615, 1628, 1648, and 1662) when civil discord over taxation arrangements repeatedly had brought about conditions of utter political paralysis.[46]

'T Hart's reliance on the formalistic distinction that troops were sent only after consent was given does not seem to be able to account for the Groningen situation; here, troops were sent precisely because there was no consent given. Also, on at least two occasions in the first half of the century, the States General did alter the structure of provincial quotas by majority rather than unanimous vote, both times in the face of opposition by two provinces. In 1616 the States General raised the quota levels due from Gelderland and Overijssel, and then for the period of 1621 to the mid-1630s (due to changed conditions from the renewal of war with Spain) they were temporarily lowered—"despite fierce protests from Friesland and Groningen," according to 't Hart.[47] Finally, to deal with Friesland's chronic nonpayment of taxes to which it had in principle once consented, the Generality (in 1636–37) imposed on it additional taxes to which it had not consented, and backed up this imposition not only with troops but also with a purge of urban government officials who opposed the tax, replacing them with officials more sympathetic to the Generality.[48]

In light of these instances when the States General prevailed, it is difficult to accept 't Hart's description of each province as "sovereign" over how much it would pay. It seems more accurate to conclude that on tax policy, as on other issues, the provinces repeatedly spoke of themselves as sovereign, and indeed the obligation to seek consensus at the States General operated as a powerful (as well as practically sensible) norm; but in fact no province really had sovereign authority such that it could refuse to pay taxes. Fiscal policy was ultimately set by as wide a majority as could be negotiated at the Generality level.

Religion, Military Loyalty, and Sovereignty

As noted, the Union of Utrecht appeared to establish provincial autonomy over religion. This appearance was somewhat complicated by the fact that each stadholder's job—as well as the job of other Dutch government officials—included the duty of maintaining "the true religion," and each stadholder served more than one province.[49] Thus, if it were to happen that two provinces (and their respective provincial states) who shared one stadholder were to arrive at conflicting understandings of the true version of the true religion, it would become unclear what the stadholder's duty then entailed. This problem did arise within the Dutch Reformed Church in the early 1600s. Moreover, since freedom for the Dutch Reformed religion had been one of the motivating forces for the revolt against Spain and the consequent formation of the Union of Utrecht, it came to pass that Dutch sentiment desired a stronger religious bond among the "allies" than is produced by a mere declaration of provincial autonomy. Unfortunately, by the time that sentiment arose, there had already been a schism within the Dutch Reformed Church.

The natural result of these developments was purges within churches and attendant political conflict. They began in 1608, with a purge of five ministers from their pulpits by the organized ministry in Alkmaar, backed by the North Holland Synod. By 1609, the States of Holland and the stadholder of Holland, Maurits of Orange, had lined up respectively on opposed sides of the conflict. The former—aligned with more liberal elements known as Arminians, later Remonstrants—canceled the purge; the latter then used his stadholder prerogative to select pro-purge—the more orthodox, Gomarist, later called Counter-Remonstrant—Alkmaar city council members from the double list of nominees in the town of Alkmaar. The Arminian civic militia in the town then seized the town hall and demanded removal of these Gomarist city council members. The Holland advocate, Oldenbarnevelt, then intervened (in violation of the stadholder's well-established prerogatives) and removed those city council members.[50]

As the truce of 1609–21 with Spain took effect, the unifying force of a common enemy was lost to the United Provinces, and adherents of the

Dutch Reformed faith then set upon each other to a degree that caused upheaval all over the land and by 1619 toppled the leader of the government (Advocate Oldenbarnevelt). Conflicts like the one at Alkmaar, but spreading to include use of Generality troops to put down mob takeovers or civic militia takeovers, spread to Utrecht, Friesland, Overijssel, and Gelderland (only Zeeland and Groningen remained religiously unified, solidly Gomarist).[51]

After a number of incidents in which Generality troops stationed near Holland's cities refused to take up arms to put down mob takeovers (due to religious sympathy with the mobs), the advocate of Holland pushed through the Holland States the Sharp Resolution in August 1617 over objections from six Gomarist cities. This resolution authorized the hiring of mercenary urban troops, known as *waardgelders,* by those city governments who could not rely on their own civic militias to keep order. (The Generality army, like most armies of the era, was also largely composed of mercenary troops).[52] The resolution declared further that units of the Generality Army stationed in Holland owed primary allegiance to the provincial States (claimed to be the true sovereign) rather than to the States General.[53]

The Union of Utrecht had simply said (in Article 7) that the soldiers of the United Provinces were to swear loyalty to the United Provinces and to the town and province where they were stationed, dodging any possible question of conflict of interest. The same article also stipulated that they were to be paid by the United Provinces; and Article 3 stated that decisions of when to defend against violence "shall rest with the confederation as a whole."[54] Prior to the Sharp Resolution no serious question had arisen over whether the army was a provincial rather than a Generality institution (although, once raised, the issue did not disappear with the calming of the religious crisis). Supervision of the military was shared among the Council of State, the States General, and the commanding officer, who was the stadholder of Holland when Holland had one, and who most of the time had the official rank of captain-general. Each regiment was on the payroll of one or another province (although the Generality stepped in to make up for shortfalls), and the provincial and city governments were responsible for troop recruitment. In addition, provincial governments were accorded certain mid-level officer appointments for the troops they paid and responsibility for troop discipline within their own territory. Usually but not always, the troops funded by a given province were also stationed in it.[55] Despite this decentralized administration, the Generality military did answer, starting in the 1590s, to a single High Military Court on disciplinary issues, a court that was a Generality, not a provincial, body.[56]

The Sharp Resolution prompted an immediate public condemnation from the stadholder and Generality military commander, Maurits of Orange, who labeled it "an affront to the true Reformed religion and our person." Cities throughout Utrecht and Holland, relying on the Resolution, hired *waardgelders,* who clashed with mobs and civic militias. Stadholder Maurits carried out a purge of the Arminians in one of the cities in Gelderland.[57]

Maurits also gave speeches in Gelderland and Overijssel calling for disbandment of the *waardgelders* and a National Synod to settle the religious divisions. By May 1618 five of the seven provinces—all but Holland and Utrecht—had voted in the States General for the National Synod. The Arminian group in Holland, led by Hugo Grotius, argued that a National Synod was inappropriate because in religion each province was fully sovereign; moreover, each province also had a duty to maintain internal order, which duty could be met by *waardgelders* and was no interference with support for the Generality army. Maurits's counterargument, presented at the States of Overijssel in May 1618, acknowledged that the provinces retained much sovereignty in religious matters but insisted that if an issue were splitting the union, then it fell into the jurisdiction of the States General "as representing the highest government of the United Netherlands by whose authority all differences and difficulties of importance over the last thirty years have been settled." In June 1618 the States General voted 5–2 that, since all military and defense matters fell under Generality authority, the *waardgelders* had to be dismissed.

At this point, Holland's Advocate Oldenbarnevelt (who had been the uncontested political leader of the United Netherlands until the religious turmoil had burst open after the Truce) sent his two close allies, Grotius and Hogerbeets, to head what they called a Holland delegation, but which represented only a minority of Holland towns. This delegation had the assignment of instructing army units in Utrecht that their first obligation was to the province that paid them—Holland—and that if there were a clash of authority they must follow Holland, rather than the States General and the stadholder (their commanding officer). (The other Holland cities sent a counter-deputation to assure the soldiers that their pay would not be cut off if they obeyed their commander, the stadholder.) This incident was the foundation of the later arrest and trial of Oldenbarnevelt, Grotius, and Hogerbeets on treason charges.[58]

Maurits then marched Generality troops into Utrecht, disbanded the *waardgelders,* and purged all the Arminian officials, replacing them with Gomarists. These new representatives of Utrecht then voted at the States General in favor of a National Synod. Holland's Arminian towns gave in and disbanded their *waardgelders;* led by Oldenbarnevelt and Grotius, Holland finally agreed to the National Synod. Maurits continued to press his advantage, pushing through the States General a secret resolution authorizing Maurits and a Generality commission to investigate the recent actions in Utrecht and Holland subversive of the union and to take actions necessary for the republic's security. Acting on this (at the time unprecedented) authority, Maurits proceeded on behalf of the Generality to arrest Oldenbarnevelt, Grotius, Hogerbeets, and the advocate of Utrecht.[59] Maurits then carried out purges of Arminians throughout the Dutch Republic. Once the government had been cleansed of all but Orangists, a special court was convened—twelve Holland judges and two each from the six other provinces, to try the former leaders now accused as traitors. Oldenbarnevelt, Grotius, and Hogerbeets were all found guilty of treason, and Oldenbarnevelt was executed; the others were imprisoned.[60]

In the middle of the seventeenth century the Gomarist/Counter-Remonstrant versus Arminian/Remonstrant split was superseded (and in a sense continued) by the (orthodox) Voetian versus the (liberal) Cocceian rift in the Dutch Reformed Church. This rift smoldered more or less quietly, dealt with by provincial government, city governments, and regional church authorities.[61]

However, political conflict over religion did erupt again in 1663 when the Holland States decreed that all Dutch Reformed prayers for the government (a standard part of the service) should eliminate references to the Prince of Orange (at this time, age thirteen, he held no office in the province) or House of Orange, and should mention the States of Holland first, "our lawful, supreme government" and "the unquestioned sovereign." The allied provinces should be mentioned second and the States General only third, for it was not the supreme government, and should not be so described in prayers. The Friesland States condemned this action, quoting Holland's own words of 1621 to the effect that "supremacy and sovereignty in the United Netherlands reside incontestably in the States General and the States of the separate provinces." Friesland demanded, and instructed its States General delegation to demand, that Holland rescind its prayer formula, because the States General was the "highest and sovereign authority over all the United Provinces." The States of Zeeland would not come forth with an outright condemnation of Holland, instead producing a statement that although the provinces have "composed themselves as if they were one body, one state, one government, and one republic," they have done so "without, however, abdicating from their right of sovereignty." Nonetheless, they have assigned the "noblest and most essential parts of sovereignty" to the Generality. Gelderland did join Friesland's condemnation of Holland's measure. Holland's pensionary (and leader of the Dutch Republic) De Witt insisted that each province was sovereign over its own territory and people, and the States General was sovereign over only the Generality Lands. This religiously linked sovereignty dispute continued to rage in pamphlets for the rest of 1663, but then the attention of governmental authorities was captured by the problem of war with England.[62]

Military Troop Numbers and Sovereignty

The clarity of the Union of Utrecht in according control over religion to provincial level government did not prove adequate for preventing Generality level intervention into religious conflict when that conflict was perceived as disrupting the unity of the Dutch Republic. Similarly, the evident allocation in the union document of defense policy to confederation-level authority also failed to prevent central versus provincial conflict over troop size.

Article 8 of the Union of Utrecht provided for a draft of all Dutch adult males into the Generality army, as well as Generality funding of the army. The draft was never implemented.[63] Instead, the States General, guided by the Council of State, assigned the number and size of troops to be recruited and paid by each province on an annual basis.[64] Since foreign diplomacy was a power reserved to the Generality, and since foreign alliances typically contained specifications of troop commitments, the Generality logically had to be the locus of decisions on troop numbers. However, since each province footed the bill for the troops allocated to its piece of the budget, provinces and sometimes even city governments felt powerful economic incentives to advocate troop reductions. When such advocacy failed at the States General, the temptation was sometimes overwhelming, in the face of inability to collect taxes or distress at burgeoning debt levels, to dismiss soldiers even without central authorization, in order to avoid paying future salaries.

On several occasions prior to 1649, such actions merely provoked warnings, scoldings, or countermands from the Council of State (the Generality body that administered taxation and military matters and advised the States General as to the annual budget needed) and condemnation at the States General. In 1623 both Overijssel and the Gelderland quarter Zutphen were warned that their unilateral troop reductions violated the Union of Utrecht. In 1626 Zeeland issued an order reducing troops by 100 men, which provoked a similar rebuke from the Council of State. Friesland, which suffered chronic difficulties from massive tax revolts, in 1630 disbanded eight of its companies, and in 1634 dismissed additional soldiers. These Frisian actions stimulated agitated debate in the States General (and the eventual, extraordinary action by the Council of State, described above, raising taxes in Friesland). Similar scoldings for similar actions were administered from the Council of State to the Gelderland quarter of Arnhem (or Veluwe) in 1643. On each of these occasions the message from the Generality bodies was unequivocal: these troops belonged to the Generality, not the province, and such measures intolerably violated "the spirit of the Union."[65]

In 1640 Amsterdam simply refused to pay several of the companies assigned to it, which forced the Generality to come up with the funds.[66] Amsterdam was not just another city; it contained a quarter of the wealth in Holland, which in turn was paying nearly 60 percent of the tax bills for the Dutch Republic. This means that the revenues from Amsterdam alone were equal to or greater than the revenues from any two of the five smallest provinces.[67]

This move by Amsterdam was the beginning of a decade-long struggle, during which (1) Holland, led by the Amsterdam delegates, insistently promoted reductions in troop numbers (as the war with Spain was winding down and Holland had a huge public debt), (2) the captain-general (and stadholder of six provinces, including Holland), Prince William II of Orange, argued for a slower rate of reduction, and (3) the Council of State and States General accepted some compromise. (Prince William II had acceded to his title and the captain-generalship when his father, Frederick Henry, died.) Between 1642 and 1648, the troops of the Dutch Republic were reduced from over 70,000 to 35,150. But Holland pushed for even greater cuts.[68]

As negotiations on the subject continued, Holland in October 1649 simply ordered the dismissal of 585 soldiers. The captain-general then countermanded the order and prevailed. Negotiations continued, but in May 1650, the States General gave up hope of further compromise and voted 6–1 with the captain-general's (and six-province-stadholder's) preference as to army size. (A cousin of Prince William II, Count William Frederick, was stadholder of the seventh, Friesland; he served as Lieutenant

General and was closely allied with William II.) On June 1, the Holland States, led by Amsterdam, voted to cut their troops below the States General allocation. On June 5, the two stadholders and the Council of State informed the States General that they would warn commanders not to permit discharge of troops without orders from them, and successfully requested that similar instructions be issued by the States General.[69]

The States General then acceded in a 5–2 vote to William II's request that he be authorized to lead a deputation to each of the eleven cities of Holland that had voted for the troop cuts, in order to persuade them to change their vote. They instructed him to maintain the preservation of the union against any efforts to undermine it. Holland protested that this violated normal procedures and interfered with their provincial autonomy.[70]

The stadholder/prince's 400-person deputation did not get very far. When the third city he visited, Amsterdam, refused to admit his deputation, since Holland had voted against it, and refused to let him give his speech, he abandoned his multicity visitation project.[71]

Holland offered a compromise that was within 350 soldiers of the number the prince wanted, but he determined that the union needed a clear assertion of Generality sovereignty over the military. So on July 30, 1650, he arrested the six leaders of the opposition in the Holland States while his cousin, Count William Frederick, surrounded Amsterdam with twelve thousand troops. The prince then traveled to Amsterdam and on August 2 received from the city council an agreement that Andrew and Cornelis Bicker (the leading anti-Orangists) would be removed and henceforth barred from political office, and that Amsterdam would vote for having Holland support the military budget desired by the other six provinces (for at least the next four years). On July 13 the entire Holland States attended the States General meeting and accepted the July 15 Council of State budget. Moreover, they agreed to the States General's proclamation that henceforth any province that unilaterally tried to reduce the army size would be in violation of the Union of Utrecht and liable to corrective action. The six prisoners of the prince were released upon their promise thenceforth to stay out of public office.[72]

The Dutch union of the seventeenth century was most concretely unified in the fact that its army had a unitary command structure, headed by the captain-general. The unitary nature of the army was not compatible with actual provincial autonomy or "sovereignty" over taxes, since more than 80 percent of the Dutch Republic's budget went toward military purposes.[73] This conflict over control of the decision as to army size in 1648–

50 lays bare the largely fictional nature of the maxim that the provinces retained sovereignty over taxation, the maxim on which Holland's case in this matter rested. That it may appear fictional in a post hoc analysis, however, does not prove that Holland's leaders were anything other than sincere in putting forth the claim.[74]

DUTCH PROVINCIAL RESISTANCE TO CENTRAL AUTHORITY IN COMPARATIVE FOCUS

Caveats

A number of caveats must preface any attempt to compare the Dutch union of the seventeenth century to nineteenth- or twentieth-century unions of states. This study purports to examine formerly sovereign states that join federal unions, but one could plausibly object that the Dutch provinces comprising the seventeenth-century union had never been sovereign states in the modern sense (indeed, that the modern conception of sovereignty had not even gelled by the time of the Union of Utrecht in 1579). It is true that, prior to and during a substantial portion of the revolt against Philip II of Spain, the provinces had been principalities or bishoprics that understood themselves to owe obligations of suzerainty to one or another Hapsburg emperor. On the other hand, under that suzerainty each of the provinces was essentially free of the control of the others, and probably thought of itself as free to control its local affairs in much the same manner as eighteenth-century American-British colonies did. As with those colonies during the later American Revolution, each of the Dutch provinces during their revolt felt itself individually free to sign onto the Union of Utrecht, in effect joining that union as an act of a free sovereign agent.

This said, it is nonetheless appropriate to concede that, to a significant degree, the understanding of sovereignty in the Dutch Republic was the medieval or feudal, rather than the modern state-focused, version.[75] Rather than emphasizing a top-down scheme in which government exercises authority over people, instead the Dutch conception of sovereignty featured a complex network of privileges and corresponding responsibilities among subject/citizens and authorities. There is much validity in this description, as there is, too, in E. H. Kossman's argument that this century was precisely a time of dramatic transition in the concept of what a sovereign is. It evolved between the 1570s and the 1690s from a sense that the sovereign is the holder of power/authority to enforce law—a "law" that is assumed to be known or knowable to all reasonable persons and is comprised of age-old customs that include recognition of what is right by nature—to the more pro-active belief that the sovereign is the wielder of power to make rules that will foster public well-being, rules that may improve upon rather than merely extend customary approaches.[76]

But here again, one finds an intriguing parallel with the American states. Morton Horwitz has argued that the American understanding of the societal role and meaning of law underwent a parallel evolution in the years 1780–1860, the very period in which those American states went from what was arguably a stage of relatively loose confederation in which the locus of sovereignty remained chronically contested (albeit simultaneously widely acknowledged) to a post–Civil War federal union whose central authority was finally accepted.[77]

Analysis of Propositions

In terms of the relative degree of resistance to central federal authority in the Dutch union as compared to the American and European unions, the fact that the claim of legitimacy for a provincial veto power was essentially continual throughout the century puts the Dutch union at one end of the scale in terms of member-state formal resistance to the legitimate authority of the central power in the federal union. This outcome renders the Dutch case useful for assessing certain propositions about the European Union put forth by other scholars.

Three such propositions suggested to explain the relative absence of member-state resistance in Europe to powerfully centralizing actions by the European Court of Justice really are not sensibly applicable to the Dutch case. The first of these asserted that the growth of an (influential) transstate interest group with a stake in the enhancement of federal authority will make state resistance to such authority less likely. One can identify groups of people whose objective interest was fostered by federal union in the Dutch Republic, and these groups wielded considerable political clout—the merchant class of Holland and Zeeland, the nobility of the inland provinces, and the federal army and navy. Nonetheless, one should refrain from trying to apply the transstate interest group hypothesis to these groupings because the Dutch polity did not clearly separate interest group membership from government membership. To be a leader among the wealthy merchants was to be a member of the local oligarchies from whom members of the provincial estates were selected (and from whom in turn the membership of the federal estates was selected). The nobility were officers in the military. Thus the term "interest group," because it implies a group outside the government trying to influence the government, is anachronistic with respect to the Dutch Republic. While there did exist in the Dutch federation transstate factional groupings, their subjectively expressed interests, in any case, tended not to align along a pro-centralization versus pro-provincial-autonomy axis, but divided rather along federation-wide lines of cleavage (peace vs. war, religious tolerance vs. religious orthodoxy, and so on). For instance, while the army (along with people whose careers were linked to the army, such as the nobility) itself was an institution of the central government and as such did have an intrinsic stake in strong federal authority, that stake did not seem to be usually conceived as federal per se; it seems rather to have been understood in terms of loyalty to the Prince of Orange, as opposed to the advocate/pensionary, or inclination toward the pro-war faction in stadholderless (non–Prince of Orange) periods.

The transstate "interest group" hypothesis, however inapplicable it may be to the nascent modern Dutch state, probably carries the following germ of truth with respect to the Dutch union (and the American as well): for any transstate union to form in the first place, there logically must be in it numerous influential people who perceive that their interest will be furthered by the transstate union. Otherwise, they would never bother to form the union. On the other hand, the existence of influential persons with both an objective and subjective interest in federal union in neither the Dutch Republic nor the American sufficed to prevent chronic province- or state-level resistance to central authority in those unions, after the union had formed.

The argument of Burley and Mattli[78] and Stuart Scheingold[79] that stresses the importance of deliberate fostering (by organs of central authority) of such subjective pro-federation consciousness among legal and judicial elites—in a manner geared to create such transstate interest groups—is also a proposition not, strictly speaking, challengeable with the Dutch example, any more than it was with the American one. This is because such a campaign did not take place in either of the earlier unions. On the other hand, the Dutch desire to have a uniform state religion to bind together the nation (although in practice it foundered on schisms within the church) seems to indicate, at least at the theoretical level, an appreciation of this proposition (as do the various conscious efforts to nurture patriotism that were launched in the early United States).

And the third proposition not testable with the Dutch case is the description (from Chapter 2) of the consequences, in modern representative democracies, of preference gaps between the citizenry (on the one hand)

and (on the other hand) accountable and nonaccountable elites. The Dutch so-called republic, by contrast, was run by self-perpetuating oligarchies without institutionalized governmental mechanisms that held them accountable to the rest of society. (Essentially, rioting developed as the primary mechanism for expressing popular dissatisfaction with government policies.) Thus, this proposition cannot be tested by the Dutch case.

One proposition in the European Union literature that can be tested by the Dutch case fails to hold up. Certain scholars have asserted that as some states within the union acknowledge the legitimacy of central authority, their example influences others to follow suit. While the EC may have exhibited this pattern, neither the early United States nor the Dutch union did. In both of the earlier instances of union, states argued variously for and against the legitimacy of central authority, depending on their interests in particular cases. A given state or province did not necessarily maintain consistency in claims about the locus of sovereignty from one issue to another or from one year to another. Thus, one can discern no pattern of unidirectional pro-federation cross-state imitation.

The comparison of the American and European Unions, and a reflection on the fate of the earlier American Confederation, led in Chapter 2 to the hypothesis that there seems to be an optimum level of confederalness—or what could be called Calhounism—for a federation. Giving a real veto power to each member state would presumably lead to paralysis, fear of which evidently pushed would-be reformers of the American Confederation to take the revolutionary step of ignoring their own veto power rule in adopting ratification procedures for the new 1787 Constitution. On the other hand, the European Union institutions present a number of features that cause authoritative decisions to look either unanimous or widely consensual, and these features seem to have helped reduce the level of member-state resistance to central authority. In the seventeenth-century Dutch federation, one encounters a peculiar situation: official lip service was paid to the rule that member states (provinces) did have a veto power over several categories of union decision. That is, the provincial officials trying to get their way against a majority would proclaim the rule. Moreover, it was "paid lip service" in the sense that officials within the majority took seriously the need to build the largest attainable consensus. In this sense, announcement of the maxim of provincial veto worked as a spur to push negotiators to work harder to extend the consensus. Still, the operative norm in fact was that union decisions would be made in accord with maximum feasible consensus rather than

unanimity. Because this was the uniformly operative norm, province insistence on the "official" line, namely that the province's veto was being
illegitimately transgressed, takes on the form—for the analytic project of
the comparison here—of official state resistance to central federation authority, and such resistance was chronic in the Dutch Republic. Basing decisions on the maximum feasible consensus goes about as far in the direction of a single-state veto power that any federation can go short of
utter paralysis, and the Dutch federation could not afford paralysis because it was at war for most of the century. The ability to act was literally
a life and death matter. The Dutch example thus seems to exemplify the
outer limits of the proposition about some optimum level of Calhounesque (or confederal) institutional features. Such confederal features
as giving equal voting powers to member states and making central decisions that appear to reflect consensus (as in the ECJ) do seem to minimize
member-state resistance. Beyond that point, the norm of legitimacy of
member-state veto can become so powerful that it produces chronic state
resistance to actions by central federation authorities. In the situation of
the EC/EU, the French Conseil d'État by the early 1990s gave up its insistence on the power to nullify ECJ decisions within its jurisdiction, not
long after the diplomatic organs of the French government had agreed in
the Single European Act that a new system of consensual ("weighted")
voting would replace the member-state veto that had been until then the
practice on the Council of Ministers.

On the other hand, some propositions derived from the observation of
differences between the European and American unions do appear to be
supported by this examination of the Dutch case. The first of those hypotheses asserts that unions that are formed—as occurred both in North
America and the Netherlands—by way of united rebellion on behalf of
local privileges against distant central authority will be more likely to have
difficulties avoiding state-level challenges to the legitimacy of union-level
decisions. Such challenges were chronic in the Dutch Republic.

Another of these difference-based propositions asserted that in societies where obedience to bureaucratic governmental authority is less routinized in general, state-level protests against the legitimacy of central
government authorities are more to be expected than in more fully mod-
ernized societies. The Dutch union might be put forth as a paradigmatic
example of this proposition. While the Dutch Republic is often described
as relatively law-abiding, peaceful, and stable compared to other seventeenth-century European societies,[80] in fact urban riots erupted repeatedly and a few of the lesser provinces underwent years on end with no

clearly established governmental authority at the provincial level, due to violent factional disputes.

Third, the analysis in Chapter 2 of Euro-American contrasts produced the proposition that integration will proceed more smoothly (other things being equal) if province-level officials have personal power incentives to foster integration of the union. Since both the Prince of Orange, who was the stadholder in several of the provinces, and the pensionary of the single province of Holland alternately led the Dutch union, it is clear that each increased his power by enhancing union strength. Indeed, without their respective leadership it is doubtful that the union could have held together as long as it did. One can conclude that the Dutch union offers at least partial support for this proposition. However, there were occasions for each leader when his personal policy preference conflicted with the will of overwhelming sentiment within the union policy-making body, the States General, on which occasions the leader in question was not above reverting to province-level power for support in resisting the trend. In those instances "strongly integrated union" translated into a loss of personal power for the provincial leader in question.

Roughly parallel situations have been observed with respect to the European Court of Justice. While that court's doctrine did empower lower-court judges in all the member states, giving them new powers of judicial review and thus encouraging their adherence to ECJ doctrine, Daniel Wincott has pointed out that one can view the decision of the German Constitutional Court (and, one might add, the Italian) on "fundamental rights" as the reverse situation. Here the member-state courts perceived a potential loss to their own prerogatives and therefore announced, in effect, that if the ECJ transgresses the fundamental rights of their state's citizens, then the constitutional court will have to overrule it.[81] Similarly, Jonathan Golub has pointed out that member-state officialdom has other kinds of incentives besides power-in-the-abstract—for instance, the securing of their own policy preferences. Thus, he has noticed differential rates across the various European member states for judicial willingness to submit cases to the ECJ, and he hypothesizes that the difference is due to the fact that some national judiciaries, particularly the British, are deliberately choosing this path because their policy preferences tend to differ from those of the ECJ.[82]

While judicial empowerment, especially as to lower-court judges of the EC/EU, constituted a dominant positive incentive that pushed member-state acceptance of central union authority, the Dutch case offers a forceful reminder that power incentives can push in either a centripetal or a centrifugal direction—for which some scholars have already begun to observe evidence in the EC/EU situation.[83] If the Dutch example is to prove instructive as to the intrinsic limits of this judicial empowerment proposition, defiance at the state level from judges in Europe will eventually be forthcoming if particular EU level decisions clash sharply with particular policy preferences of member-state judges.

In sum, the examination here of propositions derived from a comparison of the European Community and the early-nineteenth-century American union has reinforced the idea of an intrinsic limit for one of them, suggested a limit on another, and offered support for some others (see Table 5). There appears to be a definite limit beyond which Calhounesque, or more extremely confederal, features in a federation prove counterproductive, and, instead of engendering the absence of member-state resistance, end up fostering it. Likewise, providing institutional power incentives for state-level officials to bring about more cooperation with union-level decisions can work up to a point, but seem to lose effectiveness if those union-level decisions turn against the power of the official in question.

On the other hand, the Holland case strengthened the United States–based critique of one proposition about Europe found in the literature: the one on cross-state imitative influence. And it lent support to two propositions: (1) unions formed via colonial-type rebellion are likely to experience later member-state resistance, and (2) federations in societies with less routinized obedience to governmental authority are more likely to experience official governmental resistance at the state level to governmental authority at the union level.

Lastly, one must address an important contrast, with the European and American situations. The Dutch union lacked a separate federal judiciary able to claim interpretive authority for determining the rules of union and locating their bounds on federal or provincial authority. According to Article 21 of the formal document that initiated the Dutch union, issues that turned on interpretation of the Union of Utrecht document were to be settled by "general advice and consent" of the "allies" (the provinces). In practice this meant that the States General or a committee thereof would convene itself as a court of high appeal for questions that could not be settled at the provincial level.[84] However, Article 21 stipulated that when an absence of agreement among the provinces made one necessary, the final decision would be rendered by an authority composed of the stadholders or their appointees. But in fact such a quasi-judicial interpretive role for the stadholders-as-a-group or their delegates never came to be clearly es-

Table 5. The Dutch Union as Test for Hypotheses on State Resistance

Hypothesis	Confirmed	Disconfirmed	Not Applicable
Unions that appear to require unanimity from member states experience less member-state resistance to union authority.		X	
Presence of influential transstate interest group(s) who benefit from union makes resistance less likely.			X
Indoctrination campaign aimed at creating such an interest group can minimize state resistance.			X
After a preponderate portion of states have accepted union authority, state resistance from others will cease.		X	
Unions formed by united rebellion against a distant imperial power will tend to experience member-state resistance.	X		
Unions where obedience to the rule of law is less routinized will tend to experience member-state resistance to union authority.	X		
Systems in which democratically accountable elites can hand off unpopular decisions to nonaccountable elites will experience less member-state resistance.			X

(continued)

Table 5. (*continued*)

Hypothesis	Confirmed	Disconfirmed	Not Applicable
If certain member-state elites have institutionally based power incentives to uphold union authority, there will be less member-state resistance.	?	?	
If union-integrating decisions are handed down by "judges," rather than "politicians," there will be less member-state resistance.	X		

tablished. As in the later Swiss federation, high judicial authority was wielded from time to time by the union legislative body. Since this high judicial function was not separated off into an ostensibly nonpolitical body in either of the two unions, if they both proved markedly less cooperative toward federal authority than the American and European cases, that would support the argument (by Weiler et al.) about the importance of the nonpolitical "pure" image that courts of law retain. This argument will therefore be reexamined in the next chapter.

CHAPTER 4

The First Half-Century of the
Modern Swiss Federation

Numerous scholars, whether interested in the general question of what makes for a successful federation or the specific question of garnering lessons to enhance the success of the European Community, have pointed out the utility of examining the history and institutional structure of the Swiss federation.[1] None, however, has examined in any detail the question of the degree and nature of early state resistance to federal authority within that union. This chapter attempts to do just that, and to utilize the resistance pattern uncovered in nineteenth-century Switzerland as an additional test case for the propositions developed and analyzed in the preceding chapters.

INSTITUTIONAL STRUCTURE OF THE SWISS UNION

While the Swiss federation traces its roots to an oath fellowship among three German-speaking cantons for defensive purposes in the thirteenth century,[2] the twenty-two cantons that make up the foundation of modern Switzerland (plus the addition of a twenty-third in 1978–79) did not form an effective, voluntary federal union until 1848.[3] The first five decades of this union constitute an epoch more or less comparable to the early formative decades of the other voluntary federal unions examined in this study. (Of the original twenty-two cantons, three are divided into so-called half-cantons—Rhodes-Appenzell, divided into Interior and Exterior; Basel, divided into City and Country; and Unterwald, divided into Nidwald and Obwald—each of which has its own cantonal government and gets only one voting representative on the legislative chamber, the Council of States, as contrasted with two voting representatives for each full canton. This arrangement means that there were a total of 25 member-state units in the (1848–98) Swiss union examined here.)

Between 1291 and 1798, the Swiss cantons formed a variety of what were in effect international alliances with each other, waging war against one another on several occasions. In 1798, Napoleon imposed a unitary and democratic state on the Swiss. Even the French soon realized that the Swiss were not comfortable with the arrangement, and by 1803 replaced it with the "Mediation Constitution," a return to a confederacy of the cantons, but one with strong central powers. Once the Swiss were able to throw off French power, with the help of the Congress of Vienna in 1815, the Swiss reestablished, in the words of Swiss political scientist Wolf Linder, "a loose confederation of twenty-five independent cantons, who considered themselves sovereign states."[4] This confederation broke down in a twenty-six-day intraconfederation war in 1847 between the Catholic and Protestant cantons. Following the war, the Constitution of 1848 was successfully ratified.[5] Although not every canton voted for ratification,[6] each did choose to participate once the 1848 federal union had formed, much as in the United States upon ratification of the 1787 Constitution.[7]

The 1848 Constitution (which formed the foundation of the 1874 Constitution that continued until April 1999, and which in turn was the basis of the contemporary constitution) took the basic shape of its legislature from the American example. One legislative chamber, the Council of States, gives two voting representatives to each canton; the National Council bases representation of each canton on its population size. Unlike the American system, the Swiss do not have a unitary chief executive, but have an executive council of seven, the Federal Council, selected from the Federal Assembly (in a joint session after it has been elected) for four-year renewable terms. Within the Federal Council, the role of presiding officer rotates annually. The Swiss supreme court, the Federal Tribunal, does not engage in judicial review of federal legislation; the word of the Federal Assembly as to the constitutionality of its own measures is law. (It is possible, however, for a federal law to be, in effect, vetoed by popular referendum if such a referendum is requested by 50,000 citizens within ninety days of the passage of the law). On the other hand, each of the three federal-level bodies (the Federal Assembly, the Federal Council, and the Federal Tribunal), in varying contexts, has the authority to strike down a cantonal level measure as a violation of federal-level law.

These specific contexts were altered from the 1848 to the 1874 Constitution, and occasionally thereafter (e.g., 1893 and 1911), in the general direction of expanded jurisdiction, political independence, professionalization, and permanence for the Federal Tribunal. The 1848 Constitution greatly restricted its jurisdiction, leaving the vast majority of challenges to cantonal law to be settled by the executive body, the Federal Council, with appeal available to the Federal Assembly (where only a majority in both houses would be sufficient to overturn a Federal Council decision). After 1874, the Federal Tribunal became a body of full-time professional judges, housed in its own building, with original jurisdiction in all public law cases presenting conflicts between the Confederation and cantons or among the latter, and also the power to judge allegations of violations of constitutional (federal or cantonal) rights of citizens. Its judges are chosen to six-year, renewable terms by members of the Federal Assembly, but as a matter of custom the Tribunal is considered politically independent and the terms are virtually always renewed until retirement.[8] Even after the expansion of the jurisdiction of the Tribunal in 1874, however, because of the Federal Council's role as enforcer of federal law, and because of the Federal Assembly's role in deciding the constitutionality of its own statutes, these two bodies continued to exercise significant influence in challenges to cantonal laws (as conflicting with federal law). Any of the three in a specific incident (depending on the category into which such incident was placed by federal legislation and/or by constitutional interpretation) might impose limits on the exercise of cantonal power, and thus cantonal governments had opportunities to resist the authority of any of them.[9]

PATTERNS OF CANTONAL-FEDERAL RELATIONS

In contrast to the early United States, one does not find in the early decades of the Swiss Confederation repeated instances of cantonal governments openly and formally denying the sovereign authority over them of the confederation. The 1848 Constitution did face an initial, short-lived legitimacy challenge from one of the whole cantons, Uri, and from two of the half-cantons, Nidwald and Obwald. The Pact of 1815, entered into by all the cantons, contained a unanimity rule for any changes to it, as had the American Articles of Confederation. And, much as the U.S. Constitutional Convention decided that a unanimity rule for state ratification would be impractical, settling instead on a two-thirds rule, so the Swiss Diet decided (with sixteen and a half votes out of twenty-two) to declare the Pact officially replaced by the 1848 Constitution as of September 12, 1848, after the latter had been approved in fifteen and a half cantons containing 1.9 million residents and rejected in cantons containing only

300,000. This procedure did in fact violate the Pact rules, and the popular assemblies, or *"Landsgemeinde,"* of Nidwald, Obwald, and Uri so protested at the time of the election for the first Federal Assembly in October. They sent their delegates to Berne with the expressed reservations that the new constitutional system was invalid. The Federal Assembly retaliated by refusing to accept the election of these delegates as valid until they could be sent without reservations. The dissenting cantons then decided to designate their deputies without conditions, much as Rhode Island and North Carolina decided to cooperate in the American union after it had started without them.[10] After these initial months, for the next half-century the cantonal governmental authorities accepted the legitimacy of federal rule, with a single exception on the part of Ticino authorities in 1884, which is discussed in further detail below.

The stark contrast between the American states' repeated willingness to challenge the legitimacy of federal authority and the rarity of such challenges under the first several decades of the Swiss constitution perhaps stems from the fact that the Swiss constitution (in contrast to the American) followed upon the heels of, rather than preceded, the Swiss "civil war."[11] With the war among the cantons a living memory, to persist in denying the authority of the central authorities *tout court* may have appeared unthinkably reckless.

Instead of frequent open denials of the legitimacy of central authority, what one finds in the early history of the modern Swiss Confederation is a pattern of resistance to the center by cantonal governments that is best described as, on the whole, discreet and polite, but not entirely passive either. A deliberate willingness to cross central authorities is in fact evident, but one finds it cloaked typically in the language of legalistic appeals and face-saving gestures. Rather than deny outright federal authority to judge the extent of cantonal powers, a canton might instead, for instance, appeal to one federal authority on the grounds that another federal authority had erred in exceeding its jurisdiction and was treading on grounds that were covered by cantonal "sovereignty," mounting one appeal after another and all the while defying federal policy. Another version of cantonal resistance that cropped up repeatedly was that one level of cantonal authority—say, the executive council—might tell federal authorities that it was doing all in its power to comply with federal policy while at the same time a different level of cantonal authority—the constituent power of the people themselves—was continuing to resist federal law.

This cloak of legalistic "politesse" perhaps explains the divergence one finds between the typical textbook picture of essentially "peaceful constitutional development in Switzerland after 1848,"[12] on the one hand, and, on the other, the more or less chronic pattern of repeated episodes of cantonal resistance to federal rules that shows up in the records of the *Feuille Fédérale,* the Swiss analogue to the *U.S. Congressional Record.* In the textbook image, the pattern of cantonal acceptance and respect for federal authority was all but constant. In the period of this study (1848–c.1898), it was marred only by a single instance where cantonal resistance to federal authority was so intransigent as to provoke the latter to threaten the application of military force (in the canton of Ticino in 1884)[13] and by a coup of one day's duration in the canton of Neuchâtel. There, the victorious-for-a-day royalists really did reject Confederation authority out of a desire to belong to the Kingdom of Prussia, only to be quickly overtaken by the militia of the legitimate cantonal government.[14]

In stark contrast to this image of peaceful cantonal-federal relations broken only by rare and isolated instances of resistance to the center by cantonal authorities, one reads the following passage from the *Feuille Fédérale:*

> From the time the Federal Constitution went into effect, appeals should have been [expected to be] numerous, and they have been. On political subjects the battle of cantonal sovereignty against the centralizing ideas that were in part realized by our new Constitution, political passions violating constitutional guarantees and shielding themselves by them in turn, have demanded frequent intervention of federal power. [Federal] intervention has been invoked even more often on matters of private law; plaintiffs like to exhaust the jurisdictions and nothing seems to stop them, as long as a means of appeal is available. The antecedents, habits, and the diverse spirit of [the variety of cantonal and local] legislation led to continual clashes. It was difficult for judicial cantonal authorities to suddenly forget the plenitude of jurisdiction with which they had been invested before 1848. It was not less so for jurists to break with certain juridical principles inherent in their mores and in their breed in order to obey other principles in order to bend to other forms. Even resistance on the part of citizens [is evident,] where one finds always and everywhere defiance of a court which is not theirs and the desire to have the judge of their canton deal with all their business, [and] safeguard all their interests. In order to convince oneself of the accuracy of this picture, it suffices to read the accounts by the Federal Council and to analyze the cases.[15]

An additional clue that all was not peaceful and cooperative in terms of the cantonal governments' respect for federal authority comes from the most heated episode of cantonal defiance of federal authority: the government of Ticino's resistance to federal orders regarding an electoral corruption dispute in 1884. The authoritative description of this affair appears in an 1889 book by C. D. Cunningham and Francis O. Adams, the British "Envoy Extraordinary and Minister Plenipotentiary" to Switzerland. While modern works that cite Adams and Cunningham on the Ticino incident offer that incident as the lone example in the nineteenth-century union of cantonal resistance so severe as to provoke federal authorities to threaten military force and its attendant expenses, which would be visited upon the canton, the language employed by Adams and Cunningham suggests that such resistance was a more continual problem. The discussion arises in the context of an acknowledgment by the authors that if a cantonal government "declines to submit to the Federal Council's order to cancel or revoke [a cantonal measure judged unconstitutional] the latter has no direct way of enforcing its order." They continue:

> If the Canton continues refractory, [the Federal Council] can certainly send a special commissary to the spot to negotiate with the cantonal authorities, but should he be unable to settle the matter amicably, he becomes powerless. The Canton, however, *generally* gives way when the Federal Council, upon the failure of the commissary, threatens to quarter troops upon it from another Canton, thus saddling the offending Canton with a heavy expense which it is prone to avoid. So the Federal Council indirectly gets its way. [Here follows the description of the 1884 Ticino incident offered as "a case in point," the language suggesting that it was one example chosen from which several were available. Adams and Cunningham then itemize a third enforcement technique.] *Another plan to which the Federal Council has had to resort when a Canton is refractory is to keep back subsidies which are to be provided for local objects out of the chest of the Confederation, and this has been found efficacious.*[16] (emphasis added)

Indeed, while threats of military force from the central government are virtually never employed, modern Switzerland even in the late twentieth century continues to witness occasions of deliberate resistance by cantonal governments against federal governmental authority, despite the official, formal adherence since 1848 to the rule that "federal law breaks cantonal law."[17] In describing the contemporary Swiss political culture of federalism, political scientist Wolf Linder identifies a number of attributes that one can discern even in the early decades of the federation: "Official relations between the federation and the cantons [are] very delicate. Federal authorities deal with the cantons with almost as much respect as they deal with foreign states. . . . The belief of Swiss political culture that it is better to refrain both from coercive power and from direct confrontation between cantonal and federal authorities seems to be indestructible, at least among the political elite."[18]

The same cultural pattern of avoidance of direct coercive confrontations between federal and cantonal authorities pervaded the first several decades of the Swiss union. This goes a long way toward explaining the coexistence of, on the one hand, accounts of "peaceful" cantonal-federal relations, and, on the other, an image of frequent episodes of defiance by cantonal authorities of particular federal laws ("continual clashes," in the words of the *Feuille Fédérale* reporter). A closer look at specific instances of clashes between cantonal government and federal government during the first half-century of this union will convey some of the flavor of the Swiss style of nineteenth-century cantonal resistance that gave rise to these divergent descriptions.

These accounts of cantonal-federal clashes are offered not as a comprehensive rendering but as an account of those incidents readily available in the federal documentary records. A definitive, comprehensive tally of all incidents of late-nineteenth-century cantonal resistance has yet to be compiled from archival sources.[19] The sampling below of instances of cantonal resistance (as well as the more detailed narrative supplement to Table 6 that is presented below) thus attempts instead to convey their tone or style in the early decades of the union, a general sense of their scope, and the kind of responses they evoked from federal authorities in the period. Cantonal resistance to authoritative policies of the 1848 and 1874 Confederations presented a problem broader and deeper than the tip-of-the-iceberg picture given in the usual account of the single Ticino incident.

While a numerical comparison of the quantity of cantonal resistance with the level of member-state resistance in the European Union or the early American union will for these reasons not be possible here, one can, nonetheless, identify the types of resistance that show up in the Swiss records. In terms of the categories set forth in Chapter 1, in the Swiss union—apart from the isolated exceptions of three cantonal assertions of the illegitimacy of the initiation of the 1848 Constitution, and Ticino intransigence during the elections controversy thirty-six years later that provoked the threat of federal enforcement by military troops—one does not see repeated denials of the legitimacy of federal authority to interpret law (categories *b, d,* and *j* in Tables 1 and 2). Nor does one see the formal authorization by cantonal authorities for violent resistance to federal authority (category *f* in Table 1) or the appearance of open complicity by cantonal authorities in permitting violent resistance to federal authority (category *g* in Table 1). Nor, with the short-lived exception of the day-long coup by royalists in Neuchâtel,[20] does one see cantonal authorities threatening to secede from the union (category *h*). This group's success was so temporary that its actions do not really warrant consideration as those of the legitimate cantonal government. Instead, the cantonal defiance of federal authority that shows up in the first several decades of the union generally takes forms of cantonal adoption of policies that flatly contradict federal law—the federal law of constitutional provisions themselves (category *c*), of authoritative federal interpretations of these provisions (category *a*), and of federal decrees (*arrêtés*) to implement the provisions or the interpretations (category *e*). Of these sorts of "member-state" resistance in the early decades of the Swiss union, examples abound.

The instances of cantonal defiance vary in severity of tone. The most mild variant was a kind of surreptitious defiance. In this category, one finds the cantonal authorities purporting to be doing all in their power to comply with federal policy but without success, and with policy results that just happened to coincide with the reigning political sentiment within the canton.

More direct defiance involved the open adoption of policies directly contrary to federal law. These policies might have stayed in place through a series of appeals and negotiations lasting anywhere from two to forty years, until the cantonal authorities finally were moved to cooperate, sometimes only by outright federal constitutional amendment (which requires a majority vote of the population and simultaneously of a majority of the cantons).[21] In these mid-range defiance situations one discerns a posture of patient endurance on the part of federal authorities, marked by repeated "invitations" to cantonal authorities to mend their ways. The language of the Federal Council to cantonal authorities routinely employed the verb *"inviter"*—to invite—rather than verbs of command, such as *"ordonner"*—to order.

This pattern of patient endurance and polite invitations that characterizes the mid-range defiance situation occurred so typically that one is moved to wonder why the federal authorities only once in the nineteenth century were provoked to threaten military force to achieve cantonal compliance. That incident, which involved claims of electoral corruption and a dispute between the municipal authorities in Lugano and the cantonal authorities in Ticino in 1884, appears to have been unique in the respect that the Ticino authorities on this occasion had the audacity to deny the legitimacy of federal power to judge the bounds of cantonal power. Contrary to the face-saving rituals of legalistic appeals of which one reads in the mid-level defiance cases (e.g., presenting the question of jurisdictional competence before federal authorities for a decision), in this extreme act of defiance the cantonal authorities not only refused repeatedly to obey orders from the Federal Council and its Federal Commissary sent to negotiate a solution, but added insult to injury by "declaring their [i.e., cantonal] full competency in the matter."[22]

The next three sections of this chapter present an overview of each of these levels of cantonal defiance. They are followed by a section detailing the specific examples of these types of defiance. The chapter then concludes by utilizing the picture thereby developed to test the propositions about federal unions presented in the preceding chapters.

Surreptitious Defiance: Revolutionary Refugee Asylum

In the mildest version of resistance to federal authority—surreptitious defiance—cantonal authorities claimed they were in fact cooperating with federal demands; but their marked lack of success in carrying out the federal will, with results sympathetic to the preferences of political forces dominant in the canton, caused both contemporary and present-day analysts to conclude that the claims of cantonal-level cooperation were less than sincere. In other words, despite the window-dressing of cantonal claims of efforts to cooperate, the understanding was pervasive that cantonal governments in fact willfully obstructed federal policy.

One subject of cantonal resistance of this type was federal policy forbidding the harboring of active foreign revolutionaries. On this topic, federal authority was clearly indicated by Article 57 of the 1848 Constitution: "The Confederation has the right to send back from its territory foreigners who compromise the internal or foreign security of Switzerland."[23] Switzerland's neighbors from 1848 to the end of the century were experiencing intense revolutionary and counter-revolutionary ferment, and political passions within localized sections of Switzerland were often strongly supportive of one or another foreign movement. Thus, Switzerland offered an all-too-convenient place of refuge.

As a consequence, one reads of various federal regulations of the flow of political refugees as early as 1849, and of complaints at the federal level of imperfect compliance by the cantons throughout the decade of the 1850s. (Indeed, this pattern even antedates the official commencement of the federal constitution on September 12, 1848. In mid-August 1848 the military governor of Austrian Lombardy requested the government of Ticino to disarm the "organized bands of [Italian] refugees," several thousand strong, led by Garibaldi and reported to be waging guerrilla warfare against the Austrian government of Lombardy. The problematic activities of armed Italian revolutionaries extended also into Graubunden; both Mazzini and Garibaldi played prominent leadership roles from their base in Switzerland. Historian J. Murray Luck reports that by late August, "because of the failure of the cantonal governments in the Ticino and in the Graubunden to take any effective action against the militant refugees" and, further, because the Lombardian governor's threats of retaliation would have infringed on Swiss autonomy, the Swiss Federal Government dispatched troops to both Ticino and Graubunden to disarm the refugees and transport them to less sensitive locations).[24] Complaints from central authorities over the next decade included the following: "If emigrés refuse to subordinate their political tendencies . . . to the political interest of the Confederation, which wants to give them peaceable asylum, immediately energetic and efficacious measures toward them will be taken." And, "The complaints on defective policing of the refugees in Geneva are already [1858] of ancient date. . . . The Federal Council has already several times and in various epochs needed to send federal commissioners there, and to engage the authorities of the Canton to adopt more strict police control, in the interest of our country."[25]

Details of several episodes indicate that cantonal noncooperation was serious enough to cause major diplomatic incidents, including Austrian expulsion of several thousand Swiss residents of Lombardy, and threats of a Swiss-Austrian war that were serious enough to have provoked diplomatic intervention by France and Britain.[26] One can draw the following, admittedly speculative, conclusions from these. It appears that in the earliest years of the modern Swiss union, there were substantial numbers of people, even in cantonal and local governments in Switzerland, who felt more invested in various international revolutionary movements than in domestic politics of their own relatively new federation. As time went on, it appears that their national qua Swiss identity took a stronger hold, and consequently they became more willing to put Swiss national interest ahead of their hopes for world revolution.[27]

MID-RANGE DEFIANCE: CANTONAL POLICIES
OPENLY TRANSGRESSING FEDERAL LAW

It was not uncommon during the first half-century of the Swiss union for one or another canton to adopt policies that defied federal law openly rather than surreptitiously. Such flouting of federal law might persist for years, sometimes for decades, while the federal government repeatedly requested an alteration of the unconstitutional cantonal policy. All such measures of defiance of federal law that ended short of the threat of federal armed force might be considered a kind of "mid-range defiance." It appears that what distinguishes them from the most extreme version of defiance was a willingness on the part of cantonal authorities to acknowledge that, as between cantonal and federal levels of government, the authority to decide who decides (*"kompetenz-kompetenz,"* in the German formula) belonged to federal-level authorities. Within this mid-range category, however, one can impose appropriate subdivisions, marking intensity of resistance.

Defiance Supported by Legalistic Appeals

At the most mild level one sees cases where cantonal authorities flatly defied federal law for awhile, but when challenged were willing to present an appeal to federal authorities claiming a "conflict of competence," and were able therein to present at least a plausible legal argument that federal authorities were acting beyond their proper "competence" (i.e., constitutional range of authority). In the Swiss system, such appeals eventually ended up at the Federal Assembly itself—essentially the very branch being challenged—until after the 1874 constitutional revision, which allowed more of these cases to go to the Federal Tribunal. These appeals generally created a few years delay, during which the defiance of federal law might continue, but ultimately federal policy prevailed.

Two examples that fit this subset can be offered: a four-year dispute between Vaud and federal authorities over the location of a railroad line to run through Vaud, which culminated in six months of outright cantonal defiance in 1857,[28] and a dispute in 1875–77 between Neuchâtel and federal authorities over nonpayment of cantonal military taxes.[29] Each dispute was settled relatively quickly and involved at least a semi-plausible legal argument, sufficient for mounting a formal appeal against federal policy, an appeal that was treated seriously at the federal level. On the other hand, both of them exhibit cantonal resistance to federal policy that is more deliberate and formal than mere noncompliance in the "foot-dragging" sense—a noncompliance resulting from inertia, communication breakdown, or simply the presence of more pressing items on the cantonal agenda that took chronological priority. Also, although they eventually involved some degree of formal cooperation in the federal appeals process, these are not simply cases where the cantonal government decided that particular federal action was *ultra vires,* invading cantonal "sovereignty," and therefore went to the federal body in charge (generally in these years, the Federal Council and/or Federal Assembly) to request a reconsideration. Instead, they both involve official resistance first and cooperation in the appellate process only later.

Flagrant Cantonal Violations of the Federal Constitution

Moving up the scale of intensity of defiance, one arrives next at direct defiance of federal law where the canton did not bother (or felt unable) to raise a question of federal competence. It simply legislated contrary to clear federal law. Such cantonal laws might be kept in place for ten or twelve years, in the face of federal "invitations" to reform them. Sometimes the cantonal authorities would finally do the bidding of the federal authorities, but sometimes the federal authorities themselves, their patience having worn thin, simply declared that they were revoking the offending laws. Four relatively blatant examples of such cases from the early decades of the union can be described. In one, the canton Valais continued to collect a tax for years after the Federal Assembly had ruled it unconstitutional.[30] The other three (one from Basel-Country, one from Fribourg, and one from Lucerne) exhibited legislative discrimination against Swiss from outside the canton, in direct and flagrant violation of Articles 29, 41, or 48 of the 1848 Constitution.[31]

In these examples, when the canton had its law challenged for a judgment by the Federal Council, the offending canton generally did at least attempt the claim that its laws were not in violation of the constitution. The defiance in these instances, however, was so patent that the federal authorities clearly did not take the claims seriously, and simply repeated their various acts of annulment. One infers—essentially from the absence of a record of continuing litigation at the federal level—that by the 1860s the cantons ceased their resistance in this group of cases.

Chronic and Long-Term Defiance Problems

On the other hand, one subset of cantonal resistance cases did endure well past 1860. What links together this group of incidents appears to be their connection to the atom of political life: citizenship. They all involved either conflicts over who may join the citizenry of a canton (and obtain the political and commercial rights attached thereto) or conflicts over the exercise of the fundamental self-constituting act of the citizen body itself—the framing of a cantonal constitution.

This most problematic subset of the mid-range defiance category presented instances where cantons for decades on end flouted clear constitutional rules or clear mandates from the Federal Council. Numerous Swiss cantons resisted federal policy on the freedom-of-commerce constitutional rights of the Jewish Swiss and resisted federal policy on according citizenship rights to the *heimatlosen*—persons lacking the status of hometown citizenship. Moreover, some cantons persisted for years in unconstitutionally denying equality of political rights to Swiss who had moved in from other cantons. Most problematic of all were cantonal-federal conflicts involving a demand from the center that the citizen body of a canton—its constituent power—reform its constitution so as to bring it into conformity with one or another federal requirement. The last version, presenting a deeply rooted conflict between the federal principle and the principle of cantonal popular sovereignty, proved most difficult for the Confederation. While federal policy always formally prevailed, in fact sometimes cantonal resistance was so persistent that federal authorities eventually modified federal policy, compromising in the direction of cantonal preferences. This pattern, in which member-state resistance succeeded in altering federal policy, also occurred occasionally in the early American union and also in the early decades of the European Union. Some details on each of these subcategories follow.

Jewish Swiss Citizens

The first type of problematic citizens' rights cases to be definitively resolved dealt with regularization of the status of Jews—referred to in nineteenth-century Swiss legal documents as "Swiss Israelites." The terminology appears to be significant; even Jewish families resident in Switzerland for generations appear to have been viewed as in some sense foreign. The Constitution of 1848 asserted (in Articles 4, 29, and 42) that all Swiss were equal before the law and equally possessed certain fundamental rights. However, other articles—Articles 41, 44, and 48—limited the particular rights specified therein (including the right of establishing oneself in a canton as a citizen of the canton) to "all Swiss of one of the Christian confessions." This constitutional ambiguity opened the door to considerable cantonal intransigence against federal legislative efforts to secure those rights that the federal authorities viewed as included among the constitutional rights of the Jews, particularly the right of all Swiss to buy and sell freely within the federation. Overt resistance on this point was exhibited into the 1860s by the cantons of Schwytz and Aargau.[32] The problems endured until the constitutional revision of 1866 completely equalized the constitutional status of Christian and Jew in Switzerland.

Contested Electoral Rights and *Heimatlosen*

Another variant of these intractable citizenship-related cases—and one that took longer to resolve—concerned a group of incidents that concerned the somewhat intertwined issues of electoral rights in general and the rights, in particular, (political and otherwise) of *heimatlosen*. These might be permanent noncitizen residents (such as Jews) or vagabonds. The 1848 Constitution (Article 56) mandated the regularization of such persons' status under federal legislation; the legislation was adopted on December 3, 1850. In the words of constitutional commentator Christopher Hughes, despite the clear-cut federal law to the contrary, "Cantons and communes wriggled with inexhaustible resource to avoid receiving *Heimatlos[en]*, for a whole generation," and pockets of cantonal resistance on this subject survived even into the twentieth century.[33]

Electoral rights were outlined in Article 42 of the federal constitution. It mandated that "every citizen of a canton is a Swiss citizen" and "can exercise political rights in federal matters and in cantonal matters in the canton where he is established." This article allowed the canton to specify a minimum residence period before the exercise of cantonal-level voting privileges, but specified that the minimum time required could never exceed two years. Also in December 1850, the Confederation enacted a law to assure voting rights for all Swiss citizens in federal elections.[34]

Despite these clear federal provisions at both the constitutional and statutory level, certain cantons, for instance, Berne and Zug, years after the constitution went into effect, nonetheless adopted and continued to enforce electoral restrictions that clearly violated Article 42.[35]

Cantonal Popular Sovereignty versus Federal Constitution

Most problematic of all with respect to electoral rights was a pattern that pitted federal authority against the populace within a canton. The pattern essentially involved acts of resistance by the people of the canton themselves, exercising their authority as the constituent power, in continuing to enact cantonal constitutional provisions that openly contravened federal policies.[36] For instance, in Ticino and Neuchâtel violations of the federal constitutional prohibition on electoral-rights discrimination dragged on for years because cantonal institutions of direct democracy enabled the cantonal citizenry repeatedly to flout federal rules.[37]

This kind of popularly based resistance to federal authority posed exceptionally difficult problems for the Confederation. The federal constitution itself, both in 1848 and 1874, placed squarely in the hands of the cantonal majority the power to amend the cantonal constitution at will (Article 6), but this power is subject to federal limits. From 1848 on, it has been the obligation of federal authorities to "guarantee" not only the citizens' rights under the federal constitution, but also citizens' rights under the cantonal constitutions and the cantonal constitutions themselves. The latter is understood as requiring explicit federal approval of every cantonal constitution. But the direct democracies or representative bodies that comprised the constituent power at the cantonal level persisted in adopting from time to time constitutions that did not conform, in the view of federal authorities, to the requirements of the federal constitution. It was not immediately obvious how to cope with this dilemma, since federal authorities clearly were not empowered to write new constitutions for the offending canton. Leaving the canton with no valid constitution was equally undesirable. Federal solutions to this dilemma evolved over time, as illustrated in the following examples.

First of all, federal authority on cantonal electoral rights in general was not always as pro-active as it was on the *heimatlos* question. Appenzell Rhodes-Interior had a pre-1848 cantonal constitution that squarely conflicted with the federal constitution in permanently denying cantonal voting rights to any Swiss moving in from outside the canton; nevertheless, it simply did nothing to change its unconstitutional policies for more than twenty years. When the cantonal legislature (Grand Conseil) finally did draft a new cantonal constitution in 1869 to deal with this problem, the voting public rejected it. Only at that point did someone take a complaint to the Federal Assembly, which thereupon "invited" the canton to fix the problem. A properly reformed Appenzell Rhodes-Interior constitution did get adopted but not until 1872, after twenty-four years of quiet defiance of federal policy.[38]

In the earliest years of the federation, when a problematic cantonal constitution was brought to it for a "guarantee," the federation's approach was to ask that the offending cantonal constitutional provisions be revised so as to conform to the federal rules, and then to wait for compliance (which might take a few years). This approach worked with the canton of Schaffhausen: its constitution was refused a guarantee in 1852, because of two offending provisions concerning voting rights. The canton did produce an acceptable revision by the end of 1855, and it received the federal guarantee six months later.[39]

By the late 1850s, it had become apparent that a more expeditious approach needed to be developed. Fribourg, for instance, presented the following problem: the federal authorities refused its initial constitution, requesting revision in 1850 and repeating the request in 1852. Finally, in 1857 (nine years into the Confederation), Fribourg submitted a reformed version, which still contained provisions that violated the federal constitutional requirements on voting eligibility. In this instance, the Federal Assembly pioneered what was to become a frequently used approach: it agreed to guarantee the cantonal constitution with the exception of specified sections, which were to be "interpreted and applied" as though they did not violate the federal constitution.[40] Eventually, in later cases the assembly would use more direct language, indicating that specified provisions were to be considered invalid and unenforceable.[41]

This approach evidently became fairly routine practice. In 1880, the half-canton Appenzell Rhodes-Interior had submitted a newly revised constitution to federal authorities. In response to federal complaints about the failure to eliminate from the revision various patently unconstitutional provisions, the cantonal government simply pointed out that the federal government had never explicitly asked it to revise them. In this situation, the Federal Council acknowledged, "Until now one has not compelled the cantons to put their constitutions formally into harmony with the Federal Constitution."[42]

This approach—accepting a constitution as guaranteed, excluding its invalid sections—did produce certain inconsistent results (examples of which are italicized below). The revised constitution for the canton of Uri in 1888 reenacted a constitutional provision concerning convents for which the Federal Assembly had, on federal constitutional grounds, *refused* its "guarantee" in 1851, as they had *refused* it to similar clauses in constitutions of the half-cantons Nidwald and Obwald in 1850. The assembly, in their March 1877 ruling on a similar clause in the Schwytz constitution of 1876, had *accepted it but with a specific warning* of the need to avoid a potential, unconstitutional interpretation of it. Within the same year, however, the federal authorities had *accepted without comment* in December 1877 a similar provision of the revised constitution of Nidwald. In 1888, rather than follow its 1850s course of refusing to accept the offending clauses, the Federal Assembly opted merely to remind Uri of the 1851 refusal and to *warn* that the provision in question needed to be interpreted always in a way that conformed to the relevant provisions of the federal constitution.[43]

This series on convent-related constitutional provisions appears to indicate that what began as cantonal resistance to federal policy, if repeated often enough and in enough different cantons, could sometimes lead to a softening of the federal policy. In this instance the softening consisted of the shift from outright refusal of the federal guarantee, which implies that the cantonal provision is simply unconstitutional, to instead providing guidance to the canton on how to interpret the provision in a manner consistent with the Constitution.

This example should not be interpreted as indicating that the federal authorities on other subjects ceased their practice of refusing outright to guarantee other cantonal constitutional provisions that contravened the federal constitution. For instance, the Federal Assembly refused its guarantee to three articles of the same Schwytz constitution on the grounds that these three gave disproportionate electoral influence to residents of one district in the canton. Concerning these, the government of Schwytz promptly amended them in the direction desired, and the populace ratified that action. The federal refusal had been announced in a ruling of March 20, 1877; by July 4 of the same year the Schwytz government had taken corrective action.[44]

The Schwytz situation of prompt and complete cooperation in revising its constitution represents one not uncommon extreme of cantonal response to federal refusals of acceptance. The situation on convent-related provisions described above represents another not terribly uncommon cantonal response: sometimes the cantonal governments responded to local political pressures and reenacted offending provisions, which were again refused acceptance (or else "interpreted" in the correct light) at the federal level. Or, in a third alternative, the canton might simply leave untouched provisions in its constitution that the federal authorities had refused to guarantee—the popular assembly of Obwald, for instance, waited 35 years, from 1867 to 1902, before it acted on its cantonal executive's recommendation to eliminate such provisions.[45] Such inaction is not evidence per se of overt resistance to federal policy. It may simply be noncompliance concerning the formal provision as a result of political inertia, while actual practice of governing officials may have altered to conform to federal policy.[46]

When the offending cantonal clause, or other cantonal practice contrary to federal law, dealt with electoral arrangements, the federal authorities did have available an enforcement device—they could declare the election invalid and refuse to accept the elected officials into office. Federal authorities used this device in the initial months of the Confederation to pressure Nidwald, Obwald, and Uri to withdraw their reservations against the validity of the federal constitution, and then twice used the device for Ticinese elections in the decade of the 1850s, once for the 1854 elections and once for the 1859 elections.[47]

DEFIANCE LEADING TO THREATS OF MILITARY ENFORCEMENT

The lone instance when Swiss federal authorities needed to threaten the use of force against a legitimately constituted cantonal government also involved the turbulent canton of Ticino. It occurred in 1884, during a problematic twenty-year period for Ticino politics. This incident, too, involved an electoral rights dispute, one over alleged manipulation of voter eligibility lists for municipal elections pitting Lugano municipal authorities of one political party against the cantonal authorities of the opposed political party in Ticino. The cantonal authorities attempted to discipline the municipal authorities who appealed to the Federal Council for assistance. The cantonal authorities then repeatedly ignored Federal Council orders against taking this disciplinary action. Ticino persisted to the point that it provoked a federal threat of military force. The provocation included a direct assertion by Ticino authorities that they, rather than the Federal Assembly, had full competence to decide the issues of cantonal authority at stake.[48]

MORE DETAILED NARRATIVE OF CANTONAL DEFIANCE EPISODES

Table 6 details these various resistance incidents. While not a comprehensive account, it is a collation of those examples of cantonal resistance that are readily available in federal documentary records.

A supplemental narrative providing the specifics of the episodes listed

Table 6. Cantonal Resistance to Federal Policy

KEY
1 = Surreptitious defiance: cantonal authorities act directly contrary to federal policy but claim to cooperate
2 = Open defiance with plausible legal appeal: cantons resist federal policy first, but when challenged offer a plausible constitutional rationale
3 = Sheer open defiance: canton adopts and enforces flagrantly unconstitutional law
4 = Long-term or repetitive enforcement of flagrantly unconstitutional law
5 = Repetitive defiance of federal policy to the point that federal authorities threaten enforcement by armed force
6 = Denial of the legitimacy of federal authority

Date	Canton	Intensity Level	Type of Federal Policy Resisted	Topic
1848	Uri	6	Replacement of 1815 Pact with the Constitution of 1848	Validity of replacement of Pact without cantonal unanimity
1848	Nidwald	6	Replacement of 1815 Pact with the Constitution of 1848	Validity of replacement of Pact without cantonal unanimity
1848	Obwald	6	Replacement of 1815 Pact with the Constitution of 1848	Validity of replacement of Pact without cantonal unanimity
1848–51	Ticino	4	Federal constitution	Cantonal constitution discriminates by cantonal origin in voting rights
1849–50	Solothurn	1	Federal executive orders	Hiding foreign revolutionaries
1851–54	Berne	4	Federal constitution	10-year residency requirement for voting
1851–54	Ticino	4	Federal constitution	Statute discriminating by age, wealth, and cantonal origin in voting rights
1852–53	Ticino	1	Federal executive orders	Hiding foreign revolutionaries
1854	? [secret]	1	Federal executive orders	Hiding foreign revolutionaries
1851–55	Ticino	4	Federal constitution	Cantonal constitution discriminates by cantonal origin in voting rights

(continued)

Table 6. (*continued*)

Date	Canton	Intensity Level	Type of Federal Policy Resisted	Topic
1850–57	Fribourg	4	Federal constitution, federal executive order and federal interpretation of constitution	Refusal to reform cantonal constitution as requested by federal authorities
1855–58	Ticino	4	Federal constitution	Cantonal constitution discriminates by cantonal origin in voting rights
1848–59	Basel-Country	3	Federal constitution	Cantonal-origin discrimination in penal code
1848–59	Lucerne	3	Federal constitution	Cantonal-origin discrimination in penal code
1850–59	Neuchâtel	4	Federal statute	Regularization of persons lacking hometown citizenship
1848–60	Zug	4	Federal constitution and federal statute	Statute discriminating by wealth and cantonal origin in voting rights
1854–60 and 1857–60	Valais	3	Federal constitution and federal interpretation of federal constitution	Cantonal tax on commerce
March–Sept. 1857	Vaud	2*	Decree from federal legislature and federal executive order	Location of railroad
1848–63 and 1856–63	Schwytz	4	Federal constitution and federal interpretation of federal constitution	Anti-Jewish discrimination in laws regulating commerce
1848–63 and 1856–63	Aargau	4	Federal constitution and federal interpretation of federal constitution	Anti-Jewish discrimination in commercial and political rights
1848–72	Appenzell Rhodes-Interior	4	Federal constitution	Cantonal constitution discriminates by cantonal origin in voting rights

Table 6. (*continued*)

Date	Canton	Intensity Level	Type of Federal Policy Resisted	Topic
1851–88	Uri	4	Federal interpretation of federal constitution	Adoption of cantonal constitutional provision earlier judged contrary to federal constitution
1876	Schwytz	4	Federal interpretation of federal constitution	Adoption of cantonal constitutional provision earlier judged contrary to federal constitution
mid-1876– Nov. 77	Neuchâtel	2	Federal constitution and decree from federal legislature and federal executive order	Payment of military tax
1879–93	Ticino	1	Federal interpretation of federal constitution	Surreptitious refusal to exclude from electoral process former Ticinese who continued to claim tie to the canton
1884	Ticino	5, 6	Federal executive orders repeated several times and order of federal legislative official sent as commissary	Dispute over validity of electoral registry
1887–88	Zurich	1	Federal executive orders	Hiding foreign revolutionaries

*Plus attempt to rally support of other cantons.

in Table 6 follows here. They are arranged in ascending order of severity. Readers less interested in these historical details may wish to proceed to "Conclusions" below.

Surreptitious Defiance

In 1849, the "commune" (town) of Granges in the canton Solothurn accorded rights of citizenship to (and later helped hide) the Italian republican revolutionary Mazzini, in the face of an expulsion order from the Swiss federal authorities. They had received a complaint about him from the government of Sardinia dated December 15, 1849. After having helped to hide him, the cantonal police, according to Swiss statesman and historian Numa Droz, "either closed their eyes to his presence or warned him each time pressing orders came from Berne [the federal capital]." The matter was not settled until the great European powers, led by Prussia, intervened diplomatically and Mazzini was allowed to travel to England.[49]

However, he returned to Switzerland (in order to be near the Italian border) soon after and quite flagrantly made known his presence. Droz cites a lack of "loyal support from the cantonal governments" as contributing to a general atmosphere of tolerance for foreign revolutionaries, creating a need for repeated federal intervention in the form of specific expulsion orders and also orders that interned foreign emigrés from bordering countries into the interior of Switzerland. In March 1852 the Federal Council issued a declaration that no refugee guilty of dangerous machinations against a foreign power would be tolerated in Switzerland. Then in February 1853, Mazzini, back in another Swiss canton, Ticino, fomented an uprising in Milan. The Austrian government linked its suspicions about Mazzini to its annoyance at Ticino's having recently expelled twenty-two Lombardian monks, and proceeded to expel five to ten thousand Ticinese from their homes in Lombardy and blockaded the Swiss-Lombardy border. France, Britain, Swiss, and Austrian diplomats intervened to avert an outbreak of war between Switzerland and Austria; they worked out a settlement that included (again) removal of Mazzini to England.[50]

And yet again, Mazzini did not stay away. He was back in Switzerland to foment revolution in northern Italy by July 1854, at which time he bragged in a letter to the Federal Council: "Sirs, you look for me everywhere; very likely you will not find me. And [even] if you succeed, you will not dare to expel me." Droz comments that his audacity posed a less serious problem than the attitude of the cantonal authorities that made it possible.[51]

As time passed, the cantonal authorities generally became more fully cooperative on the issue of harboring foreign revolutionaries, but at least one more problematic incident emerged in the late 1880s.[52] In 1887 an issue of the Zurich-based socialist journal *Sozialdemokrat*, which had "violently libeled" the royal family of Germany and the prince of Bismarck, was smuggled into Germany. This created international tensions, and, in response to federal efforts at a crackdown, the Zurich police claimed to be unable to find the authors of the journal. It turned out that the chief of the Zurich police was himself involved with German socialists, helping them to expose the fact that Germany had sent "agents provocateurs" into Zurich. This revelation intensified the international turmoil, causing the Federal Council to "invite" the journal to cease its provocative tone. In response, the journal became even more strident. Finally, on April 18, 1888, the Federal Council issued a decree expelling the publishers of the journal from Switzerland (an order that proved popular and thus was enforced).[53]

Mid-Range Defiance: Cantonal Policies
Openly Defying Federal Law
Defiance Supported by Legalistic Appeals

Two examples of cantonal defiance of federal policy, in which the cantonal authorities employed legalistic appeals to prolong their resistance, should suffice to convey the flavor of this mild subset that I call mid-range defiance. Such incidents were not unusual.

One early incident concerned the canton of Vaud. Vaud had granted a "concession" permitting construction of a railroad line through its territory linking Yverdon and Berne via Payerne, Marat, and Laupen.[54] In early August 1853 the Federal Assembly ratified the concession. But Fribourg, a neighboring canton through which the line needed to pass, refused to grant a concession and instead decreed construction of a line linking Thörishaus, Fribourg, Payerne, Estayer, and Yverdon. In February 1856, the Federal Assembly ratified Fribourg's line and decided "for the moment" that, despite the request of interested railway companies and of the government of Vaud in repeated letters, federal authorities would not force a concession from Fribourg for the Vaud-favored line. In July, it requested a study of the issue and a recommendation from the Federal Council. On the basis of these, in September 1856, the Assembly decreed its approval of the Fribourg line, ordered mediation by the Federal Council in order to obtain approval from Vaud for the details of the Fribourg-preferred route through Vaud territory, and mandated that, failing successful mediation, the Assembly would determine the details of the concession within Vaud. The Federal Council was authorized to "approve definitively" both the path and construction plan within Vaud and to so use the federal expropriation power. The Assembly decreed further its definitive rejection of the Vaud request to force a concession from Fribourg for Vaud's preferred line. Acting on this authorization, the Federal Council on March 9, 1857, approved construction plans for a railroad line in

Vaud, indicating that the government of Vaud was refusing to examine and consider the plans, and it authorized the application of federal expropriation law to carry out the plans.

Vaud then defied federal authority outright. The Vaud authorities refused to permit the filing of the subsection plans in any of the communes, and prohibited any expropriation for the project. According to the reporter R. E. Ullmer, the Federal Council four and a half months later "invited the government of Vaud 'in a pressing manner to report the orders that it had given in this regard to the commune authorities and to direct them to conform to the requirements of the expropriation law.'"[55] The Vaud government replied quickly, arguing that the Federal Council's plans for the line were merely a preliminary draft since they had not been approved by Vaud, and as such they could not be filed. The Federal Council responded within a few weeks that the plans were not simply preliminary, and were complete enough in their detail that they must be filed. The government of Vaud eleven days later prohibited continuation of the work that had begun, until the plans for the work were submitted and received its approval. A few days later, on September 2, 1857, the Federal Council issued an edict (*arrêté*) annulling this prohibition and setting the deadline of September 15 for Vaud to approve the plans. The government of Vaud protested that this was not enough time for it to decide whether to approve the plans. On September 18, the Federal Council appointed a commission to attempt an amicable resolution, but failing that authorized the commission to provide for execution of the will of the federal authorities. The mode of defiance—to put it in terms familiar to American readers—involved the equivalent of a governor, backed by his state legislature, acting in direct defiance of a presidential order that had been authorized by Congress. This defiance lasted for six months before the canton moved to the legally sanctioned route of raising a conflict of competence question, at which point it also ceased its defiant behavior.

At this point, six months after the resistance had begun, the legislature of Vaud authorized its executive arm to raise a "conflict of competence" question at the Federal Assembly (in its judging role), and to refrain during settlement of the question from any "material act opposing the acts of the Federal Council," although they did not concur with the latter.[56] The resolution of the Vaud legislature argued that its "cantonal sovereignty" had been invaded by the various actions of the Federal Council and that it was going to send a copy of this resolution to all the cantonal governments. The federal commission issued a majority report by December 15 to the effect that the federal legislature had acted within its constitutional competence, as had the Federal Council, and that Vaud's "cantonal sovereignty" had not been violated by the federal insistence that it permit the railroad construction. The Federal Assembly let the matter rest there, and refrained from ruling on whether the Federal Council had acted beyond its competence.

A second example of using legalistic appeals while flatly defying federal law can be drawn for the post-1874 period, as an illustration that some cantonal recalcitrance continued after the adoption of the new constitution. Article 42 of the 1874 constitution indicated that federal revenues would include, among others, "(e) The income from half the gross yield of the [military] service exemption tax levied by the Cantons." Article 18 of the same document stipulates, "The Confederation shall lay down unified provisions on [the] service-exemption tax." In March 1875 the Federal Council sent a circular to the cantons advising the use of existing cantonal laws for collecting the military service tax. Another Federal Council circular on December 27, 1875, invited the cantons to send to the federal treasury, during the month of January 1876, half of the gross proceeds collected in 1875 on this tax, as well as any back taxes they may have owed. The circular stated in emphatic terms, "There cannot be any doubt at all" (*Il ne peut y avoir aucun doute*) that one half of the military tax collected for 1875 should enter the federal treasury.

The canton of Neuchâtel began the year 1876 making regular payments in accord with these federal instructions. Several other cantons, however, were late in sending their payments, in response to which the Federal Assembly issued an invitation to the Federal Council to compel the cantons to send half the gross product of the military tax before they completed their annual accounts. On July 9, 1876, the Swiss people rejected the first proposed federal law on the military tax, which would have carried out the expectation of Article 18 for a uniform prescription of the federal tax. Consequently, the Federal Council on July 28 "invited" all the cantonal governments to proceed to the collection of the service exemption tax for 1876, under their existing laws, and to send half to the federal treasury by February, as per Article 42 (e), along with any back taxes on this item that they still owed.[57]

At this point (on August 28, 1877, still not having completed its payments from the 1876 collections), Neuchâtel formally resisted the "invitation" of the Federal Council, announcing that "by the power of their office" (*par office*) they would not cooperate until the federal government complied with the Article 18 prescription of uniform taxes on this subject. In return, by the power of its office, the Federal Council again "invited" (on September 18, 1877) the Neuchâtel government to send one half of its 1876 exemption taxes proceeds. When this did not bring results, the federal executive extended Neuchâtel's "deadline" for the payment of what it owed for 1876 from the coming October 15 until the coming November 28. In this extension, the Federal Council offered the (perhaps face-saving) alternative that the canton furnish proof that it had appealed to the Federal Assembly to challenge the constitutionality of the Federal Council's actions. On November 22, 1877, the legislative Council of Neuchâtel approved such an appeal, and on November 27, the executive of the canton took the appeal to the Federal Tribunal. In mid-1878 a federal law on the subject did get adopted to take effect in October, but the dispute over back taxes from 1876–77 remained to be resolved. The Federal Tribunal did resolve it in favor of the federal government, in light of the clear language of Article 42, supported by the Article 113 statement that the highest authority for interpretation of federal powers is the Federal Assembly. While it is beyond the capacity of this American researcher to determine how much of its back taxes Neuchâtel ever paid, it is clear that the cantonal government of Neuchâtel chose in a formal capacity for a year and a half to resist a clear order from the federal executive branch, and one that had explicit sanction in Article 42 of the constitution.

Flagrant Cantonal Violations of the 1848 Federal Constitution

A number of the more flagrant cantonal violations of federal constitutional rules involved cantonal laws that discriminated on the basis of cantonal origin; three described in this section fit that category. Article 29 assures to all Swiss citizens "freedom of purchase and of sale of [all] . . . products of soil and of industry," and guarantees their free import and export and transport among all the Swiss cantons, subject to cantonal police regulations. The latter are forbidden to discriminate between citizens of the canton and Swiss citizens of other cantons *and* are required to be submitted to, and approved by, the Federal Council before being put into effect. Article 41, Section 4, reiterates that once any Christian Swiss citizen is established in a canton, he enjoys "all the rights of cantonal citizens . . . particularly freedom of industry and the right to buy and sell real property." Article 48 reemphasizes the nondiscrimination rule of Articles 29 and 41, guaranteeing that all Christian citizens of Switzerland, irrespective of home canton, must be treated alike "both in matters of legislation and in all that concerns juridical proceedings." Finally, Article 4 of the Transition Provisions section of the constitution makes clear that any preexisting provisions of cantonal constitutions that conflict with this federal constitution "will be abrogated as of the day on which the present Constitution is ratified."

The canton of Valais clearly defied the Article 29 and Article 41 freedom of commerce provisions six years after the constitution took effect, in adopting a law in February 1854 that essentially taxed all wood cut for commercial purposes (literally, all wood not used in construction or for heating fuel). In response to a series of petitions complaining of this violation, the Federal Assembly so ruled in August 1857, and it "invited" the government of Valais to abolish the collection of this tax. Instead, in October the government of Valais issued a new decree claiming that it was complying, while in fact it reinstated the tax as a tax on exported wood. In mid-1859 Valais notified the Federal Council that it had complied, and the latter requested a copy of the complying decree. The Federal Council then ruled on the last day of December that the new decree, like the earlier law, still violated both Article 29 and the Federal Assembly's ruling of August. By July 1860 the Federal Council reported that Valais had eliminated its defiant law.[58] This incident reveals a canton acting in defiance of the constitution over a period of six years and of the Federal Assembly's authoritative interpretation of the constitution for three years.

Similarly, when the half-canton Basel-Country adopted a law late in 1855 imposing a special license tax on peddlers from outside the canton, it did so in flagrant opposition to the provisions in Articles 29, 41, and 48 of the federal constitution. In response to an appeal three years later against this law, the Federal Council "invited" the government of Basel-Country to suspend immediately its enforcement of several parts of this unconstitutional law, to replace these offending sections of it, and to submit the reformed version to the Federal Council for approval, as per the explicit requirements of Article 29, before implementation. This September 1858 ruling asserted that if the cantonal government persisted in defying the federal constitution, the Federal Council would have to annul all convictions under the invalid law. By 1861, the now six-year-old cantonal law was still being unconstitutionally enforced in flagrant defiance of the Federal Council's order. On November 25, 1861, the Federal Council, responding to an appeal against the canton from a merchant, declared in frustration, "The provisions of Article 29 of the Federal Constitution have not at all been observed by Basel-Country." The federal authorities again ruled the 1855 law unconstitutional and unenforceable.[59]

While in the first few years of the operation of the constitution, there may have remained some legitimate doubt as to the fate of newly unconstitutional provisions sprinkled among cantonal statute books (as distinguished from cantonal constitutions, explicitly covered by Transition Article 4), all such doubt should have been removed by an utterly unambiguous 1852 ruling of the Federal Council acting in its role as interpreter of the federal constitution for public law questions. There the council declared void a paternity ordinance of Lucerne that flatly discriminated (contra Article 48) between cantonal citizens of Lucerne and other Swiss citizens in the canton. In doing so, the federal authority ruled plainly that all relevant provisions of the 1848 federal constitution took direct effect the moment the constitution was ratified and that thenceforth all preexisting cantonal laws contrary to it were immediately void under the implications of Transition Article 4 and could not be followed by cantonal judges.[60]

Nonetheless, more than a decade into the operation of the 1848 Constitution similar flagrant violations of the proscriptions against cantonal-origin discrimination were still going on in other cantons. The Federal Council in 1859 settled an appeal from an 1857 conviction of two Swiss men banished from Fribourg under a criminal statute that applied this banishment penalty for the offense in question only to people from outside the canton. The federal body declared that the article of the Fribourg penal code that the Fribourg judges were still enforcing had become null and void as of ratification of the Constitution of 1848 (due to conflict with Article 48), and that the convictions under it could not stand.[61]

The evident clarity of Article 48 on this subject did not preclude similar problems in other cantons. In 1858 the Federal Council was called upon to annul the criminal penalty of expulsion imposed by Lucerne upon an Aargau citizen on the basis of a longstanding law that specified this punishment only for persons who were not citizens of the canton, in clear violation (again) of Article 48. The Federal Council declared void this aspect of the law, and, in July 1859, the Federal Assembly implicitly ratified this decision by removing from its agenda Lucerne's appeal requesting that it be overturned.[62]

Chronic and Long-Term Defiance Problems

Violations of the Rights of the Jewish Swiss. The constitutional ambiguity on rights of Jews in the early years of the Confederation gave rise to several appeals to the Federal Council by various Jewish merchants against discriminatory cantonal legislation, only some of which were upheld.[63] By 1856, the Federal Assembly attempted to provide clear guidance to the cantons on this subject in a ruling of September 24. It stipulated that (1) the sovereignty of the cantons in regulating the position of those "Israelites" who are not established as citizens in (*"non ressortissants du"*) the canton is not limited—this meant, essentially, a canton was permitted to keep Jews from establishing themselves as a member of its citizenry or even as a long-term resident—except that the regulations may not interfere with the rights guaranteed to all Swiss in the federal constitution; (2) these rights guaranteed in Articles 29 and 42 of the constitution require that "Israelite Swiss" have equally with all other Swiss citizens the right to buy and to sell freely the objects designated in Article 29, as well as to exercise political rights, be it in the canton of origin or in the canton where they are established as citizens.

The Federal Council was charged with executing this ruling (*"arrêté"*); it communicated the ruling to the cantons and invited them to reform their laws so as to comply with it in the shortest possible time, and, pending the reforms, to refrain from enforcing any laws that violated Articles 29 or 42. Further, the Council explicitly interpreted the ruling: those cantons that had "Israelite" citizens were obliged to treat them, according to Article 4 of the constitution, as "equal under the law *in all respects* to other citizens of the canton, except in directly church-related affairs."[64]

Despite these clear instructions, fifteen years into the Confederation, some cantons were still in the process of removing from their statute books ordinances that violated Articles 29 or 42. Two reported doing so in 1861, one in 1862, and one in 1863.[65] Although remarkably lethargic, these at least were not overtly resisting federal authority. The same cannot be said of all the cantons.

Swiss legal chronicler R. E. Ullmer admits that at least "a few cantons... persisted with a great obstinacy in refusing civic equality to Jews." He cites an 1863 case where the Schwytz government simply refused a request from the Federal Council that it stop discriminating against the Jews in the granting of peddler licenses. The canton admitted that it had no legal foundation for its actions but stated that it simply "could not resolve itself to give the peddling license in the future" to the people in question.[66]

Similarly, he describes a lengthy encounter between the federal authorities and the canton of Aargau. In May 1862, the legislature (Grand-Conseil) of Aargau put forth a law that would finally comply with Articles 4, 29, and 42 of the federal constitution (not to mention the federal ruling of 1856) by equalizing the legal status of Jewish Aargauvians with the other citizens of Aargau. This law was then voted down in a popular referendum. Leaders of the two Jewish communities of Aargau then appealed to the Federal Council, which acknowledged that as a legal matter, the 1856 ruling should be enforced, but as a political matter, it might need to suspend enforcement of the legal rights of the Jews "until a new [political] order." The Aargau legislature then passed a new law that took no account of the formal legal recommendations of the Federal Council. The latter requested a copy of this new law, and sent it in turn to the Federal Assembly.

The Federal Assembly considered the problem for two weeks and produced the following ruling: the Federal Council was "invited" to suspend all parts of the 1863 Aargauvian law that were in conflict with the 1856 Federal Ruling and to see to it that the canton of Aargau no longer refuse the exercise of federal or cantonal political rights to Aargauvian Jews; the Federal Council also was invited to see to the inclusion of Jews in the rights of local community members in Aargau, in accord with the December 1850 law on *heimatlosat*. In August 1863, the Federal Council notified the canton that its 1863 law was suspended, that it was required to treat the 1856 federal ruling as the equal of any cantonal law already in effect—that its implementation required no further local enabling legislation—and that the cantonal government should notify the Federal Council as to its "manner of viewing the question" of the incorporation of Jews into its local communes, so that the Council could give the subject its "profound examination."[67]

These various cantonal "obstinacies" on the subject of the Jews eventually ended by clear constitutional amendment in 1866 that explicitly mandated equal treatment. The federal government precipitated the amendment by agreeing in 1864 to a treaty with France under which all French Jews (along with all other French citizens) were accorded, upon moving to Switzerland, all the legal, political, and economic rights of a Swiss moving in from another canton.[68] This resulted in French Jews' having a higher legal status than Swiss Jews in Switzerland, an anomaly that was two years later rectified by federal constitutional amendment.

Contested Electoral Rights and the Heimatlos *Problem.* Berne had adopted a law in 1851 stipulating a ten-year residency requirement for cantonal voting rights, in blatant defiance of Article 42, which specified that the minimum requirement could not exceed two years; Ticino, too, openly defied Article 42 by adopting a law in December 1851 that imposed special age and wealth qualifications for voting upon any Swiss moving in from other cantons. Federal authorities uncovered these violations as a result of their inquiry late in 1854 surveying the *heimatlosat* problem.[69]

Even as late as 1860, Swiss factory workers (from outside the canton) domiciled in the canton of Zug had to appeal for a decision from the Federal Council because the laws of Zug kept them from voting in federal elections, again in flagrant violation of express provisions of the federal constitution (Articles 48 and 63) and of the federal election law of 1850.[70]

The 1850 federal law for settling the citizenship of *heimatlosen* goes on for ten pages in the *Recueil Officiel;* it required essentially the following:[71]

1. Except for the elderly and the equivalent of convicted felons, all Swiss persons had to receive citizenship both in their canton and commune (local community) of residence.

2. The Federal Council with the aid of the cantons was to survey the number and situation of *heimatlosen* in Switzerland, and to assign people to a particular canton. Cantons would have a right of contesting these resolutions before the Federal Tribunal.

3. The "naturalization" of all the *heimatlosen* was to take place within the time limit of one year, unless, "for exceptional circumstances or particular difficulties," the Federal Council saw a need to extend the time limit.[72]

4. Cantons were obliged to grant citizen rights in a "commune" to all the actual residents who did not otherwise have an official hometown (which involved both local voting rights and certain economic welfare benefits and obligations) upon the payment of a specified fee. (Evidently, if the individual *heimatlos* could not pay the entrance fee, the federal government helped.)[73]

In flagrant defiance of these federal provisions on citizenship and voting rights, the citizenry of several cantons for years on end exhibited a desire to keep out certain newcomers from their electoral body. Despite the one-year implementation period specified in the federal law of December 1850, the Federal Assembly in 1854 was still trying to learn whether the cantons had appropriately reformed their laws on electoral rights and on the right to establish oneself in the canton. Consequently, in October 1854, the Federal Council sent a circular to the cantons requesting them to report back on the situation. As a result, one learns that several cantons retained pre-Confederation provisions that were either clearly unconstitutional or arguably so. For the former, the Federal Council ruled them unenforceable and requested that the cantons adopt suitable replacement provisions that would conform to the federal constitution. For the doubtful provisions, the Federal Council indicated the required interpretation and application so as to assure conformity with the federal constitution.[74]

Federal authorities continued to express concerns about cantonal defiance of these rules at least into the 1860s. One reads a July 1857 decree from the Federal Assembly "inviting" the Federal Council to "insist" that cantons who have not yet put into execution the law on *heimatlosat* or have done so only partially now should enforce it fully.[75] At the same time, the Assembly asked that the council set time limits on cantonal appeals against the federal *heimatlos* allocation decisions.[76] (Typically in such appeals two or more cantons would dispute where a particular *heimatlos* belonged, each arguing that he belonged in the other canton.) Such cases were still being taken to the Federal Tribunal throughout 1858.[77] In July 1858, one reads of the Federal Assembly repeating the "invitation" to the Federal Council. This time the Federal Council decided in September 1858 to "invite the cantons in a pressing manner" to provide a detailed response to the inquiry it had sent them a year earlier, if they had not yet done so.

Despite repeated requests in the previous year, only three cantons had responded to the 1857 inquiry. In light of this problem, which the council labeled "passive resistance," and in consideration of the fact that some cantons were really trying to cooperate in the situation and were having difficulties completing the task, the council resisted setting a fixed time limit. By September 1862, as the problems dragged on, the Federal Council had finally begun setting time limits for the contesting of *heimatlos* assignments, and even at this late date, the limit provoked protests by individual offending cantons.[78]

Cantonal Popular Sovereignty versus Federal Constitution. By 1859, according to a federal inquiry, only twelve, or about half, of the cantons had replied to the council's "pressing" invitation of 1858. Among them, there appeared to be general cooperation with the exceptions of Neuchâtel and Ticino. The details of the difficulties with these two cantons reveal the pattern that was to continue to pose problems for the Confederation long past the first decade of the 1848 Constitution. The pattern essentially involved acts of resistance by the people of the canton themselves, exercising their authority as the constituent power, in continuing to enact cantonal constitutional provisions that openly contravened federal policies.[79]

Just a few years into the Confederation, Ticino's legislature had declared certain of the cantonal constitutional provisions no longer in force because of their conflict with the Federal Constitution, but the population revoked this decision, in effect reenacting the offending provisions, in 1851. Then in 1854 the Federal Council expressed concern that certain provisions of the cantonal constitution presented the potential to be applied in ways that conflicted with the federal one, but the Ticinese people re-adopted all the questioned provisions again in 1855. Finally, in October 1858, the Federal Council did officially "suppress" one of the suffrage restrictions from the 1855 Ticino Constitution.[80]

Neuchâtel engaged in a revision of its cantonal constitution in 1858. An initial draft included a provision mandating the immediate "naturalization" of all *heimatlosen* of the canton within a certain commune that would be created for that purpose. The voting populace of Neuchâtel vetoed this effort to comply with the now eight-year-old federal *heimatlos* statute. After the final draft of the new cantonal constitution, minus this provision, had been ratified, the Federal Council did what it could: it reminded the government of Neuchâtel that cantonal law to deal with *heimatlosen* was still needed, and that federal authorities expected it to be one of the first projects of the newly constituted Neuchâtel legislature.[81]

It does appear that the voting populace in Ticino appears to have been unusually willing to flout the authority of the federal constitution. In addition to the 1850s resistance involving the Ticino Constitution described above, a new wave of clashes between Ticino and federal authorities took place between 1879 and 1896. At the core of the dispute was disagreement over what it meant to be Ticinese. The Ticino voting populace wanted to permit persons of Ticinese origin who had left the canton and/or Switzerland, but who perhaps intended to return for permanent residence some day, to be counted in the allocation of representatives and to participate in elections if they returned to the canton for the occasion. The federal authorities repeatedly acted to counter this inclination, sometimes insisting that cantonal constitutional clauses be reworded, sometimes simply insisting that they had to be interpreted in particular ways.[82] The federal concern was that if a former Ticinese had in fact moved his domicile out of the canton, he should not continue to have an impact on Ticino elections.

On the surface, the Ticino authorities cooperated with the various federal requests as to constitutional rewording, but contemporary commentators indicate that in implementation Ticino repeatedly followed its own inclination rather than federal guidelines.[83] (The situation appears to have been complicated by the fact that 1870–91 was a period of extreme political turbulence in Ticino. Ticino authorities needed the assistance of federal authorities to maintain or restore order in 1870, 1876, 1889, and 1890–91, and the assistance was not always sent as a result of a request from Ticino authorities. Interestingly, the other time period when Ticino was resisting federal constitutional rules, 1851–58, was also punctuated by a federal intervention to maintain order, in 1855.)[84] The issue finally came to a head in 1893–96. In 1893 the Ticino citizenry expressed overwhelming support for a cantonal constitutional revision that frankly gave voting rights to anyone "registered as a member of a Ticino household in the registry of households of a Ticino commune," irrespective of where the person actually lived (as long as he was not exercising voting rights in more than one Swiss commune/canton).

Federal authorities pondered this reform for two and a half years (November 1893–March 1896) before finally approving it. While leading constitutional analysts opposed it as contrary to the federal constitution, federal authorities somehow needed to come to terms with the fact that it had been supported in a referendum with nearly 95 percent in favor: 13,620 to 739.[85] This seems to be an instance where resistance within a canton that was both intense and widespread prevailed by bringing about an alteration of the official federal interpretation.

Defiance Leading to Threats of Military Enforcement

Under these circumstances, it is not particularly surprising that the lone instance when Swiss federal authorities needed to threaten the use of force against a legitimately constituted cantonal government also involved the turbulent canton of Ticino. The need occurred in this same problematic period for Ticino politics, in 1884.

According to the classic account of this incident by Francis O. Adams and C. D. Cunningham, the conflict originated in a dispute over the validity of the voter registry in a municipality in the Lugano district.[86] Municipal authorities were of the Radical Party and cantonal authorities of the Conservative Party. Conservatives in Lugano took their appeal over the heads of municipal authorities to the cantonal authorities, where their party was dominant. The cantonal government on the day before national elections ordered the municipal voter lists changed, and imposed a stiff financial penalty (equivalent to one hundred British pounds) on any failure to do so. The municipality appealed to the Federal Council by telegraph against this order, and then ran the elections ignoring the order. The Federal Council ordered the cantonal government to suspend action against the municipal authorities and to report its side of the story to the council. During the next two weeks the Federal Council had to repeat the request several times by telegraph and post, but the cantonal government opted for open defiance. It declared its "perfect competency in the matter," ordered the municipality to pay its fine, and, upon its refusal, ordered the prefect of Lugano to take possession of a garden that was the private property of one of the municipal officers and to sell it at auction to pay off the fine. The Federal Council then sent a federal legislative official as the federal "commissary" to the cantonal capital where the Ticino government refused to heed any of his instructions. Moreover, despite his telegraph to the prefect of Lugano to prevent the auction, the prefect ignored him and auctioned off the garden.

Once the federal commissary had informed the Federal Council of these events, they immediately notified the cantonal government that if disobedience continued, a battalion of troops from Lucerne would be sent into Ticino to restore federal authority, and the expense of quartering the troops would have to be borne by Ticino. At this news, the Ticino government backed down, although protesting the federal action. Cantonal authorities annulled the sale of the garden and ordered the fine remitted.

CONCLUSIONS
The 1848 Swiss Union in Comparative Context

Despite the noncomprehensive quality of this collation of incidents, one can, nonetheless, draw certain comparative conclusions from this available record about the nature of cantonal resistance in the early decades of the modern Swiss union.

Readers familiar with the early American union will recognize in some details of the accounts of cantonal resistance parallels to the American situation. First, the Vaud story, concerning placement of a railroad line, echoes the Virginia Resolutions of 1798, in that Vaud, too, circulated its protest to all the cantonal governments seeking their support for its interpretation.

Second, in the action by some cantons to adopt cantonal constitutional provisions that had previously been adjudged by federal authorities unacceptable for other cantons, one can discern a pattern similar to the action in the United States, when, for instance, Ohio attempted to enforce a state law identical to the one that the Supreme Court had just struck down from Maryland in *McCulloch v. Maryland* (1819). Ohio, like a number of Swiss cantons, took its efforts to the highest federal court of appeal, where it too lost (*Osborne v. Bank of the United States,* 1824; cf. Uri in 1851, following the 1850 decisions against Nidwald and Obwald).

Third, a number of the accounts carry something like the tone of the American dispute treated in the *Fairfax's Devisee v. Martin* (1813) and *Martin v. Hunter's Lessee* (1816) litigation, in that these reveal the willingness of the canton to insist after a purportedly "definitive" ruling from authoritative branches of the federal government that it, the canton, had authority to defy the ruling.

Still, the Swiss picture is distinguished from the American in that in these instances, the cantons virtually always acknowledged that the ultimate authority to decide-who-decides rested at the federal level. This combination—resistance to a "definitive" federal ruling combined with a cantonal willingness to let the conflict of competence be decided at the federal level—looks strange to the American observer because the same federal body issuing the "definitive ruling" that the canton had resisted—namely, the Federal Assembly—was the highest source for hearing the canton's appeal that this body was in the wrong. Moreover, the body with original jurisdiction to hear the "conflict of competence" appeal—the Federal Council—was the body enforcing the very ruling that the canton was challenging in its appeal. (Hardly any of the cases examined here ended up at the officially "judicial" arm of the Confederation—the Federal Tribunal.) This unusual combination gives Swiss cantonal resistance its peculiar flavor; in general, even as the cantons resisted federal policy, however flagrantly, they nonetheless maintained a posture of acceptance, in principle, of federal authority to settle the dispute in the end.

Thus, in terms of the other cases examined in this book, the Swiss union contrasts with both the seventeenth-century Dutch union and with the early-nineteenth-century American union in not having experienced repeated challenges to the legitimacy of its authority. In this attribute, it bears comparison to the formative decades of the European Community. Admittedly, the latter did experience a sustained challenge to the legitimacy of one of its central organs (the European Court of Justice) from a single source, the French Conseil d'État; Swiss history (even discounting the three legitimacy challenges in its very first year of operation) does contain the Ticino incident of 1884, where federal authority was flatly denied. Still, on the whole, both unions present cases where the tone of member-state resistance can be described as muted, since the legitimacy of central authority was basically accepted from the start.

In contrast to the muted tone of cantonal resistance in Switzerland, one has to acknowledge that the quantity of resistance to federal policies, even as taken from this incomplete account, was rather high. Moreover, it was widespread; while Ticino certainly stands out as unusually recalcitrant, Table 6 shows a substantial majority of cantons engaged in at least some defiance of federal policy in the early decades of the union.[87] Of twenty-five member states (counting the six half-cantons and the nineteen full cantons), seventeen appear in Table 6.

Overall, in terms of the four unions examined in this work, the Swiss case seems to fit between the American and the European. The seventeenth-century Dutch union was at one extreme, experiencing continual challenges to its legitimacy in that the provinces never abandoned the idea that they had retained their sovereignty in the form of a veto power over federal policy. The American union experienced for its first seventy years intermittent but quite frequent challenges both to the legitimacy of federal authority to tell states what they could do, and to actual federal laws. Although the early decades of the modern Swiss union were characterized by virtually constant acceptance of the idea that the federal authorities in the final instance may legitimately determine the bounds of cantonal power, nonetheless, as Table 6 summarizes, a sizable number of cantons fairly often engaged in open defiance of federal policy. In the European Community, since the ECJ turned it into a quasi-federal polity by legal doctrine in the early 1960s, open member-state defiance of either ECJ legitimacy or ECJ policies has been remarkably rare.

As for the types of resistance to federal authority in the Swiss union, the incidents of cantonal resistance to federal policies described here can be sorted in terms of the categories set forth in Chapter 1, as indicated in Table 7. The available Swiss federal historical records are too lacking in detail to give definitive numbers, but a rough sense of scale, at least, can be discerned.

Unlike the situation in the American union where the most powerful issues provoking state resistance to the center varied from one state to another and varied over time, one message that comes through powerfully from the various accounts of cantonal resistance available in Swiss federal records is that there was a dominating type of issue that fueled the most and the most intense cantonal resistance to the center. While one does see some variety in the type of issue that led to cantonal-federal disputes in the early decades of the union, there is a discernible dominance by issues related to who belongs to the cantonal citizenry, who gets to vote, and who gets to be a part of that power that constitutes the can-

Table 7. Categories of Cantonal Resistance

Type	Number of Incidents
a. Defiance of specific federal interpretation of federal law	7+*
b. Rejection of authority of federal body to decide in cantonal-federal dispute (1848: Nidwald, Obwald, Uri; 1884: Ticino)	4
c. Defiance of the evident meaning of federal law	25+
e. Defiance of order to comply with federal interpretation of law	?†

*This counts as "one-plus" incident the 1879–93 period during which Ticino evidently engaged in surreptitious defiance of the federal rule that emigrés not be counted for representation and not vote in Ticino elections.

†While such defiance was sometimes evident, this category cannot be itemized separately because the executive authority in the period examined was the same authority as the interpreter of the federal constitution (i.e., there was not a separately functioning judicial authority) for most of the cases examined. Moreover, in certain incidents that show up as a single item in Table 6, the actual number of executive orders defied is simply listed as "several" in the best extant source.

ton.[88] This is an understandable pattern, for these issues would seem to go to the heart of sovereignty; to be a part of the citizenry in a democratic republic is to be a part of the sovereign. It is understandable that as the center of gravity of Swiss sovereignty shifted from the cantonal to the federal base in 1848, this shift would be accompanied by a lag period of various contests over the details. That Swiss authorities encountered more persistent difficulty in dealing with these issues than with others is not particularly surprising. The Swiss pattern, however, underlines just how startling was the European member states' acceptance in Maastricht of the principle giving voting rights in both European and municipal elections to all nationals of EC member states in whichever EC country they reside.

Swiss Union as a Test Case for European Union Scholarship

One attribute that characterized both the American and Dutch cases—the cases presenting more chronic patterns of member-state resistance—and lacking in both the European and Swiss cases is a shared recent history as colonies of a distant imperial power. The Swiss experience as part of the Hapsburg empire was such a remote memory by 1848 that it was hardly likely to have been an influential force in the nineteenth-century federation.

On the other hand, both the cantons and the European nation-states had lengthy traditions of prizing their independence of action—much longer than was true for the Dutch provinces or early American states (each of which united into a confederation format shortly after their respective colonial rebellions). This lengthy tradition of independence is the very reason that the overly tight, French-imposed union of early-nineteenth-century Switzerland was an immediate failure. Thus, the relative frequency of cantonal willingness to resist centrally mandated policies (as distinguished from federal legitimacy itself) in the early decades of the modern union is not terribly surprising, although the relative placidity of the European member states on this score remains in need of explanation.

It may be that one of the major and underrated causal forces for the high degree of acceptance of federal authority that one observes in the European Union is World War II itself. Although the motive of avoiding intra-European war was much discussed in the early years of the EC, modern scholarship very much discounts it as compared to economic explanations.[89] The example of the Swiss union should be viewed as suggestive in this regard. Both the Swiss and the European unions were precipitated by a war among the member states. Such a war would, naturally, be cause for caution in regard to a legitimacy challenge. World War II was far more devastating, to put it mildly, than the four-week Swiss Sonderbund War of 1847. The desire to avoid another such conflict surely operated as a powerful disincentive to resistance to centrally mandated policies of the European Union. The Dutch and early American unions, where official state-level denials of legitimacy of federal action were relatively frequent, pose a clear contrast to the EC/EU and to the Swiss union in this regard. Indeed, after America's "War between the States," challenges to the legitimacy of federal authority all but disappeared.

In terms of other explanatory factors suggested for the relative absence of member-state resistance in the European Union, three seem to be particularly relevant for understanding the Swiss situation. First, the point was made (in Chapter 2) that the appearance of unanimity in the format of opinions from the European Court of Justice contrasts sharply with that in the U.S. Supreme Court, and that it made more likely member-state acceptance of the decisions. Commentators on Swiss institutions have noted as well the appearance of unanimity in rulings from the Federal Council and Federal Assembly. (Rappard notes that the expression of disagreement within reports of the council are "very rare."[90] Ullmer draws attention to the appearance of unanimity that prevailed in the style of reports issued by the Federal Assembly.)[91]

To the degree that the appearance of unanimity did prevail, it may well have fostered cantonal adherence to federal policy, but it is worth pointing out that in a given dispute over a cantonal exercise of power, one might see as many as five different authoritative reports, in mutual disagreement with one another. The Federal Council would issue a report on original jurisdiction. Then an appeal could go to both houses of the federal legislature, each of which could appoint a commission to investigate the question and issue a formal advisory report. Then each house would separately vote on the subject, and could issue a report to explain its vote. These five viewpoints did not necessarily cohere, and this potential for disagreement as to the import of federal law may have encouraged some cantonal defiance.[92] As Switzerland moved closer to the twentieth century, a larger portion of the cases contesting cantonal power went to the Federal Tribunal (rather than the Federal Council/Federal Assembly combination). Since the Tribunal issues unanimous decisions also, this development would support the decline in frequency of cantonal resistance to federal policies that did indeed transpire over time.

Two other explanatory variables discussed in the European Union scholarship deserve mention, because they do seem to shed light on the early Swiss union. A number of scholars (e.g., Weiler and Burley and Mattli) have attributed the extraordinary success of the ECJ in securing member-state acceptance of federal authority in the EC to the fact that the ECJ is a judicial body issuing legal opinions that appear to be neutral and above politics. An exaggerated version of the point would be to say that this fact made any potential member-state resistance to ECJ centralizations of federal authority look vaguely criminal and therefore to be avoided. It may be that part of the willingness of Swiss cantons to defy federal decisions in the first few decades after 1848 was fostered by the fact that "judgments" of the unconstitutionality of cantonal policies or even of cantonal constitutions were coming not from courts but from political bodies—the federal executive and the federal legislature. Over time, as noted, this distribution of jurisdiction shifted toward the Federal Tribunal, and also the frequency of cantonal resistance diminished.

On the other hand, this argument of the causal power of the judicialization of decision-making may be a circular one. It may be that judges in the nineteenth century in Switzerland and in the United States were not trusted to make the right decision. Thus, the supreme judicial body of the United States until the Civil War of the 1860s was frequently defied by state authorities, and (in the United States) was defied even more blatantly than were nonjudicial officials in Switzerland. It may be that in Switzerland, the parallel expression of distrust of judges is to be found, until later in the nineteenth century, in the narrow restrictions on the Federal Tribunal's power to tell elected cantonal authorities what to do. Over time, judges may have come to be more trusted, and it may be for this reason that in the United States, the Supreme Court came to be routinely obeyed by state authorities[93] and in Switzerland was given more authority (that had previously belonged to legislative or executive bodies) to interpret the bounds on cantonal power. The ECJ did not come into being until the mid-twentieth century, when judges and the rule of law were already held in high esteem, and in this temporally limited Euro-American culture there may be some validity to the argument of Joseph Weiler and others (described in Chapter 2) that the specifically judicial features of the ECJ played a big role in causing its judgments to be accepted by member states. In other words, as the rule of law became more deeply embedded in the culture of these societies, the fact that a given decision came from a judge (rather than a "politician") may have come to be more salient for enhancing the likelihood that it would be respected as binding authority.

Alternatively, however, the twentieth-century willingness to accept judgments from a central federal court in Switzerland, the United States, and the EC/EU may all be evidence of a more generalized phenomenon: the cultural routinization of obedience to all lawfully constituted authority, not just that of judges—a routinization that was not yet so firmly entrenched in mid-nineteenth century Switzerland. In the first half-century of the Swiss federal union, federal troops were sent to help cantonal authorities maintain order against domestic eruptions of political violence on several occasions.[94] The frequency of such outbursts of violent opposition to authority waned as Switzerland moved into the twentieth century, in a time period that coincided with Swiss willingness to accord more and more categories of cases to the jurisdiction of the Swiss Federal Tribunal.

Finally, one of the leading arguments for explaining the success of federal integration of the European Community has been the argument that integration has mainly been pushed by transstate commercial interest groups who are interested in transstate trade and therefore promote the breakdown of state-erected barriers to trade. To these groups, over time, have been added the congeries of groups who have professional interests in "doing" European law—lawyers, law professors, law book publishers, and so on.[95] Chapter 2 indicated that this argument does not seem to fit the case of the early American union, for many commercial interests in that era too were proponents of federal integration as a way to eliminating trade barriers, but this fact did not prevent considerable state resistance to federal authority.

Both Myron Tripp and Thomas Hueglin have noticed similar business interest alignment in nineteenth-century Switzerland, and likened its pro-integration political impact to the pattern in the United States.[96] In addition, Andre Eschet-Schwarz has argued that the growth of fifteen trans-cantonal interest groups (e.g., a music association, a gymnastic association) in Switzerland between 1800 and 1848 played a significant role in "promoting the federal state." These groups met in a different canton each year, promoted patriotic trans-Swiss sentiment, and recruited members from political, economic, and social elites.[97] These groups would not have had an exact analogue in pre–Treaty of Rome Europe or in the American states in the decades prior to 1787. Still, their well-entrenched existence in Switzerland for many years prior to the Sonderbund War among the cantons seems to underline the point that the mere existence of transstate pro-federal interest groups does not per se suffice to prevent state-level resistance to a federal central authority. It may well be that in both the Swiss and American unions such interests did exert influence strengthening central authorities, but that in both unions, nonetheless, other centrifugal forces were powerful enough to support significant levels of cantonal resistance to federal policies.

Tripp, incidentally, also notes that in both Switzerland and the United States the pattern of lobbying by commercial interest groups changed over time; as the federal government became stronger in each union and began itself to regulate business interests, business interests in both places began to remember what they liked about "states' rights."[98] It is possible that this development could come to pass in the European Union, if central authorities seriously begin to flex their legislative muscles.

In sum, while this examination of cantonal defiance of federal policies in the early Swiss union has not answered all questions about member-state cooperation in early decades of federal unions, it has added new dimensions to the comparative critique of hypotheses espoused elsewhere for explaining the coherence of integrative unions, particularly the modern European. The next chapter will attempt to draw together the insights from this four-case study for some helpful generalizations about formative epochs in modern, voluntary federal unions.

CHAPTER 5

Conclusions: State Behavior
in Suprastate Unions

"Confederations . . . are usually stepping-stones to a federal state" (Murray Forsyth).[1]

"Federation, as opposed to unitary government, is only alive where there is an underlying confederative situation, a submerged ethnicity, . . . or a passionately held allegiance to past 'history' as a cantonal state amounting to an ethnicity" (Christopher Hughes).[2]

"It is unclear whether the motive of trade restriction is sufficient to replace the military motive in creating a European federation" (William Riker).[3]

FRAMING THE PROBLEM

Attempts to generalize about confederations and federations as abstract categories have produced diametrically opposed conclusions, as the preceding quotations, produced within a span of fifteen years, illustrate. Murray Forsyth perceives a dominant tendency toward increased centralization, a tendency that Christopher Hughes sees as contributing to the extreme of unitary government save for the rare instances where truly powerful, countervailing cultural forces preserve citizen loyalty to regional units. William Riker, by contrast, sees a general tendency for federations to break apart whenever the military alliance motive—or trade-war-substitute motive—fades in importance.

Studies in comparative politics face the alternative dangers of foundering on either the Scylla of generalizations so abstract as to be of little practical import in specific situations, or the Charybdis of immersion in particular details specific to a single polity to a degree that makes generalization impossible. This study has attempted to steer between these problems by examining a specific subcategory of federated union—those formed voluntarily, by independent states, in the modern Euro-American cultural context. This work has attempted to avoid entering the categorization debate over whether the European Union is best understood as a confederation, a federation, or a consociation.[4] What is clear is that the form of the union has evolved rapidly in its first forty years; what is not clear is what the stopping point will be of what its own members agreed in Maastricht to call "an ever closer union." Several scholars have asserted that it is already "a polity," and should be analyzed as such (although typically the label is qualified by some adjective, as in "contested polity," "multilevel polity," or "compound polity.")[5]

The goal here has been to ascertain what forces, in a nonconquest situation, cause formerly sovereign states to continue to maintain their willingness to cede sovereignty to a suprastate unit after their initial decision to join that unit. The question is particularly salient of late, in part because of the continued strengthening of the European Union, but also, more broadly, because modern states around the world are exhibiting an increased willingness to engage in multilateral commitments to be rendered enforceable by new suprastate courts.[6]

It is certainly plausible that some of this impetus toward joining larger governmental units is an attempt to form countervailing power blocs suitable for coping with the enormous consolidations of economic power visible in multinational corporations, and formations such as the International Monetary Fund. Not only do trade, finance, and labor forces cross state borders; so do environmental problems. Multigovernmental cooperation and the use of transgovernmental authorities for coping with those issues have already been going on for years.

Indeed, the most recent works on what motivates transstate regional formations have stressed the fundamental motor force of responses to transstate economic forces—whether via domestic political leaders' responding to domestic economic groups, or via interactions directly between transstate economic groups and EC supranational institutions, or both.[7]

Not only economic forces, however, have been at work. The more powerful nations of the world increasingly display an interest in establishing some sort of basic human rights regime, as evidenced by the strengthening of the European Court of Human Rights, the trial of Pinochet, the United Nations efforts in Bosnia, and the NATO effort in Kosovo.[8] The recent explosion of suprastate free-trade regimes and human rights regimes has, naturally, produced a new wave of scholarship that emphasizes economic motives for the former and ideological motives for the latter.[9] This development contrasts with an earlier generation of scholarship on federated formations that tended to emphasize military or defense motives.[10] Still, military and diplomatic concerns have not been entirely absent from scholarly analysis of motives for joining, for instance, the EC/EU. The 1995 timing of the entry into the EC/EU of Cold War–neutral countries Austria, Finland, and Sweden was at the very least facilitated by the collapse of the Soviet Union.[11]

Regardless, however, of the impetus for joining suprastate unions, behavior of states once in them has shown a wide range of variation over time. An improved understanding of the nature of that variation has been the goal of this study.[12]

Ordinary citizens, as Aristotle pointed out long ago, obey laws basically out of habit.[13] Just as most Americans, when they see a speed limit sign do not pause to ask themselves if the ordinance was adopted in Washington, D.C., their state capital, or their city council chamber, citizens in the EU countries do not generally seem to worry much whether the rules about additives in their automobile fuel came from Brussels or their national capital. By contrast, it is not obvious what one should expect of governmental officials in state units that have formally and voluntarily (acting in the name of the population in their unit) ceded parts of their sovereign authority to a larger unit. Whether or not the same officials, a specially elected body, or the people themselves voted to accede to the federating pact, the question arises what future officials in those state units will do. Will ingrained political habit stemming from the former independence of their unit, given the ambition that tends to characterize officials in general (as in Krasner's maxim that "rulers want to stay in power")[14] promote continued assertions of unit independence when disagreement with the policies of the central authorities arises? Or will the fact of the compact somehow operate to bind official behavior into the future? Or, to put it another way, what happens when government officials whose offices have been the depository of sovereign authority lose part of that authority to officials of larger units? Under what sorts of conditions is the relationship among the units likely to remain cooperative or become conflictual?

In a recent survey of scholarly approaches to these questions as they apply to integration in the European Union, Paul Pierson has suggested that they can be conveniently divided among four categories:[15]

1. *Intergovernmentalists* (or *neorealists*) (e.g., Geoffrey Garrett and Barry Weingast) view the EC/EU as essentially a "forum for interstate bargaining." (In this picture, the policies adopted by EC authorities basically reflect the will of the member nation-states, so the latter would have no sound reason to resist these policies.)[16]

2. *Comparative federalists* (my term; Pierson leaves the category untitled) treat the EC/EU as a single "quasi-federal system" (e.g., Fritz Scharpf and Renaud Dehousse), and analyze the union as a "single (if highly fragmented) polity."

3. *Neofunctionalists* (e.g., Alec Stone Sweet and the mid-1990s work of Anne-Marie [Burley] Slaughter and Walter Mattli) stress the degree of independence from member-state control that has been exhibited to date by both the European Commission and the Court of Justice and suggest that these institutions are in fact serving the desires of transnational interest groups to a significant degree against the wishes of powerful member-state governmental leaders.[17]

4. *Historical institutionalists* (among whom Pierson places himself) observe political development "as a process that unfolds over time" and view the "implications of these temporal processes as embedded in institutions—whether they be formal rules, policy structures, or norms." (He cites as other exemplars of this approach K. Thelen and S. Steinmo and also unpublished work by G. John Ikenberry.) Historical institutionalists emphasize "how the evolution of rules and policies along with social adaptations creates an increasingly structured polity that restricts the options available to all political actors."[18] Writing a few years later, Karen Alter groups Fritz Scharpf's work together with the historical institutionalists Pierson and Mark Pollack, in order to further develop a historical institutionalist analysis of the ECJ.[19] Mattli and Slaughter, also writing in 1998, appear to place themselves within this broad stream of scholarship, which abandons the rigidly intergovernmentalist-functionalist dichotomy and focuses instead on the interactions among institutional norms and structures and subnational, national, and supranational actors.[20]

In the few years before Pierson's piece was published, a group of British scholars also specifically endorsed the historical institutionalist approach as the best way to understand what has been happening in the European Union. These included Simon Bulmer, Jo Shaw and Gillian More, Kenneth Armstrong, and Daniel Wincott.[21]

Most recently, Andrew Moravcsik has himself been defending an eclectic blend of approaches, a fifth category, which he calls *liberal intergovernmentalist*. It shares with neofunctionalism an emphasis on transstate economic forces, but it shares with intergovernmentalism the insistence that such forces take on their most significant political momentum when they are perceived as salient domestically by dominant domestic political actors. (Thus political leadership figures prominently in his theory.) Moreover, while Moravcsik criticizes some of the more rigid versions of historical institutionalism, he grants that a "weak" version of it helps explain the process of European integration. (What he rejects is its overemphasis on unintended consequences, although he does acknowledge that the important assertions of power by the ECJ were in fact unintended by the treaty signers).[22]

To the degree that this book fits into any of these categories, it too would seem to fall largely into "historical institutionalism," in that it heeds the import of institutional change over time and also is attentive to the variety of incentive structures created by differing institutionalized arrangements. However, like the work of Fritz Scharpf, this work has also stressed the value for historical institutionalist insight that can be gained by comparison with other *federal* (in the sense of formed by a federating pact) polities.[23] This book has thus built on the perception of Johan de Vree that federal integration and international integration are parts of the same continuum, and can usefully be examined together.[24]

Hence, in addition to careful reflection on the likely impact of particular institutional arrangements over time, this study has provided a comparative dimension. While numerous analysts have attempted to explain the phenomenon presented by the European Union—a situation in which territorial states, independent for lengthy periods, have now voluntarily and relatively placidly ceded considerable portions of their "sovereign powers" to the central authority of the union—few of these EC-focused analyses have tested their suppositions by comparison with other cases.[25] In contrast, the comparative dimension in this study has provided the opportunity to attempt to verify a number of assumptions made by those scholars of the European integration process who have actually addressed the curious absence of resistance to centralizing moves by the ECJ. Some of their conclusions about how particular institutions function, which seemed intuitively appealing on the basis of the single case they examined, have proven less persuasive now that they failed to hold up in other cases involving parallel institutions.

Despite a substantial fifty-year literature on the topic of comparative federalism, which began with K. C. Wheare's first edition of *Federal Gov-*

ernments in 1946 (the most recent edition of which was the fourth in 1963), and which continues into the late nineties, little has been done before now to test systematically how the European Community fits the propositions that have evolved from this literature. This literature tends to focus on two questions: What sorts of governmental institutions properly warrant the designation "federal"? (The answer varies according to the definition of "federal" posited in each work.) And under what conditions are federal arrangements of government likely to endure? The answer to this latter question features the condition of a powerful will, at least among the politically active class, to retain the option for diversity among the member states and yet to be united with other states for reasons of military-diplomatic strength and/or economic advantage.[26]

Because this study has examined only voluntary unions, to the exclusion of those imposed by imperial authorities or by conquest, the matter of a will to form a union has been treated as a given rather than a variable (although there has been variability in reaction to specific policies announced by union authorities). Whether one calls the European Community "federal," "confederal," "quasi-federal," or "consociational," what seems clear is that it is yet another example of a union of freely federating states that retain a great deal of the power to govern the residents of their respective territories and that have nonetheless ceded important degrees of governing power to central institutions. (Until 1994 these were the Council of Ministers, the European Court of Justice, and the European Commission. After 1994, the European Parliament became an additional important actor.) The European Community has already endured for more than forty years, and was much more centralized in 1999 than in 1958. No one is predicting its imminent breakup. The question animating this study, therefore, is not whether it would "succeed," in the sense of enduring with some discernible mix of central and member-state division of power. Rather, the question is: How has it managed to endure to this point with such a low degree of member-state resistance to central authority, in clear contrast to other unions of states of comparable cultural settings during their formative epochs?

By comparing the degree of member-state resistance to central authority during the early decades of four unions that formed voluntarily from independent states, this study has uncovered a number of postulates derivable from one of the cases that would have seemed generalizable for other federal unions but that did not hold up for other cases in the sample. This inductive, comparative approach is not one that can feed either of the two competing grand theories of regional integration within international relations literature—neofunctionalism and (neorealist) intergovernmentalism. It does, however, comport well with the insights expressed recently by Mattli and Slaughter: "The story of European legal integration cannot be told without an account of the interrelationship between neofunctionalist and intergovernmentalist factors. Neither framework is fully satisfactory on its own terms." And, "At this point the debate [between these two grand theories] has reached the limits of its usefulness. [More recent scholarship on legal integration within the EC] challenges neofunctionalists and intergovernmentalists to leave their paradigms behind and work toward a set of mid-range hypotheses."[27] Just such mid-range theorizing has been the goal of this study, by means of which it has been possible to render questionable hypotheses that would have seemed plausible based on a one- or two-case study, and also to suggest more durable hypotheses that appear to characterize tendencies within such unions.

For instance, one might have thought that the degree of clarity in the constitutive document on the allocation of powers between the center and the subunits—because it is the document to which all member-state governments had deliberately assented—predicts a later absence of conflict between the two. The Union of Utrecht of 1579 exhibited a marked ambiguity on this matter, and indeed for two centuries one saw chronic conflict over the bounds of sovereignty of the member provinces. The Swiss Constitution of 1848 was much clearer: all powers not listed as belonging to the federation remain with the cantons. The federal legislature has final authority to decide that its own acts are constitutional, but anything it enacts (other than emergency measures) can be vetoed by popular referendum. Certainly by comparison to the Dutch case, the Swiss union was relatively nonconflictual on the matter of federal authority. While there were numerous cantonal enactments that contravened clear federal policy, there were nonetheless hardly any of the kind of outright member-state denials of federal power to act that were so frequently evident in both the Dutch and the American unions.

On the other hand, if one makes a comparison between the European and American federations, the intuitive importance to be put on the clarity of the founding document disappears. The American Constitution, ratified (eventually) by every state, with a clear supremacy clause and a clear specification that jurisdiction for every case "arising under" the Constitution would go to one supreme federal court, nevertheless engendered a union where state governmental units repeatedly challenged federal supremacy over a wide range of issues. In Europe, by contrast, the Treaty

of Rome said nothing about its own authority to negate future, conflicting laws adopted by signatories to the treaty, but the European Court of
Justice successfully interpreted the treaty as carrying this implication and
provoked relatively little state resistance to the move.

Caution is warranted in drawing conclusions from even a four-case
study. To conclude that founding documents—that is, initiating intergovernmental agreements—do not matter at all would be going too far. Yet
one can now reliably judge it an error to credit the clarity of the 1848
Swiss founding document as *the* cause of the relative absence of member-
state rejection of federal authority within that union, since such clarity
neither prevented state resistance in the United States, nor was needed to
prevent it in the European Community. A sensible approach to the un-
covering of conflicting examples of this sort would seem to be to acknowledge that the variable in question (here, clarity of the founding document) did not itself determine the outcome (absence of later member-state
rejection of federal authority), and to search further to uncover other, like-
lier causal variables. (Such has been the general approach in this work.)

The surprising ease with which the European Court of Justice asserted
its authority to establish "supreme law" for the European Community
creates an example that also calls into question other plausible hunches
as to variables that might make unlikely member-state resistance to central authority in newly formed unions—hunches, that is, that would have
seemed plausible except that they do not hold true when the EC is compared to other cases. One would have thought, for instance, that the
longer states functioned as independent sovereigns, the more likely they
would be to resist central authority within a union that they later joined
(on the grounds that a deeply embedded habit of wielding independent
authority is harder to break than a few years experience of independence).
One could also have assumed that the more cultural heterogeneity across
the member states within a union, the more they would be likely to resist
central union authority. This latter hypothesis is common in comparative
federalism literature (although William Riker, for one, shares the conclusion of this study that it is invalid).[28] Neither of these intuitively plausible hypotheses holds up as a predictor of which union, the American or
the European, would experience more member-state resistance.

CONCLUSIONS

The histories of the four unions discussed here has exhibited partial
transfers of sovereignty toward federated unions as basically long-term

processes of negotiation, where the negotiation not uncommonly takes the form of official acts of defiance at the member-state level. By "official acts of defiance," I refer not to the kinds of noncompliance that are more or less routine in any large-scale society, that is, noncompliance resulting from inertia or inattention or prudential delay (with the intent to comply as promptly as feasible). I refer instead to open, official, and public acts of member-state resistance, that is, actions by state-governing authorities relying on their official capacities—formal public pronouncements by the governing executive, majority decisions of state appellate courts, or official legislative resolutions.

From the foregoing study, one can rank the four unions under discussion in their level of resistance to federal authority, taking into account the depth as well as the frequency of member-state defiance. Thus, the Dutch provinces would rank as the most chronically resistant, followed by the American states, the Swiss cantons (although they resisted more than is generally acknowledged), and finally the European Community.

The seventeenth-century Dutch union was at one extreme, in that the union experienced continual challenges to its legitimacy because the respective governments of the member provinces never abandoned the claim that they had retained their sovereignty in the form of a veto power over federal policy. This was so even though this provincial claim flew in the face both of the wording of the constitutive document, the Union of Utrecht, and the consistent practice of the federal legislature.

The American union, too, experienced for its first seventy years intermittent but quite frequent challenges both to the legitimacy of the federal authority to tell states what they could do, and to actual federal laws. Official legislative, executive, and judicial state bodies during this period engaged openly on numerous occasions in one or another of the following: defiance of specific federal court interpretations of law, rejections of the authority of federal courts to interpret law, defiance of the evident meaning of federal law, formal acts of nullification of federal law, defiance of federal court orders, authorization of forceful resistance to federal law enforcement, and threats to secede from the union. Unlike the Dutch union, however, at any given time in the United States (until the Civil War) there was a clear consensus among a large majority of the states as to the legitimacy of the federal decision-making authority.

In contrast to the Dutch and American situations, the early decades of the modern Swiss union were characterized by virtually constant cantonal acceptance of the idea (with only a small handful of isolated exceptions) that federal authorities in the final instance may legitimately determine the bounds of cantonal power. Nonetheless, a sizable number of cantons fairly often engaged in open and official defiance of federal policy. These actions of cantonal defiance of the union government generally took the form of cantonal adoption of policies that flatly contradicted federal law—the federal law of constitutional provisions themselves, of authoritative federal interpretations of these provisions, and of federal decrees (*arrêtés*) to implement the provisions or the interpretations. Of these sorts of "member-state" resistance in the early decades of the Swiss union, examples abound.

In the European Community, since the ECJ turned it into a quasi-federal polity by legal doctrine in the early 1960s, open member-state defiance of either ECJ legitimacy or ECJ policies has been remarkably rare. While some such defiance has occurred (which fact may cause observers who lack a comparative framework to exaggerate its importance), it has been quite limited both in number of instances and in intensity. As in the Swiss union, outright challenges to the legitimacy of EC authority have been extraordinarily few, coming only from a single source (viz., the French Conseil d'État, following the advice of its Commissaire du Gouvernement, and officially abandoning its rejection of ECJ authority only in 1989). But in contrast to the Swiss union, overt member-state defiance even of EC policies (as distinguished from authority per se) by the first six countries to join the EC has also been quite limited both in terms of the number of instances and number of member states involved. While national authorities in France on several occasions openly defied EC law (and did so for sustained periods of time), the only other country where such defiance took place was Germany. But there, the two authorities engaging in such behavior—the Supreme Tax Court and the Ministry of Finance—were promptly overruled by German higher authorities.[29] Thus, both in terms of relative frequency and relative stridency, the EC ranks at the other extreme from the Dutch union in this study. Its member states exhibited the least official resistance to central union authority of the four unions I examined.

On the basis of this ranking, one can assess a variety of hypotheses to explain the relative frequency of member-state resistance to federal authorities. The virtue of a four-union comparison for assessing such hypotheses is not that it enables one to reject the explanation *tout court*, for it is always possible that a given explanation might in fact perceptively describe any single idiosyncratic case. What comparative analysis can provide is the opportunity to assess the generalizability of the explanation. For instance, increasing numbers of supranational courts are exercising authority to enforce increasing numbers of multilateral normative commitments;[30] thus the assertion in EU literature that judges can more effectively or more quickly or more smoothly bring about integration toward tighter unions than politicians can is an important one, particularly if it is generalizable beyond the case of the EU.[31]

A catalogue of these hypotheses is presented in Table 8. (One hypothesis about the nature of federal unions that is omitted from the table and not discussed in this book is the contention of William Riker that the nature of a "federal bargain" is determined by the structure of political parties within the federal union.[32] He seems to have been heavily influenced by the fact that he included in his study nonvoluntary, authoritarian unions, such as the Soviet and Yugoslavian unions, where the role of authoritarian political parties dominated political life. Although the absence of federation-wide political parties in the EU is probably of some importance in slowing the integration process, the subject matter of this book has been voluntary federal unions, concerning which Riker's hypothesis is not particularly useful.)

As Table 8 highlights, certain hypotheses about avoiding member-state resistance in the integration process have shown a durability across several examples of multistate unions, while others seem to fit only the cases that gave rise to them. Hypotheses 1, 2, and 3 stand out as having been particularly well confirmed by this study: (1) Unions formed in the crucible of revolt against imperial power will be more likely to experience state resistance to central power. (2) Unions where obedience to the rule of law is more routinized in general will experience less resistance by member state officials to the rule of federation-level authorities. And (3) a union precipitated directly by a war among its member states will be less likely to undergo overt member-state rejection of its authority. These will be more fully discussed below. Moreover, with an important clarification, the fourth hypothesis could be added to this group as well-confirmed propositions.

On the surface, hypothesis 4 applies successfully to all the unions except the Dutch. In fact, however, the failure of the fourth proposition with respect to the Dutch case is an artifact of its having been expressed in terms of an absolute: namely, the more confederal the union structure, the less member-state resistance. Numerous concrete illustrations of confederal features adopted in the EC and unsuccessfully sought by several early American states were described in Chapter 2. Since the Dutch union is at a far extreme in degree of decentralization of authority, and is also at an extreme in member-state resistance (in that the provinces continually in-

Table 8. Hypotheses on Member-State Resistance

KEY
+ = applies successfully to explain this union's rank in degree of member-state resistance;
− = fails to conform to this union's rank in degree of resistance;
0 = appears inapplicable to this union (i.e., the union does not contain the feature crucial to the hypothesis).
DU = Dutch union
AU = United States of America
SU = Swiss union
EU = European union

Hypothesis	DU	AU	SU	EU
1. Unions formed in the crucible of revolt against imperial power will be *more* likely to have state resistance to central power.	+	+	+	+
2. Unions where obedience to the rule of law is more routinized in general will experience *less* resistance by member-state officials to the rule of federation-level officials.	+	+	+	+
3. A union precipitated directly by a war among its member states will be *less* likely to experience overt member-state rejection of its authority.	+	+	+	+
4. Unions that *appear* to honor the sovereignty of the members by assuring each an equal voice in the body that determines the bounds of federal power—by having that body *appear* to decide by unanimity, although in fact what prevails may be merely consensus, and by retaining a formal separation between federal- and state-level judicial systems—will be *less* likely to experience member-state resistance to the center.*	0	+	+	+
5. If there are institutional (power or status) rewards to member state officials to promote obedience to federal authority, there will be *less* member state resistance.[†]	−/+	0	0	+

Table 8. (*continued*)

Hypothesis	DU	AU	SU	EU
6. In unions that require staying in, or promptly returning to, state-level office for the exercise of federal-level authority, there will be *less* state resistance.[‡]	0	0	0	+
7. A well-financed, well-organized pro-union socialization campaign aimed at legal/political elites can *reduce* state resistance.	0	0	0	+
8. Where elites prefer union and masses do not (in democratically representative systems), allowing integration by non-accountable elites at the member-state level can *reduce* state resistance.	0	0	0	+
9. If the union-integrating decisions are made by judges rather than politicians, there will be *less* resistance to integration.	+	−	−	+
10. The existence of transstate interest groups with an objective interest in fostering a tighter union will lead to *less* member-state resistance to federal authority.[§]	0	−	−	+
11. After a sizable number of member-states have abjured resistance to union authority, their example will influence other states to do the same.	−	−	−	+

*In the Dutch union, a body with authority to judge the bounds of federal/province-level power never clearly developed; each province had one vote in the federation level legislature, but the legislature generally did not act until it could attain widespread consensus. Provinces claimed a veto power but in fact did not have one.

In the Swiss union, the federal judiciary can directly override cantonal-level courts; thus there is not a separation of the two judicial systems. Nor do cantons have an equal voice within the Federal Tribunal. But the bounds of federal level power are decided legislatively: one of the two legislative chambers gives an equal voice to each ("whole") canton and no law can pass without the consent of this house. Moreover, it is commonly observed that Swiss political culture highly values consensus even within legislative politics. This combination of features puts Switzerland in a mid-level category in degree of confederalness; since it is in a middle rank on degree of state resistance, it is assigned a plus sign.

†In the Dutch union, it sometimes enhanced the power of province-level officials to foster obedience to federal authority, but sometimes doing so would have the opposite result. For the

(continued)

Table 8. (*continued*)

latter situation, the hypothesis gets a plus, but for the former a minus. In short, the Dutch example does not offer a clear test-case for this proposition.

‡The Dutch union alternately gave supreme federal power to a single province-level official, either the pensionary/advocate of Holland or the Prince of Orange. On the other hand, the other federal level legislators could seek their office without holding state-level office; thus again the Dutch structures do not comfortably fit the hypothesis (derived from the Euro-American comparison).

§There were transstate interest groups in the Dutch union, in a sense, such as the merchant class and the military, and sometimes they would benefit from tighter union, depending on policy preferences of the union consensus. It is anachronistic, however, to apply the term "interest group" here, because membership in these groups meant being a part of the government in the seventeenth-century Dutch union.

sisted that they should each have a veto power over major union decisions), this union seems to defy the proposition.

On the other hand, if the proposition were restated more cautiously—that there seems to be an optimum level of confederalness that will allow successful union functioning while minimizing state resistance—then the Dutch case would fit the thesis, in effect illustrating its outer bounds. Such unions that fail to establish clearly and definitively which body holds the "*kompetenz-kompetenz*" power (the power to decide who decides) over the location of the dividing line between central and member-state power will encounter repeated legitimacy challenges. Nonetheless, short of the point of giving a member-state veto to every federal-level decision, the likelihood of member-state resistance can be minimized by increasing the number of confederal features in a given union. Such confederal features in the European Community included such institutions as supermajority decision-making at the federal level and institutional formalities (such as the appearance of unanimity in all ECJ decisions) that honor the appeared retention of sovereignty in the subordinate units.

This confederalism proposition directly conflicts with an earlier claim by comparative federalist William Riker in Chapter 6 of his 1987 book, but his claim—that centralization maximizes stability of federations—relied on a methodology with a number of serious flaws (some of which he himself acknowledged in the book):

1. The Riker data set lumped together voluntary unions with ones maintained by party dictatorships or by imperial conquest.

2. Instead of counting length of durability to measure stability of the federation, the chapter coauthors (Riker and Jonathan Lemco) used the

arbitrary measure of continued existence in federal form as of 1980, the date of the original research.

3. The authors acknowledge, "We are not entirely sure we can define exactly what we have found . . . [because] 'centralization' and 'peripheralization' are very complicated and ill-defined notions."

4. Without explanation, the study counts the United States of 1776–81—joined together by only a military alliance—as the same federation as the Confederation of States of 1781–88, and as the same federation as the one established by the post-1787 Constitution. It is hard to understand how someone could arrive at a single, appropriate ranking of degree of centralization of authority that fit these three remarkably different constitutional arrangements.

5. Finally, Riker, the senior author, himself acknowledged seven years after he coauthored this chapter that "we may well have erred" in constructing the basic methodology that treated as "unstable" a federation that experienced an attempted secession, even though it succeeded in putting down the secession and continuing in federal form thereafter. He cites for his error the early United States, but his acknowledgment could apply as well to the fact that his analysis omitted the Swiss Confederation of 1815, beginning only with the post–Sonderbund War Federation of 1848.

While all these render his a flawed analysis, the first and second in the list would seem to make Riker's study particularly inapt for understanding the EC (which, incidentally, he does not include in his list of federated unions).

Hypotheses 5–8 in Table 8 must be judged as neither confirmed nor denied by this study. They postulate that (5) if acceptance of union-level authority offers power/status rewards to state-level officials (i.e., as happened for judges in EC member states), then there will be less member-state resistance; (6) in unions where one must hold state-level office (Council of Ministers) or return to it shortly (ECJ) in order to wield union-level authority, there will be less member-state resistance (because state-level officialdom will contain some pro-union voices); (7) the presence of a well-financed, well-targeted pro-union socialization effort that produces an influential pro-union interest group will minimize state-level resistance; and (8) in unions of democracies, if elites at the state level favor the union more than masses do, a device for handing decision-making authority over to nonaccountable state-level elites (i.e., non-elected judges) will minimize state-level resistance. Each of these postulates is derived from a feature unique to the European Union, was induced from or supported by the Euro-American comparison, and attributes causal force to the European institutional feature for the difference in degree of member-state resistance between the two unions. All four propositions may well be both correct and generalizable, since the EC was at one extreme in exhibiting a minimum of member-state resistance to central authority, and because it was the only case examined that really had this particular institutional feature. Still, before one could place confidence in these propositions, a more wide-ranging research effort would be appropriate—ideally one that included other cases where the causal institutional variables were in fact present—to learn if the hypotheses hold up in other contexts.

Hypothesis 5, in particular, the suggestion that member-state defiance of union authority can be minimized by providing power/status incentives to member-state officials for cooperating with union-level authority—which happened in the EC via judicial empowerment at the member-state level—faced certain limits in Chapter 3. In the Dutch union, at least two province-level officials, the stadholder and the advocate of Holland, also served as the primary leader of the union as a whole (during differing periods), the former as Prince of Orange and leader of the union army, and the latter as the leader of the union legislative body. Because of their respective union leadership roles, each of them enhanced his power by acts that strengthened union authority. On the other hand, each also faced other incentives that caused certain policy preferences. When majority forces within the union opposed those policy preferences, each resorted to asserting (without success) the legitimacy of his province-level veto power, against union-level authority. While the empowerment thesis probably has merit for partially explaining why these men supported a strong union as much as they did, nonetheless, the Dutch case suggests (at least on the basis of these two officials) that power and status incentives sometimes can push in centrifugal as well as centripetal directions, and also that they can be outweighed by other sorts of incentives. Scholars who have considered differential rates at which EC member states support union authority, or differential rates within particular countries at which particular courts support union authority (e.g., Daniel Wincott and Jonathan Golub), have similarly concluded that the judicial empowerment thesis has already started to exhibit these limits within the EC context.

The set of unions examined here did permit a more thorough testing of a number of other propositions about minimizing conflict in integrating federal unions. Hypotheses 9–11, which attempt to explain the remarkable ease with which the European Court of Justice has pulled together the European Community, all failed to hold true in other evidently comparable cases.

Hypothesis 9 asserts that if union-integrating decisions are made by judges rather than politicians, there will be less member-state resistance to union authority. However, the fact that judges made the bulk of the integrative decisions in the early United States did not prevent that union from ranking among the more-resistance-experiencing half of the cases studied. Nor did the fact that nonjudges in Switzerland during the period studied made virtually all the country's integrative decisions keep the Swiss union from ranking in the less-resistance-experiencing half of the cases.

As to hypothesis 10, transstate interest groups of considerable clout did promote federal union in the early decades of both the Swiss and American unions. Many of these were commercially oriented, but others focused on building one or another aspect of a federation-wide national culture. Nonetheless, their efforts were not adequate to prevent a substantial degree of member-state resistance in both unions.

Regarding hypothesis 11, in none of the unions, other than the modern European, did the force of emulatable example of several provinces/cantons/states that accepted federal authority function successfully to prevent later resistance to such authority by the other member units. Both this hypothesis, however, and hypothesis 9 about decisions made by judges via formalistic legal reasoning—although they did not hold true for unions in the past—may have a more limited generalizability for certain federated unions in the contemporary world. This point will be more fully explicated below.

On the other hand, this study does provides robust support for a few hypotheses concerning the successful voluntary integration of formerly independent states. One of these has already been discussed: there appears to be an optimum level of confederalness in institutional arrangements for avoiding state resistance to union authority. This optimum, while not going so far as to allow an actual member-state veto over union actions, is approximated by arrangements that maximize consensus-based decision-making and the appearance of unanimity for union-level decisions.

More than three centuries ago, Samuel Pufendorf, in an analysis of the nature of confederations, explicated the psychological mechanism by which confederations that formally require unanimous consent of member states for making certain categories of decision tend in practice to evolve toward consensus-based arrangements. Since the members were linked by an overall commonality of interest, if all the members but one (or, arguably, all except any tiny fraction of the membership) were united in a common course of action, an obstinate and intractable persistence in an isolated opinion against the general consensus would appear as "perverse stubbornness" likely to be viewed as "unreasonable" (in the way that outlaws are unreasonable) and therefore a violation of the pact by its other members.[33] This assessment of group psychology sheds considerable light on how the member states of the Dutch union of Pufendorf's day managed to maintain a two-hundred-year confusion as to whether their decision rules really required unanimity rather than consensus. Moreover, it explains how independent states that enter federal unions with a predictable desire to retain veto power over such profound decisions as wars, treaties, or taxation can end up with a certain comfort level over substitutions that approximate consensus with decision rules of two-thirds, three-fourths, or "weighted voting."

Second, federations formed in the crux of a revolt against distant imperial power are likely to experience a good deal of member-state resistance to the union, as did the Dutch and American unions (and, outside the scope of this study, the India-Pakistan-Bangladesh union). State resistance to more distant central authority will resonate with the patriotic pride in the anti-imperial struggle, and consequently is likely to crop up more often in such unions.

Third, federations formed shortly after, and in response to, a war among the member states are likely to benefit from a subdued degree of conflict once the union has formed. The memory of World War II probably helped to pacify relations within the European Union (notwithstanding the skepticism about such claims from those EC scholars who focus singlemindedly on economic motivations), just as the Sonderbund War tempered potential resistance tendencies in the Swiss cantons. Indeed, one could add the American union after the Civil War to this picture: after the war, open resistance to federal authority by state officialdom all but disappeared in the United States (at least until a brief flare-up in the 1950s). A war among the member states immediately preceding union appears to render more threatening the secession option and thus make proclamations of union illegitimacy less palatable.

Fourth, and perhaps most important for the fate of future voluntary federations (and less tight multicountry unions), this study has uncovered what appears to be a direct correlation between the degree to which a society has internalized the rule of law, or the degree to which it has experienced the routinization of obedience to lawfully constituted authority, and the acceptance by state-level authorities of the rule over them by duly constituted federal-level authorities. The routinization of the rule of law has emerged as the variable most clearly (negatively) related to the degree of state resistance to federal authority in these unions, in that the unions'

ranking in degree of resistance correlates exactly inversely with their ranking on the degree to which the rule of law had manifestly been internalized in the society of each union. This finding, incidentally, offers support
to Andrew Moravcsik's parallel argument about where suprastate human
rights regimes are likely to succeed.[34]

The Dutch union was by far the most turbulent of the four examined
here. In it, political transitions were often accompanied by violence,
purges, and the threat of armed force. Moreover, it contained entire
provinces where for certain years one could not determine where or who
the government was for purposes of collecting taxes. It also experienced
the deepest level of resistance to union-level authority.

The early decades of the American union were also quite turbulent by
contemporary standards. Numerous symptoms can be identified. Violent
state resistance to federal authority on occasion proved too much even for
federal troops. The threat of armed force (in this era that predated the secret ballot) is known to have sometimes swayed elections. The question
whether judges should follow public opinion rather than their honest assessment of law was considered a legitimate subject of political debate,
and juries were not legally obliged to follow judicial instructions as to
what law meant until 1850.

The Swiss union in the latter half of the nineteenth century, too, was
plagued by outbreaks of mass violence, where cantonal governments
called in federal troops on several occasions to restore order. Still, in
Switzerland the federal troops were at least able to quell the violence at
the cantonal level, and the eruptions of violence do not seem to have been
as endemic as during the early decades of the United States. Moreover, the
gradual expansion, over the first several decades of the union, in the jurisdiction accorded to the Federal Tribunal (as distinguished from the political bodies of government) appears to have signified a gradual increase
in respect for the rule of law as such.

By the late twentieth century, when the European Court of Justice began declaring a "supreme law" of the European Union, its declarations
could take root in fertile soil. Member states of the EEC (and later the EC,
then EU) by then either honored long traditions of the rule of law (as in
the United Kingdom, the Netherlands, Belgium, and Luxembourg), or (as
in Italy, West Germany, and France) deliberately and forcefully turned
their backs on fascist regimes of World War II, by establishing not only
democratic republics but also constitutional courts to uphold the republican constitutions.

Lest the reader suspect that this emphasis on the routinization of the rule of law is some sort of accidental surrogate for "modernity"—in that the regimes furthest back in history are dubbed the most turbulent, and the most recent are dubbed the most accepting of lawfully constituted authority—it is worth clarifying that the claim here is not one of linear "progress" through time. The breaking apart of both the Soviet Union and Yugoslavia in recent years—although, to be sure, these were imposed rather than voluntary unions among states—should prove a cautionary example. These two were clearly cases where the rule of law was unfortunately not a deeply or widely internalized norm. The sheer fact that union had originally been imposed on some or all member states rather than freely chosen by all of them did not itself necessarily presage future state resistance to the point of break-up, as could be illustrated by numerous examples, such as Germany or Australia. On the other hand, the absence of a strong societal norm of obedience to the rule of law does seem to presage resistance at the member-state governmental level to authority exercised from the center in federal-style unions. The powerful presence of such a norm within the signatory states of the Treaty of Rome, then, seems in large part to explain their acceptance of the legal integration of the European Community wrought by the European Court of Justice.

The strength of this norm in the EC also may help to explain why hypotheses 9 and 11 functioned effectively in the EC but not in the other unions examined here. In a society where the propriety of following law versus following public opinion is considered an open and debatable question, as it was, for example, in the early-nineteenth-century United States, the fact that judges rather than elected politicians prefer a given policy does not appreciably strengthen its legitimacy. Similarly, the fact that most member states at any given moment recognize the legitimacy of union authority will count for much less in a union where the rule of law is not well entrenched. These two hypotheses from EC scholarship that did not hold up to the test of the cases studied here may nonetheless have a certain strength in the future for describing likely patterns of governmental behavior in those societies where the rule of law is well entrenched.

At the same time, the relative weakness of rule-of-law norms among the former Eastern Bloc states that have expressed interest in joining the EU presents ground for serious caution. A precipitous eastward expansion of the EU, if the conclusions of this study prove correct, would make likely a substantial rise in the level of member-state resistance to central authority within that union. Even in politics, bigger is not always better.

State Resistance to Federal Authority
in the United States

For the reader interested in the empirical foundation of the analysis of American state resistance patterns provided in Chapter 1, Appendix A simply provides a more comprehensive narrative account of state resistance to federal authority in the first several decades of U.S. history. The sources for these narratives appear in the notes to Table 3.

[1790] After delaying ratification of the U.S. Constitution until after the First Congress convened, NORTH CAROLINA eventually did ratify in November 1789, but evident discomfort about submitting to federal authority showed up in both the legislative and judicial branches in 1790. State legislators in the Assembly voted down a proposal that they and all other state officers be required to take an oath to uphold the U.S. Constitution, despite the clear command of Article 6, Section 3: "Members of the several state legislatures, and all executive and judicial officers . . . of the several states, shall be bound by oath or affirmation to support this Constitution." In the same year, the highest court of North Carolia (called the Superior Court) refused to obey a writ from a federal court to turn over a case for a federal decision. The case involved a land dispute between British subjects and executors of a North Carolinian estate. The North Carolina legislature formally ratified the state court's refusal to comply with the federal order.

[1793–98] In February 1793 the U.S. Supreme Court handed down its first decision, *Chisholm v. Georgia*. The decision allowed state governments to be sued by creditors. GEORGIA refused to let the verdict be executed, legislating the death penalty for any attempt to do so. The Court's decision was so unpopular that the U.S. Constitution was amended by 1798 to overturn it (through a two-third's vote in each house of the federal Congress and ratification by three-quarters of the states).

[1794] In Pennsylvania, nongovernmental armed resistance to the federal tax on whiskey—the Whiskey Rebellion—caused the president to call up more than 12,000 troops from the militia of four neighboring states to quell the rebellion.

[1796] In *Ware v. Hylton,* the U.S. Supreme Court declared unconstitutional a Virginia law that had authorized payment of the commonwealth's Revolutionary War debts in depreciated currency. Virginia delayed complying with the decision, thereby evading its consequences until the more sympathetic, post-1800 (Jeffersonian) Congress paid off the debts.

[1798] In *Respublica v. Cobbett,* the Pennsylvania Supreme Court refused to allow the removal of a case to a federal appellate court, claiming there existed "no common umpire but the people" who can amend the Constitution to resolve disputes over the boundary between state and federal power. The case concerned a British subject of Federalist Party sympathies who had been charged in state court with libeling Jeffersonian politicians. The state supreme court explicitly denied that the U.S. Constitution authorized the U.S. Supreme Court to control state courts (despite the constitutional wording evidently to the contrary, as described in Chapter 1), and the state judges likened the Constitution to an international treaty that, short of war, would have to be renegotiated if the parties differed as to its meaning.

[1798–99] In response to the federal (and Federalist Party–sponsored) Alien and Sedition Acts regulating seditious libel, the Jeffersonian legislatures of Kentucky and Virginia issued resolutions declaring it the right and duty of each commonwealth to determine the bounds of federal power under the national Constitution and to protect those bounds by interposing state authority between the citizens and the federal government, nullifying the illegitimate act within state borders. Kentucky declared these federal laws "void and of no force," and Virginia declared them "palpable infractions of the Constitution." Kentucky strengthened and reissued the resolution in 1799. Seven other states condemned the resolutions. The controversial federal laws were allowed to lapse by the post-1800 Jeffersonian-dominated Congress.

[1803–9] The U.S. District Court in 1803 decided *Olmstead et al. v. Rittenhouse's Executrices,* a dispute over property seized by the state during the Revolutionary War. The Pennsylvania legislature then enacted a law contrary to the court decree and authorized the governor to use the state militia to oppose enforcement of the federal court order. In *United States v. Peters* (1809), the U.S. Supreme Court condemned the state assumption of power to nullify federal court decrees. The Pennsylvania legislature then "nullified" the U.S. Supreme Court order and recommended a constitutional amendment setting up an "impartial tribunal" to settle state-federal constitutional disputes, and the governor called out the state militia to keep the order from being served. (Ten states then passed res-

olutions of disapproval, stating that the U.S. Supreme Court in fact was the impartial tribunal already established).[1] Eventually, Pennsylvania complied with the U.S. Supreme Court order.

[1808] Legislatures of MASSACHUSETTS and CONNECTICUT in 1808 issued resolutions endorsing interposition and nullification with specific regard to the Embargo Act of 1807. The federal District Court (in Massachusetts) upheld the Embargo Act as constitutional in October 1808 (*United States v. The William*). Congress repealed the embargo in March 1809.

[1812–13] The legislatures of MASSACHUSETTS, RHODE ISLAND, VERMONT, and CONNECTICUT declared unconstitutional the president's use of state militias in the War of 1812, as did the Supreme Court of Massachusetts.

[1814] The Hartford Convention of 1814, attended by delegates from MASSACHUSETTS, RHODE ISLAND, NEW HAMPSHIRE, VERMONT, and CONNECTICUT, endorsed state interposition theory with respect to the federal military draft laws for the War of 1812 (see 1798–99). The legislatures of MASSACHUSETTS and CONNECTICUT then endorsed the Hartford Convention report, but those of nine other states specifically rejected it.

[1815] The VIRGINIA appellate General Court refused in *Jackson v. Rose* (1815) to carry out the terms of a federal statute which mandated that financial penalties for violation of the statute were recoverable by a federal lawsuit in state courts. The General Court claimed that these terms violated state sovereignty.

[1815] The VIRGINIA Supreme Court in 1815 claimed to overrule the U.S. Supreme Court decision of *Fairfax's Devisee v. Hunter's Lessee* (1813), in *Hunter's Lessee v. Martin.* The VIRGINIA Court declared unconstitutional the federal law giving the U.S. Supreme Court appellate jurisdiction over state supreme courts, Section 25 of Judiciary Act of 1789. The U.S. Supreme Court overruled that decision in *Martin v. Hunter's Lessee* (1816), upholding Section 25, and issued an order not to the rebellious appellate court but to the inferior state court, which complied.

[1817] The MASSACHUSETTS Supreme Court, in *Wetherbee v. Johnson,* declared unconstitutional a federal customs statute that allowed appeals from a state court to the federal circuit court, and treated as still unsettled the dispute in *Martin v. Hunter's Lessee* about the parallel provision, for appealing from state supreme courts to the U.S. Supreme Court, in Section 25 of the Judiciary Act of 1789.

[1819] In apparent response to the U.S. Supreme Court decision *McCulloch v. Maryland* (1819), declaring unconstitutional a (Maryland) state tax on the national bank, the VIRGINIA legislature in 1819 instructed its federal senators to propose a constitutional amendment to create a special tribunal for deciding lines between state and federal power.

[1819–20] Also in response to *McCulloch v. Maryland,* the executive branch in OHIO refused in 1819 to obey a federal circuit court order acting on the Supreme Court ruling. The OHIO legislature followed by rejecting both this Supreme Court holding and the rule of *Martin v. Hunter's Lessee* (1816) upholding Section 25 of Judiciary Act of 1789. This legislature endorsed and circulated to Congress and the other states the Kentucky Nullification Resolution of 1798 and 1799. The KENTUCKY legislature reendorsed the resolution, and the Massachusetts legislature in direct response endorsed the U.S. Supreme Court's power in 1822. Ohio's action was then declared unconstitutional in the U.S. Supreme Court's ruling in *Osborn v. Bank of the United States* (1824).

[1821] The VIRGINIA legislature in 1821, in condemnation of an appeal from state court to the U.S. Supreme Court concerning a criminal conviction under a state antilottery law, issued a resolution denying the appellate jurisdiction of the U.S. Supreme Court over state courts, and ordered counsel for the state to refrain from arguing any substantive questions at the U.S. Supreme Court other than the jurisdictional one. The U.S. Supreme Court took jurisdiction of the case, *Cohens v. Virginia* (1824), and there reiterated the rule of *Martin v. Hunter's Lessee* (1816) as to its appellate authority over the states, but it upheld the Virginia Supreme Court on the merits concerning the validity of the lottery statute.

[1821–28] The KENTUCKY legislature "remonstrated" against the 1821 U.S. Supreme Court decision, *Green v. Biddle,* which had declared void on contract clause grounds a set of Kentucky laws (making more difficult the eviction of "squatters" from land they did not own) on the grounds that the Kentucky laws conflicted with a prior interstate compact between Kentucky and Virginia regarding land titles. Here the Supreme Court was not overruling state judges; the case came on appeal from a federal circuit court. Thus the sole basis of state complaint was that federal courts claimed a power to declare state laws unconstitutional. The legislature claimed the decision was "incompatible with the constitutional powers of the state," and the state executive and judicial branches continued to enforce the (voided) state laws. In 1822 KENTUCKY repeated the legislative resolution. The case was then reappealed to the U.S. Supreme Court, which in 1823 again held the state laws unconstitutional. In December 1823, the KENTUCKY legislature again protested the opinion as "erroneous" and "subversive," and urged Congress to require a two-thirds judicial vote for any Supreme Court decision of unconstitutionality. In 1824 the KENTUCKY legislature repeated its denunciation of the Supreme Court, called for reform by Congress, and passed a law in effect giving a land reward to persons who defy the Supreme Court decision. In 1825 the lawmakers repeated the resolutions again, and requested guidance from the governor as to the best method for disobedience to erroneous U.S.

Supreme Court decisions, as well as guidance on whether physical resistance was advisable. In 1825 a popular convention declared erroneous the U.S. Supreme Court decisions of that year which had voided Kentucky's laws postponing the execution of debts (*Wayman v. Southard;* and *Bank of the United States v. Halstead*) and called on Congress to reform the Supreme Court. In 1828 the KENTUCKY Court of Appeals, in *Bodley v. Gaither,* declared that *Green v. Biddle* had not "settled any constitutional question" (on the factually erroneous premise that it had been decided by only three of the seven Supreme Court justices), and refused to treat it as law.[2] *Green v. Biddle* went substantially unenforced in Kentucky courts.

[1821–32] On a more or less annual basis various members of the U.S. CONGRESS offered proposals to alter the Supreme Court's power to throw out state laws. One suggested giving power to the Senate for all questions where a state may be a party; some proposed limiting the term of office of federal judges (so as to make them more attuned to political opinion); one proposed making the justices removable by the President upon a request endorsed by both houses of Congress (again, to render the justices more sensitive to public opinion); some urged requiring that all decisions be made by a majority of the full Supreme Court (as distinguished from a majority of those sitting on the case); several suggested requiring a two-thirds rather than a simple majority for declaring void a state law; some simply called for repeal of Section 25 (which gave such jurisdiction to the Court). None of these proposals proceeded very far.

[1822] The VIRGINIA House of Delegates voted on a proposed constitutional amendment to deprive the U.S. Supreme Court of its authority to declare void state statutes, which barely failed; a Virginia congressman then introduced a bill in the U.S. House of Representatives to repeal Section 25 of Judiciary Act (see 1815, above). The bill died.

[1823] The GEORGIA legislature (responding to Ohio; see 1819–20) adopted a resolution denying the appellate jurisdiction of the U.S. Supreme Court over the states and requesting reform by constitutional amendment.

[1824] The SOUTH CAROLINA legislature adopted a resolution denying all jurisdiction of federal courts to declare void state laws, in response to a federal circuit court decision striking down a state regulation of free blacks (*Elkinson v. DeLiesseline,* 1823). The federal court decision went unenforced.

[1824] In an apparent effort to restrict the impact of the federal Fugitive Slave Act of 1793, INDIANA legislated that persons adjudged fugitive slaves under the federally specified procedures could appeal the decision to a state court jury trial.

[1826] PENNSYLVANIA legislated in 1826 to restrict the federal Fugitive Slave Act of 1793, creating procedural protections for accused fugitive slaves that were not present under the federal rules; these prohibited low-level state magistrates from certifying accused fugitive slaves for rendition to claimants (contravening the terms of the federal legislation), and it prohibited using force or violence to detain a Negro "as a slave" (see 1842, below).

[1827] GEORGIA Governor Troup wrote in his official capacity to his state's U.S. senators and representatives that state/federal conflicts were wholly a matter of negotiation because no "competent tribunal" had yet been assigned by the Constitution to decide them.

[1830] The SOUTH CAROLINA legislature, in response to the federal tariff, issued in 1830 a resolution of interposition and nullification.

[1829–30] The GEORGIA legislature in 1829 passed laws nullifying (not on interpretive constitutional grounds, but as an act of sovereign power) the federal treaties with Cherokee Indian tribes. The state basically allowed whites to use violence to seize Indian property. Then it proceeded to arrest, try, convict, and sentence to hang for murder an Indian, Corn Tassel (in some accounts, the first name is George, and in some the last name is Tassels). *Tassel v. Georgia* was appealed to federal court (on the grounds that under the treaties, Indian courts not state courts had jurisdiction over Tassel). The U.S. Supreme Court subpoenaed the governor of Georgia, George Gilmer, who informed the legislature that he would resist with force any attempt to enforce the subpoena. The legislature then ordered Governor Gilmer and every official of the state to disregard any federal process served on them. Tassel was executed.

[1830] NEW YORK (in letters from its attorney general) twice refused to honor U.S. Supreme Court subpoenas for the case *New Jersey v. New York* on the grounds that the Supreme Court was mistaken in believing that it had authority to settle interstate controversies without express authorization from Congress.

[1831] MARYLAND's House of Delegates called for a constitutional amendment that would have required a two-thirds vote in the U.S. Senate for declaring any state law unconstitutional. The proposal made little progress.

[1831–32] The governor of GEORGIA, Wilson Lumpkin, was served two federal writs from two different Cherokee Indian cases in 1831, *Cherokee Nation v. Georgia*, 5 Peters 1 (on March 11), and *Worcester v. Georgia*, 5 Peters 515 (on November 27). (See above, 1829–30, on Georgia's Cherokee legislation.) He ignored the first and announced of the second that the governor "will disregard all [such] unconstitutional requisitions." The Georgia legislature declared that it would "resist and repel" any attempt by outsiders to interfere with the criminal processes of the state. In 1832 the U.S. Supreme Court decided *Worcester v. Georgia,* declaring the state law unconstitutional and ordering the release of prisoners being held under it. Governor Lumpkin called the decision "an attempt to prostrate the sovereignty of the State" and pledged "determined resistance" to it. The Georgia legislature called for a national convention to reconsider the jurisdiction of the U.S. Supreme Court. In 1833, the governor pardoned the prisoners in exchange for their withdrawing their appeal from the Supreme Court.

[1832] A bill that was introduced in Congress to stiffen sanctions for persons resisting Section 25 of the Judiciary Act (see 1815, above, for a discussion of *Hunter's Lessee v. Martin*) failed to pass.

[1832–33] In 1832 the SOUTH CAROLINA legislature called a popularly elected convention for the purpose of considering the constitutionality of the federal Tariff Acts of 1828 and 1832. The convention did so, declared the acts unconstitutional and void, prohibited enforcement after February 1, 1833, declared that any person attempting to appeal to the U.S. Supreme Court would be "dealt with as for contempt of court," and announced that any attempt at coercion by the federal government would be met with secession from the union. The SOUTH CAROLINA legislature then passed a number of implementing laws for these declarations, including authorization of the governor to call up the militia if force were required. In 1833 U.S. Senator Henry Clay of Kentucky came up with a compromise tariff. In response, the SOUTH CAROLINA legislature rescinded its tariff nullification bills, but then it proceeded to nullify (on constitutional grounds) the federal Force Act, which had been adopted in the tariff crisis to authorize the president to use the army to collect revenues if needed.

[1833] In ALABAMA, armed nongovernmental groups successfully resisted the federal troops sent to protect the treaty rights of Indians, causing the federal army to withdraw and leave the Indians at the mercy of violent marauders.

[1834] The SOUTH CAROLINA Supreme Court in 1834 held unconstitutional the (already rescinded) state nullification legislation that had been adopted with respect to federal tariffs in 1832.

[1834] GEORGIA's Governor Lumpkin and the legislature in 1834 announced that they would treat as a nullity a writ of error from the U.S. Supreme Court, and instead went ahead to execute one James Graves, whose execution the writ would have blocked.

During the period 1829–37, the federal political context of state resistance changed dramatically, because the Supreme Court composition shifted to yield a strong 7–2 "states' rights" majority by 1838. This shift decreased the number of occasions for overt state resistance in the period from 1838 to the Civil War, but—as the discussion below illustrates—could not eliminate them.

One major (though not the only) federal policy provoking resistance during this period was that toward runaway slaves. Slaves ran to northern states for freedom; southern masters wanted them recaptured; Congress in 1793 (acting on the authority of Article 4, Section 2, Clause 3 of the Constitution)[3] had enacted a Fugitive Slave Act that made recapture relatively easy. Federal, state, or local judges or magistrates, upon testimony from the person claiming ownership, could issue a writ certifying a given black person as a fugitive from servitude, which writ would then authorize taking him or her South, by force if necessary. As antislavery feeling in the North heated up, several states, beginning with Indiana in 1824, passed laws to provide procedural protections, such as trial by jury, so that free blacks would not be kidnapped with the use of this federal law. Some of the laws also forbade state officials to aid in the capture of persons accused of being fugitive slaves. (See discussion of Indiana [1824] and Pennsylvania [1826] above.)

In *Prigg v. Pennsylvania* (1842), the U.S. Supreme Court ruled that the procedural protections were unconstitutional in that they interfered with the procedures mandated by Congress (which had to be supreme under Article 6, Clause 2, of the Constitution), but that the refusal to let state officials help in the federal project was constitutional, as a "sovereign" prerogative of the states. Thus from 1842 to 1850 the northern states busied themselves with laws taking their officials and their jails out of the slave-catching business. Since federal judges were very sparsely distributed around the country, this now-lawful development succeeded in making slave capture both difficult and expensive, so northern state governments had little incentive to resist congressional authority on fugitive slaves in more legally questionable ways. Southerners, because of ensuing difficulties of recapture, eventually pushed through Congress the Fugitive Slave Act of 1850, which created numerous federal commissioners, who would serve to certify accused blacks as fugitive slaves. Now that the federal government had put in place another efficient slave-catching mechanism, northern states again had incentive to resist federal authority on this topic by passing laws that gave procedural protections to the accused, and they proceeded to do so in substantial numbers after 1850.

[*1837*] MASSACHUSETTS legislated to "restore the trial by jury on questions of personal freedom," restricting the procedures of the federal Fugitive Slave Act of 1793.

[*1838*] CONNECTICUT legislated to restrict the federal Fugitive Slave Act of 1793 by (contrary to its terms) forbidding state magistrates and judges to aid in the certifying of fugitive slaves (for return to their claimants) and by providing an appeal from such a federally granted certificate to a state court trial by jury.

[*1840*] The VERMONT legislature, in apparent defiance of the federal Fugitive Slave Act of 1793, made it a crime for any citizen to aid in the capture of a runaway slave and also mandated, as did NEW YORK in the same year, that persons

adjudged fugitive slaves under the federally specified procedures could appeal the decision to a state court jury trial where the state would provide a defense lawyer.

[1846] The MASSACHUSETTS House of Representatives adopted a resolution that the Mexican War (which the federal government had already declared and begun) was unconstitutional. (The U.S. House of Representatives followed with the same resolution!) The Massachusetts legislature then openly refused to cooperate with the troop recruitment process.

[1850] The GEORGIA legislature resolved in 1850 to secede from the union if the Wilmot Proviso (restricting increase of slave states) were adopted by Congress or if California were admitted to the union as a free state. The proviso, or provisions similar to it, was included in the platforms of the Free Soil Party in 1848 and later the Republican Party. It passed in the House of Representatives twice in the 1840s but never made it through the Senate.

[1850] Despite the *Prigg* decision, which had declared such measures unconstitutional due to their conflict with federal statute (see discussion above), the VERMONT legislature enacted a rule to secure state court jury trial for accused fugitive slaves.

[1853–56] OHIO resisted the 1853 U.S. Supreme Court decision voiding one of its laws, *Piqua Branch v. Knoop*. The state law in question had reversed an earlier state legislative grant of a tax exemption to a particular corporation, and the Supreme Court ruled this an unconstitutional impairment of the prior "contract" between the legislature and the corporation. First, Ohio tried overruling the U.S. Supreme Court by amending the state constitution. In *Dodge v. Woolsey* (1856), the U.S. Supreme Court rejected this approach. Meanwhile, the Ohio attorney general argued that the state supreme court should refuse officially "to enter" the *Piqua Branch* mandate into Ohio law. The Ohio supreme court delayed enforcing the federal mandate for three years, but finally did so (3 Ohio St. 342).

[1854] The GEORGIA Supreme Court in *Padelford v. Savannah* (1854) took up a claim that a Georgia sales tax violated the U.S. Constitution as it had been interpreted by the U.S. Supreme Court in *Brown v. Maryland* (1827). The Georgia court ruled unanimously that the tax did not violate constitutional doctrine set forth in *Brown v. Maryland* (*Padelford* at 445). Then the judge went on to explain that it was his own opinion (one on which he had not consulted his fellow judges) that the U.S. Supreme Court has no jurisdiction over Georgia courts, that its precedents are not binding on them, and that the two federal laws, of 1789 and 1833, respectively, that gave federal courts appellate jurisdiction over state courts are both unconstitutional.

[1854] The CALIFORNIA Supreme Court in *Johnson v. Gordon* (a case that originated in an alien's effort to transfer a case from state court to a federal district

court) declared unconstitutional Section 25 of the federal Judiciary Act of 1789, and refused to honor a writ to allow an appeal to the U.S. Supreme Court, insisting that the federal courts have no legitimate jurisdiction over the state courts, even on federal questions, and that the contrary view would be "in derogation of [state] sovereignty." (In 1855 the California legislature forbade its judges to act on this doctrine and ordered impeachment if they defied Section 25 of the federal law).

[1854, 1855, 1857, 1858] In 1854 the legislatures of CONNECTICUT and RHODE ISLAND followed Vermont's 1850 example, defying the U.S. Supreme Court's *Prigg v. Pennsylvania* (1842) decision by providing state court jury trials for accused runaway slaves. In 1855 MASSACHUSETTS and MICHIGAN followed suit, and in 1857 OHIO and MAINE did the same. In 1858 VERMONT and MASSACHUSETTS reenacted these laws, and WISCONSIN and KANSAS adopted similar ones.

[1855] The chief justice of the OHIO supreme court, sitting with a state district court in *Stunt v. The Steamboat Ohio* (a case dealing with a claim that an Ohio tort law violated the "inviolability of private property" under the U.S. Constitution), refused a motion in aid of an appeal to the U.S. Supreme Court. The chief justice declared that the U.S. Supreme Court did not have jurisdiction over state courts, despite the federal Judiciary Act 1789, which he adjudged unconstitutional.

[1854–59] The WISCONSIN Supreme Court in 1854, on the grounds that the federal Fugitive Slave Act of 1850 was unconstitutional (because slavery itself violated norms implicit in the Constitution), released Sherman Booth on a writ of habeas corpus after he was charged before a federal official for helping a fugitive slave, in direct violation of the federal act. In 1855 the Wisconsin Supreme Court again released him by the same writ with the same ruling after he had been found guilty in federal district court on the same charge. Wisconsin authorities then refused to process the writ of error from the U.S. Supreme Court to permit an appeal, and these authorities were reinforced by a formal order from the Wisconsin Supreme Court in 1857. The U.S. Supreme Court then took the case anyway on the basis of a copy of the state court record in the possession of the U.S. attorney general. The case was argued in 1859, but Wisconsin refused to send counsel to participate. Then Wisconsin refused to act on the mandates of the U.S. Supreme Court handed down in *Ableman v. Booth* (18 Howard 476 and 21 Howard 506, 1859) because its own Supreme Court was evenly divided on the question.

The Civil War (or War between the States), which lasted from 1861 to 1865, essentially settled the question of state subordination to federal authority. The open resistance so common in the antebellum decades all but vanished, save for one last sputter in the 1870s.

[1872] In a land-patent case, *Tyler v. Maguire,* the MISSOURI Supreme Court responded to the U.S. Supreme Court's order, "We reverse and remand for proceedings in conformity to our opinion," by reversing itself but then reenacting the same decree. The U.S. Supreme Court, on a second appeal, then announced that its order was being "in effect evade[d]" and therefore it reversed (again) and awarded execution directly to the prevailing party.

In the following years, official state resistance (as distinguished from occasional evasion and foot-dragging) to federal authority ceased, until a brief flurry in the 1950s and 1960s in response to racial desegregation was put down by federal troops.

European States' Resistance to European Community Authority

The following is a comprehensive narrative account of instances of open resistance by member states to the federal authority of the European Community) supplemented by a chronology of abjurations of such resistance. Also, as in Appendix A, this account highlights dates and names of member states. Sources for the narratives of each incident appear in the notes to Table 4.

[1966] The GERMAN Finance Ministry formally issued this edict: "We hold the decision of the European Court to be invalid. It conflicts with well-reasoned arguments of the Federal Government and with the opinions of the affected ministers of the European [Community]." The ministry instructed customs officials to ignore the ECJ decision and to reject all claims based on the ECJ decision. In response, a lobbying group, the Association of German Exporters, organized a writing campaign to attack the ministry's position. Members of the Bundestag (one of the two legislative chambers) then challenged a representative of the ministry as to whether his behavior was not in fact inappropriate in a state meant to be governed by the rule of law. The Finance Ministry then gave in and accepted the ECJ decision.

[1968] In *Syndicat Général de Fabricants de Semoules* (the *"Semoules"* case) the FRENCH Commissaire du Gouvernement admitted that a full analysis of the legal issues involved would require referral to the ECJ, but argued that an acceptance by French judges of the supremacy of European law over French legislation would violate the judges' "place within [French] institutions." The French Conseil d'État (hereafter, Cons.d'E.) then decided the case itself, which action, in light of what the Commissaire had said, was in blatant violation of the Treaty of Rome's Article 177 requirement that any national court of last resort refer questions of interpretation of European law to the ECJ. See description of the *Nicolo* case under 1989 below for reversal of this doctrine.

[1970] The FRENCH Cour de Cassation (hereinafter, C. Cass.) on October 22 appeared to accept the superiority of EC regulations over French statutes in the *"Ramel"* case. This began two decades of a split between the jurisprudence of the French civil courts system, headed by the Cour de Cassation, and the French Administrative courts system, headed by the Conseil d'État (See above at 1968 for the position of the Cons.d'E.; and see *Rothmans* and *Phillipp Morris, 1992,* cases below for a description of the recent end of this split.)

[1973] The ITALIAN Constitutional Court in *Frontini v. Ministero delle Finanze* acknowledged a theoretical basis for future possible defiance of European law, claiming that fundamental values protected by the Italian Constitution set outer limits on what European law could do and that the Italian Constitutional Court would be the judge whether such violations occurred. This doctrine was to be repeated in the 1984 *Granital* decision and in the 1989 *Fragd* decision (see below).

[1974] The GERMAN Constitutional Court (also) announced a theoretical basis for future possible defiance of European law in the so-called *Solange I* decision, insisting that fundamental rights under the German Basic Law are supreme over European law, in principle, and that the German Constitutional Court considered itself responsible for maintaining these fundamental rights so long as the European Community did not adopt a written Bill of Rights to protect them. The decision evoked a warning from the European Commission of possible charges for violating the treaty, and also quiet negotiations between the commission and the German Government. The same Constitutional Court abandoned this doctrinal position in 1986 (*"Solange II,"*) on the grounds that the ECJ now gave adequate protection to the fundamental rights of Europeans. So long as such protection continued, Germany would be able to follow European jurisprudence. But see also 1993 (below) for an apparent return to a modified version of the *Solange I* position.

[1975] In the *Jacques Vabré* case of 1975, the C.Cass. explicitly endorsed the supremacy of EC law and of ECJ case law in France. (The doctrine of the C.Cass. and C.d'E. remained split on this point until 1992.)

[1975] One house of the BELGIAN legislature, the Senate, in June endorsed a bill to forbid judges to strike down Belgian laws, but the other house ignored the bill, so it never became law.

[1978–79] The FRENCH Assemblée Nationale debated a proposal to censure and nullify ECJ interpretation of the Euratom Treaty (one of the three founding treaties of the European Community), as an example of an "illegal decision." The proposal was eventually tabled, but see 1980 below.

[1978–1979] On October 22, 1978, in *Minister of the Interior v. Cohn-Bendit,* the FRENCH Cons.d'E. blocked a request from a lower French administrative court for an ECJ preliminary ruling, in direct defiance of the command in Article

177 of the Treaty of Rome that any lower court may at its discretion request from the ECJ an interpretation of European law needed for a pending case. Moreover, the Cons.d'É. announced an interpretation of the direct effect of part of a European Community directive that was flatly at odds with the interpretation previously given by the ECJ (in *Van Duyn v. Home Office*, at 1348). *Cohn-Bendit* in fact was mooted, by the minister's giving Cohn-Bendit the order he requested two days before the Cons.d'E. decision. Nonetheless, the Legal Affairs Committee of the European Parliament proposed a treaty amendment to prevent future such occurrences in national courts. The European Commission debated bringing charges against France (according to the procedure described in Article 169 of the treaty) at the ECJ for failure to meet its obligations under the treaty, and also proposed amending the treaty to allow a direct right of appeal to the ECJ when a court of last resort refuses to request a preliminary ruling.

[1979–80] The FRENCH government announced that it would not comply with the ECJ decision in the so-called *Mutton War* case, until a mutually acceptable solution to the conflict dealt with in the case could be politically negotiated in Brussels. The European Commission brought second and third noncompliance charges against France in 1980.

[1980] In *Office Nationale Interprofessional de Céréales* (ONIC) on May 9, the FRENCH Cons.d'E. rendered a decision flatly contrary to the rule of law handed down by the ECJ interpreting the same European regulation in a (German) case on October 4, 1979: *D.G.V,* Cases 241, 245–250/78.

[1980] The FRENCH Parliament adopted a law on July 25 concerning nuclear energy containing "provisions manifestly incompatible with ECJ doctrine" interpreting the Euratom Treaty, according to Buffet-Tchakaloff *France devant la Cour,* 366, citing Law 80–572. The relevant treaty provision was revised in EC negotiations shortly thereafter.

[1980] The FRENCH Assemblée Nationale on October 9 adopted a bill (the Aurillac Amendment) to forbid French courts to declare void French legislation on grounds of conflict with European law or treaty; the Senate refused to pass it.

[1980–1981] The FRENCH Cons.d'E. in *Société Sovincast,* on November 20, and again in *Société civile Centre international Dentaire,* on February 25, reiterated its *Cohn-Bendit* doctrine that European directives do not have direct legal effect in the sense of creating actionable individual rights; such rights can come only from national implementing legislation. As early as 1974 in *Van Duyn* the ECJ had ruled, to the contrary, that directives can have direct legal effect under specified circumstances.

[1981] In the *Value-Added Tax Directive Case,* the GERMAN Supreme Tax Court ruled flatly contrary to the ECJ doctrine on the direct effect of directives, claiming to follow instead the French Cons. d'E. doctrine of the *Cohn-Bendit* case

(1978–79, above). However, the ECJ had not yet ruled that the particular directive at issue did have direct effect, so the defiance was as to legal theory, not application of a specific law. (See 1985–86, below, for later developments of German law on this point.)

[1983–88] The ECJ condemned FRANCE for breach of EC law with respect to the direct effect of a European directive on tobacco pricing, in *Commission v. France* on June 21, 1983; the French Cons.d'E. then confirmed the government action as legal, on December 13, 1985 (Rec. Lebon at 377); the ECJ then again condemned France for breach of the same community law, on July 13, 1988, in *Commission v. France.* (This incident evidently prompted a letter from the French prime minister to the Cons. d'E., which then brought about a change of jurisprudence in 1989. See 1989, below, on the *Nicolo* case.)

[1984] On September 28, in the case involving the *Sociétés de protection des animaux,* the Cons.d'É. started treating European directives as having direct effect in France, thus accepting the doctrine rejected in *Cohn-Bendit.* (See also 1989, below, on the *Nicolo* case.)

[1984] The ITALIAN Constitutional Court reiterated the theoretical basis for future possible defiance of European law, repeating its *Frontini* position (see 1973 above) in the *Granital* decision of June 8.

[1985–1987] The GERMAN Supreme Tax Court in *Value Added Tax II* (1985) reiterated its defiant doctrine of the 1981 decision (see above) with regard to the same VAT directive. However, between the two decisions the ECJ had interpreted the specific directive as having direct effect. The GERMAN Constitutional Court therefore overruled the Tax Court and affirmed the ECJ doctrine on the direct effect of directives as valid in Germany.

[1989] The ITALIAN Constitutional Court again reiterated the theoretical basis for future possible defiance of European law, repeating its *Frontini* position (see 1973 and 1984, above), in the *Fragd* decision of April 21 (at n. 232). In this instance the Constitutional Court detailed the types of fundamental values that check European law in Italy; they include fundamental rights, the principle of democracy, the unity of the Italian state, and certain other organizational principles.

[1989] In the *Nicolo* decision of 1989, the FRENCH Cons.d'E., having been urged by the French prime minister in 1988 to reconsider its jurisprudence on the relation between French and EC law, accepted the supremacy of the European Treaty of Rome over French law.

[1990] The FRENCH Cons.d'E. continued in the new direction it had launched with the *Nicolo* decision by, in the *Boisdet* case, accepting the supremacy over French law of regulations adopted by the European Council of Ministers.

[1992] In the *Rothmans* and in *Phillipp Morris* decisions of 1992, the FRENCH

Cons.d'E. accepted the supremacy of EC directives over French law, ending a twenty-year period of differing with the C.Cass. over acceptance of the supremacy of ECJ jurisprudence in French law.

[1993] The GERMAN Constitutional Court again (see 1974) endorsed a theoretical basis for future possible defiance of European law, in the *Maastricht II* decision (on October 12, 1993). The court reasoned that a fundamental (so in German Basic Law, nonamendable) right, the right to vote, implied the right to elect a German Bundestag with sovereign legislative powers; therefore, this right operates to restrain powers that EC institutions may someday claim. The German Constitutional Court reserves to itself the power to decide whether such a conflict between German sovereignty and European law is present.

Abbreviations of Public Documents

ATF = *Arrêts du Tribunal Fédéral* (Lausanne, Switzerland; annually since 1876)

CMLR = Common Market Law Review

ECR = European Court Reports

FF = *Feuille Fédérale* (records of the Swiss Federal Assembly; volumes appear three or four times a year, beginning in 1848)

RO = *Recueil Officiel des Pièces Concernant Le Droit Public de la Suisse des Lois Fédérales, Traités, Décrets, et Arrêtés* (Berne, Switzerland: A. Fischer, 1864)

Notes

INTRODUCTION

1. *International Herald Tribune,* March 25, 1999, p. 1.

2. Fox, "New Approaches," 105–21; Gow, "Shared Sovereignty," 170–75; Jackson, "International Community."

3. Both quotes appear in Fowler and Bunck, *Sovereign State,* 66–67.

4. Habermas, "European Nation-State," 35; see also Kavanagh, "Beyond Autonomy?"; Murphy, "Political-Territorial," 107; but cf. Krasner, *Sovereignty,* 220–23, insisting that the "degree of change from the past" with respect to economic globalization is "often overstated".

5. Journal Officiel, Débats de l'Assemblée Nationale, Paris, May 6, 1992, p. 936.

6. Comments (both from 1989) cited in Malcolm, "Sense on Sovereignty," 342.

7. Ibid., 351, 362–63.

8. Forsyth, "Political Science, Federalism, and Europe," 19.

9. Mattli, *Logic of Regional Integration,* 87–88.

10. B. Friedman, "Valuing Federalism," 365–66, 378 n.265; Fox, "New Approaches," 108.

11. Scholarly critics on record prior to the notorious anti–World Trade Organization street demonstrations in Seattle in 2000 included Rabkin, *Why Sovereignty Matters,* and Casey and Rivkin, "Against an International Criminal Court."

12. Volcansek, *Law above Nations;* Moravcsik, *Choice for Europe;* B. Friedman, "Valuing Federalism," 327 n. 29; 365–66 nn. 208–12; 378 n. 265. Friedman points out that a little-noticed GATT ruling has had remarkable impact of restricting even the U.S. Constitution. The Twenty-first Amendment to the Constitution states unequivocally, "The transportation into any state . . . of intoxicating liquors in violation of the laws thereof is hereby prohibited." Nonetheless,

a GATT panel ruled in 1993 that American state laws that put special taxes on the importation of non-American beverages had to give way in light of the GATT treaty, and this ruling, at least as a formal matter, has prevailed (378 n. 265). See also Mills, *Human Rights;* Krasner, *Sovereignty,* 113–21.

13. Bodin, *On Sovereignty.*

14. Gow, "Shared Sovereignty," 166–67, 177–79; Close and Ohki-Close, *Supranationalism.*

15. Merriam, *Theory of Sovereignty,* chaps. 9–10; Forsyth, *Unions of States,* chaps. 4–6. But cf. Elazar, *Exploring Federalism,* 108–9, describing the federal principle as a "radical attack upon the modern idea of sovereignty."

16. Merriam, *Theory of Sovereignty,* 30–31.

17. E.g., Philpott, "Sovereignty"; Hashmi, *State Sovereignty,* "Introduction"; Shaw, "Theory of State Transformation"; Delsol, "Souveraineté"; Mills, *Human Rights;* Elazar, *Constitutionalizing Globalization,* 17–20, 65; but cf. Krasner, *Sovereignty,* 24. Thomas Biersteker and Cynthia Weber attest to a "virtual explosion" of both scholarly and media interest in sovereignty since 1986 (*State Sovereignty,* 1 and n. 1 at 18–19 and citations therein). Fowler and Bunck note a sharp rise in the number of scholarly challenges to the concept of sovereignty beginning in 1985 (*Sovereign State,* 2 at n. 12).

18. Camilleri, "Rethinking Sovereignty"; Elshtain, "Rethinking Sovereignty"; MacCormick, "Beyond the Sovereign State"; Ward, "Identity and Difference"; Krasner, "Sovereignty," 67, 86–87.

19. Authors were Bertrand Badie and Neil MacCormick, respectively.

20. Arendt, *Between Past and Future,* 164–165; Brecht, "Sovereignty"; Laski, *Authority,* 119–20.

21. Merriam, *Theory of Sovereignty;* De Jouvenal, *Sovereignty;* Hinsley, *Sovereignty;* Forsyth, *Unions of States,* chaps. 4–6; Philpott, "Sovereignty"; Murphy, "Political-Territorial."

22. *Nicomachean Ethics,* bk. 1, chaps. 1–2, para. 1094a-b; *Politics,* bk. 1, chap. 2, para. 1253a; bk. 3, chap. 9, para. 1280a-b.

23. Merriam, *Theory of Sovereignty,* 11, citing *Institutiones* 51, pt. 2, sec.6.

24. North, *Structure and Change,* 125, chap. 10.

25. Gierke, *Political Theories;* Kantrowicz, *King's Two Bodies;* Wilks, *Problem of Sovereignty;* Black, *Monarchy and Community;* Myers, *Medieval Kingship.*

26. To assert that "the" modern understanding of the sovereign state emerged in seventeenth-century Europe is not to insist that it has remained fixed in every detail since that time. Robert Klein, for example, in *Sovereign Equality,* traces certain important evolutions in the concept as it has operated in international relations in the nineteenth and twentieth centuries.

27. North, *Structure and Change,* chaps. 10–11; Tilly, "Warmaking and Statemaking."

28. Burch, *Property.*

29. Hinsley, *Sovereignty,* chap. 3; cf. Henshall, *Myth of Absolutism.*

30. Nathan, "New World Order."

31. Krasner, "Sovereignty," 67, 86–87.

32. Krasner, *Sovereignty,* borrowing from Fowler and Bunck "basket of attributes," *Sovereign State,* chap. 4.

33. Krasner, *Sovereignty;* see also Skidelsky, "Rothschild," 24. Krasner borrowed the term "organized hypocrisy" from Brunnson, *Organization of Hypocrisy.*

34. Krasner, *Sovereignty,* 119, 125–26, 7, 235–37.

35. Ibid., 7.

36. These tendencies are amply documented in Elazar, *Constitutionalizing Globalization.*

37. Murray Forsyth, *Unions of States,* examines the same four but he adds the German Empire of 1871 into the mix. The German Empire resulted essentially from conquest by Prussia, and thus has been excluded here. Forsyth's study ends where this book begins; he examines the process of transforming confederal forms to federal unions. This book looks at state resistance within federal formations.

38. Close and Ohki-Close, *Supranationalism,* 75.

39. Moravcsik, *Choice for Europe,* 79.

40. Ibid.

41. Riker, *Development of American Federalism;* Riker, *Federalism: Origin, Operation, Significance;* Lemco, *Federal Governments.*

42. For instance, in Riker's federalism theories, unions without a military motive cannot endure. Thus, in 1996 (in "European Federalism"), he expressed skepticism that the EU could endure past the collapse of the Soviet threat. So far, he has proved wrong.

43. Wheare, *Federal Governments;* Watts, *New Federations.*

44. Riker, *Development of American Federalism,* 20.

45. Ibid., 24, citing Rutland, *Papers,* 9:346.

46. 14 Georgia 440. This statement was issued as dicta, concerning which the rest of the judges had not been consulted.

47. Quoted in Charles Warren, "Attacks," 184–85.

48. Lenaerts, "Faces of Federalism," 210.

49. Schermers, "Comment," 2530.

50. Merriam, *Theory of Sovereignty,* chaps. 9–10; Forsyth, *Unions of States,* chaps. 4–6; Eugène Borel, *Étude sur la Souveraineté.*

51. The one who seems to have come closest to such an anticipation, because

he was trying to grapple with the new reality of the League of Nations, was Carl Schmitt, writing in 1926, *Die Kernfrage des Völkerbundes* (Berlin), cited in Forsyth, *Unions of States,* 224 n. 38. Carl Schmitt then proceeded to examine extensively the relation between sovereignty and federal unions in Part 4 of *Verfassungslehre* (Berlin, 1928). See discussion in Forsyth, *Unions of States,* 146–55. The latter work of Schmittt's is available in French as *Théorie de la Constitution* (Paris: Presses Universitaires de France, 1993) (but evidently not in English).

52. Krasner, *Sovereignty,* 228–35.

CHAPTER 1: THE MEMBER-STATE RESISTANCE PARADOX

1. Two exceptions to the general neglect of this story are Jessup, *Reaction and Accommodation,* 172–82, 355–74, 429–30; and B. Friedman, "Counter-Majoritarian," 390–413.

2. Scheingold, *Law in Political Integration,* 49; Rasmussen, "Towards a Normative Theory," 135–36.

3. For recent examinations of noncompliance in the EC/EU, see Krislov, Ehlermann, and Weiler, "The Political Organs in the Decision-Making Process in the United States and the European Community," in Cappelletti, Secombe, and Weiler, eds., *Integration Through Law;* Snyder, "Effectiveness of European Community Law"; Gallagher et al., *Representative Government in Modern Europe,* 102–4; and Shaun Bowler, David Farrell, and Ian Holliday, "Building a European Union." According to Bowler et al., as of 1994 the European Commission had taken twenty-one cases to the ECJ to request that fines be imposed on member states for "failure to comply with" (in the sense of "carry out") an ECJ decision (33–34, 39).

4. For a discussion of Madison's various positions, see Edward Corwin, "National Power and State Interposition," 544–47.

5. Madison, "Number 39," in *The Federalist Papers,* 245–46.

6. *Costa v. ENEL* (ECJ ruled EC law supreme over subsequent legislation in 1964); *International Handelsgesellschaft v. EVGF* (1970) and *Simmenthal II* (1978) (EC law supreme over national constitutional provisions).

7. Stein, "Lawyers, Judges," 1.

8. *ERTA; Re: The Draft Treaty on a European Economic Area.*

9. Lenaerts, "Some Thoughts," 119–20; Stone, "Ratifying *Maastricht,*" 70.

10. *Commission v. Denmark* (1988).

11. Lenaerts, "Some Thoughts," 118–19, and cases discussed therein.

12. Aggestam, "Crossroads."

13. Mattli, *Logic of Regional Integration,* 100.

14. *Francovich v. Italy* (1991).

15. Rasmussen, "Towards a Normative Theory," 138.

16. Mattli, *Logic of Regional Integration,* 101.

17. Chryssochoou et al., *Theory and Reform.* The Council of Ministers consists of ministers relevant to particular issues from each member state. Its membership fluctuates from issue to issue, and each state has one vote on the Council. Until 1994 (when the European Parliament received additional powers), it was the main legislative body within the European Union. Under the Maastricht Treaty its name became "Council of the European Union." It should not be confused with the European Council. The latter began informally as a thrice-yearly summit meeting of the heads of state plus their foreign ministers; under the Single European Act it was officially mandated to convene twice a year and is optionally attended by the president of the European Commission. The European Council is a diplomatic session without formal rule-making authority for the union. Penelope Kent, *European Community Law,* 14–15; Freestone and Davidson, *Institutional Framework;* Aggeston, "Crossroads," 85–87.

18. Some of these new jurisdictional areas were qualified by special restrictions. For details, see Albors-Llorens, "Changes in the Jurisdiction"; Ehlermann, "Différenciation, Flexibilité, Coopération Renforcée"; and Chryssochoou et al., *Theory and Reform,* 55–80. For a somewhat speculative discussion of the political concerns underlying the changes, see Alter, "Who Are the 'Masters'?," 141–42.

19. Lenaerts, "Some Thoughts," 93.

20. By the 1990s the publicity accorded to the Maastricht Treaty and to the debate over whether the U.K. should join the euro raised the level of heat in Parliament, such that M.P.'s of a Eurosceptical bent took to blaming the ECJ for "a tendency to encroach far too much into areas that are properly within the sovereign authority of this Parliament" (e.g., *Hansard, Commons,* 6th Series, vol. 250, col. 93, Nov. 16, 1994; vol. 263, col. 515, July 6, 1995; vol. 265, col. 12–13, October 30, 1995; vol. 301, col. 1132–49, Nov. 27, 1997). These belated protests evoked this sensible reply—which implicitly applies to all the late-joining countries—from a long-time M.P., Sir Kenneth Clarke:

The idea that the [European] Court is supranational has always been established and was accepted as part of our membership. It has been known for twenty-five years—ever since we entered the European Union—that legislation of individual national Parliaments can be set aside if it is inconsistent with a judgment of the European Court. [It was "fiercely debated" before we joined.] The idea that we supposed that we were entering only a trading arrangement is one of the great myths of our time.

Parliamentary Debates, [Hansard] House of Commons, 6th Series vol. 302, col. 197, Dec. 2, 1997.

For a description of the adaptation to the principle of the supremacy of European law within the legal systems of the six later-joining states (Ireland, Denmark, the United Kingdom, Greece, Spain, and Portugal), see van Empel, Schermers et al., *Leading Cases,* 159–60, 203–5, 228–39.

21. Cf. Forsyth, *Unions of States* (arguing that, despite the formal independence of the individual thirteen states from 1776 to about 1780, in combat against the British, a kind of "spontaneous political unity" prevailed), 54–55. While there are historians who argue against the idea that the thirteen states were individually independent entities (e.g., Richard B. Morris, *Forging of the American Union,* chap. 3), it is by now well documented that a number of them conducted an independent foreign policy both before and after the Articles of Confederation. See Van Tyne, "Sovereignty in the American Revolution," 539–41; Levitan, "Foreign Relations Powers," 478–90.

22. Rasmussen suggests that the answer to both these questions is that states rebelled when the judges exercised too much "activism," idiosyncratically defining judicial activism as judicial rulings out of touch with those values that "enjoy consensual support from the body politic" (*On Law,* 124, 301–2). While his book contains many other thoughtful insights, this particular suggestion deserves the simple response that it does not fit the evidence, either for the nineteenth century United States or for the European Community. Cappelletti concurs in this response to Rasmussen's suggestion, "Running Wild?," 7–8.

23. Cf. Volcansek and Rasmussen on the French Conseil d'État's *Shell Barre* decision; Volcansek on the same court's *Ets. Petitjean;* Rasmussen's characterization (accepted in Alter, "Court's Political Power,") of the German Supreme Tax Court's response to the ECJ's decisions in *Lutticke* and *Molkerie;* and Volcansek's discussion of the Italian Constitutional Court's slow response to the ECJ's treatment of *Costa v. ENEL* (1964) and the *Simmenthal II* case (1978), both of which reversed earlier decisions of the Italian Court.

The Italian Court did not overtly contradict the ECJ's reversal of the Italian Court's own ruling. It did, however, wait some time before officially endorsing the ECJ position, doing so, for the *Costa v. ENEL* position in December of 1973, in *Frontini v. Ministero delle Finanze,* and for the (1978) *Simmenthal II* rule in its *Granital* decision of 1984. See Volcansek, *Judicial Politics,* 48–51, 62–68, and 150–51; Rasmussen, *On Law,* 310, 323, 454–56, 463 nn. 63–67; Adelina Adinolfi, "Judicial Application of Community Law"; and Marta Cartabia, "Italian Constitutional Court."

In my view the two German cases present problems of imperfect compliance,

NOTES TO PAGES 21-31 185

and the Italian cases, slow compliance. The two French cases involve differences over interpreting Article 177 of the EC Treaty; its terms require the court of last resort in a country to refer for a preliminary ruling all cases to the ECJ that "raise" a "question" of treaty "interpretation." Thus when French (or any other) courts have felt their interpretation was obviously correct or necessary, and the challenge asserted by the litigant therefore frivolous, they have refrained from referring the case, relying on the so-called "acte clair" doctrine. Although some commentators (Volcansek, Bebr, Alter) do treat refusals to refer under the "acte clair" doctrine as "resistance" to the treaty, it is arguably a practical necessity, and the ECJ itself eventually endorsed a version of the "acte clair" doctrine in 1982 in *C.I.L.F.I.T. v. Ministero della Sanita*. As of 1994 the backlog of cases at the ECJ was causing a preliminary ruling to take two years from request to decision.

Finally, Karen Alter describes an additional instance of legislative resistance to ECJ doctrine in France concerning automobile registration fees, but the book she cites to document the event does not contain such a reference, so it is not included in Table 2 here or Table 4 of Chapter 3 (Alter, "Court's Political Power," 475, citing Buffet-Tchakaloff, *France devant la Cour*).

24. Warren, "Attacks," 15–16; McDonald, *Constitutional History*, 102–3.

25. Alec Stone[-]Sweet, "Constitutional Dialogues," 21; Alter, "Explaining National Court," 22. Both these scholars rely on the factual account in the report by Hervé Bribosia for their claims that the Belgian court has asserted, in principle, a potential limit on the EC/EU. But Bribosia himself indicates that if EC/EU law specifically came before the Belgian Court, that court might well carve out an exception from what it had said about international law as such. See Bribosia, "Report on Belgium," 26–33.

26. For material in this and the following two paragraphs the sources are Campbell, *Slave Catchers*, chaps. 1–2, and McDougall, *Fugitive Slaves*, chap. 5.

27. Warren, "Attacks," 5–12.

28. A brief narrative for all of the incidents listed in Table 3 is provided in Appendix A.

29. Material in this and the next paragraph comes from McDonald, *History*, 105–6; Warren, "Attacks," 168–75; Bobbitt, *Constitutional Fate*, 109–14; Kelly et al., *American Constitution*, 211–12.

30. Warren, "Attacks." An additional court-curbing proposal omitted from this list did garner some scattered support but never official endorsement in a state or federal branch of government. This was the suggestion in 1830 by a former U.S. senator from Delaware that U.S. Supreme Court justices be removable by the president upon a request endorsed by two-thirds of the state legislatures. B. Friedman, "Countermajoritarian," 391 n. 228, 407.

31. McDonald, *History,* 98–99, 106–9; Kelly et al., *American Constitution,* 150–53; Powell, *Languages,* 230, 239–48; Tipton, *Nullification,* 36–39; Warren, "Attacks," 175; Campbell, *Slave Catchers,* 17.

32. Warren, "Attacks," 5–16, 175–77; McDonald, *History,* 98–109; Kelly et al., *American Constitution,* 150–53; Tipton, *Nullification,* 32–39; B. Friedman, "Countermajoritarian," 410–13.

33. The Missouri Supreme Court responded to the formulaic U.S. Supreme Court order, "We reverse and remand for proceedings in conformity to our opinion," in a land-patent case, by reversing itself but then reenacting the same decree. The U.S. Supreme Court on a second appeal then announced that its order was being "in effect evade[d]" and therefore it reversed (again) and awarded execution directly to the prevailing party. *Tyler v. Magwire* (1872); Warren, "Attacks," 185–86.

34. *Van Gend en Loos v. Netherlandse Administratie.*

35. *Costa v. ENEL.*

36. *International Handelsgesellschaft v. EVGF.* The rule that national constitutional provisions must give way to supranational EC law was reiterated in *Simmenthal II* (1978).

37. See van Empel, Schermers et al., *Leading Cases,* 159–60, 203–5, 228–39. See also Schermers and Waelbroeck, *Judicial Protection,* 127–38. For a detailed account of how the legal order in one of the later joining nation-states with a strong tradition of Parliamentary supremacy adapted to ECJ supremacy, see Craig, "Report on the United Kingdom."

38. Steven Bibas, "Fundamental Rights," 253–70.

39. Albors-Llorens, "Changes in the Jurisdiction," 1277, 1285–86.

40. Alter, "Court's Political Power," 475.

41. After the Maastricht Treaty of 1993, the European Parliament took on a more coequal role as legislator, and the Council of Ministers' official title changed to the Council of the European Union.

42. *Grad v. Finanzamt Traustein* (1970) and *Van Duyn v. Home Office* (1974).

43. *Value Added Tax Directive Case,* German Supreme Tax Court (1982) (case later known as "*VAT I*").

44. This has not been the case with the other two of France's three high courts. The Constitutional Court, which acts as an advisory body to Parliament on whether pending French laws violate the national constitution, has avoided involvement with European law cases. Similarly, the Cour de Cassation (Supreme Civil Court) has not resisted European authority; indeed, it has openly accepted it even during the era of overt resistance by the Conseil d'État.

45. *Syndicat Général de Fabricante de Semoules* (hereafter, *Semoules*).

46. Rasmussen, *On Law,* 351, citing remarks of French Prime Minister Regis DeBray; also cited in Alter, "Who Are the 'Masters'?," 132.

47. Alter, "Court's Political Power," 464–67; Bebr, "Rambling Ghost." See also n. 24 above.

48. In 1978, *Minister of the Interior v. Cohn-Bendit* (hereafter *Cohn-Bendit*); in 1980, *Office Nationale Interprofessional de Céréales* (hereafter *ONIC*); and *Société Sovincast;* in 1981, *Société civile Centre international dentaire* (hereafter *Dentaire*); and in 1985, *Commission v. France* (tobacco pricing cases). The latter had been decided by the ECJ on June 21, 1983, whose ruling (a condemnation of France for illegal behavior) was then rejected or defied by the French Conseil d'État on Dec. 13, 1985, *Recueil Lebon,* 377. (The ECJ then reiterated its condemnation of France in Case 169/87, July 13, 1988.)

49. *France devant la Cour,* 366.

50. Dutheil de la Rochère, "*Société . . . Rothmans.*" The so-called "Mutton War" cases of 1978–80 were called *Commission v. France,* as were the tobacco pricing ones of 1983 to 1988.

51. Dutheil de la Rochère.

52. That France, particularly via its Conseil d'État, has been uniquely recalcitrant is widely acknowledged. See, e.g., Mauro Cappelletti and David Golay, "Judicial Branch," 311–15.

53. For a brief account of each one of these incidents, see Appendix B.

54. "*Solange I*" is *Internationale Handelsgesellschaft v. Einfuhr-und Vorratsstelle.* "*Solange II*" is *Wunsche Handelsgesellschaft.*

CHAPTER 2: STATE RESISTANCE IN THE UNITED STATES AND THE EUROPEAN COMMUNITY

1. At least one existing federation, the Canadian, does permit nullification by individual provinces of Canadian Supreme Court decisions that declare a provincial law in violation of the Charter of Rights.

2. This veto power system was a matter of de facto practice, adopted via the Luxembourg Accords upon the insistence of France in January 1966. These accords have no formal legal status. Freestone and Davidson, *Institutional Framework,* 102–3.

3. See, e.g., Calhoun's *Disquisition on Government.*

4. Warren, "Attacks," 27, 188.

5. In December 1823, the Kentucky legislature adopted a resolution urging Congress to pass such legislation. In March 1824 Martin Van Buren reported such a bill out of the Senate Judiciary Committee; it was tabled a month later. In May 1824 the House Judiciary Committee debated but rejected a bill that would have

required a two-third's Supreme Court vote to overturn state legislation. In 1824 and again in 1825 Congressman Robert Letcher of Virginia introduced a resolve to do the same. No action was taken on it. In 1826 Senator Rowan of Kentucky proposed the same as an amendment on a pending bill altering the size of the Supreme Court. Both the amendment and the bill went down to defeat. In 1827 Congressman Wickliffe of Kentucky introduced a bill in the House that would require such a two-third's vote. It was not adopted. And in 1829 such a bill was reported out of the House Judiciary Committee. It went no further. Ibid., 22–33.

6. In this system as of 1994, France, Germany, the United Kingdom, and Italy each had ten votes; Spain had eight; Belgium, Greece, the Netherlands, and Portugal each had five; Denmark and Ireland each had three; and Luxembourg, two. Measures needed fifty-four votes out of the seventy-six total to pass. The Single European Act extended voting by this system to cover most legislation for the internal market, leaving out (for the unanimity requirement) only fiscal measures, free movement of persons, and the rights and interests of employed persons. Kent, *European Community Law,* 14–15. The parallel drawn in the text is inexact in the sense that voting in the EU is proportional to size while voting in the U.S. Supreme Court is one per justice.

7. *DeFrenne v. Belgium.*

8. *Society for the Protection of Unborn Children v. Grogan* (1991); Bowler et al., 18–19; Coppel and O'Neill, "Taking Rights Seriously?"

9. Lenaerts, "Some Thoughts," 105–6.

10. Paul Pierson also notes this similarity in "Path to European Integration," 133.

11. Kelsen, *Law and Peace,* 145–50. See also Hinsley, *Sovereignty,* 224–25; Strayer, *Medieval Origins,* 102; and Fowler and Bunck, *Sovereign State,* 6, for the same point.

12. Warren, "Attacks," 26, 188; B. Friedman, "Countermajoritarian," 407.

13. In a variation on the one-state, one-justice proposal, one reaction to the American pro-South *Dred Scott* decision was the emergence of suggestions that justices be selected in a more geographically representative way. B. Friedman, "Countermajoritarian," 430 n. 392. It became informal practice in the United States, until the term of Ronald Reagan (1981–89), to aim for at least regional (albeit not state-by-state) representation in the Supreme Court appointment process. Reagan seems to have initiated a trend to focus more narrowly on ideology and to ignore geography. Perhaps this is because the United States is more regionally homogeneous of late.

14. Weiler, "Transformation," 2425.

15. Warren, "Attacks," 165. The 1830s proposals came from Senator Joseph

Lecompte of Kentucky and were defeated, respectively, by votes of 115–61 and 141–27.

Technically U.S. judges serve for "good behavior," which amounts to lifetime tenure unless they are impeached. As early as 1808, when the issue of judicial power itself had become a subject of partisan debate between Federalists and Jeffersonians, the latter demanded in the Pennsylvania legislature that the U.S. Constitution be amended to limit the tenure of office of federal judges. A bill to do so was introduced by Senator Tiffin. B. Friedman, "Countermajoritarian," 370.

16. Anne-Marie Burley and Walter Mattli, "Political Theory," 65; Plötner, "Report on France," 31–33.

17. Burley and Mattli, "Political Theory," 64–65.

18. See also discussion of the case in Gerald Gunther, *Constitutional Law,* 29–32., and Powell, *Languages,* 296–302; and discussion of similar arguments in the lesser known case, *Jackson v. Rose* (1815), in Powell, *Languages,* 295–96, 301–2.

19. This assumption was embodied in Supreme Court precedent as official law in *Hans v. Louisiana* (1890). Until then, it had not been prominently challenged.

20. In *Ex Parte Young* (1908), the Supreme Court allowed a lawsuit from a private citizen for an injunction to be issued by a federal court to keep state officials from carrying out an unconstitutional law. The various contradictions of contemporary Eleventh Amendment doctrine are explored in *inter alia* Vicki Jackson, "Eleventh Amendment"; and Suzanna Sherry, "Eleventh Amendment and Stare Decisis."

21. Martin Shapiro, "European Court of Justice," 126–27.

22. The number of Article 177 cases brought to the Court mushroomed dramatically from a single case in 1962 to 119 in 1978, stabilizing after that to about one hundred per year (but with additional cases being handled by the Court of First Instance after 1988). Scheingold, *Political Integration,* 30–36; Burley and Mattli, "Political Theory," 58, citing Rasmussen, *On Law,* 245.

23. There was, for a time, considerable controversy over the flexibility with which one might legitimately interpret the phrase "raise a question of interpretation." See Chapter 1 discussion of the "acte clair" debate.

24. Weiler, "Journey," 421–30; Burley and Mattli, "Political Theory," 64–65.

25. Pinder, "New European Federalism," 48–49. Charles Merriam, writing a century ago in *Theory of Sovereignty,* noted a parallel phenomenon concerning European familiarity with the classics of American political thought, *The Federalist Papers* and John C. Calhoun's *Disquisition on Government.*

26. B. Friedman, "Things Forgotten," 755–56 nn. 98–99.

27. The first two proposals were raised in the U.S. Senate, having emerged in 1808 from a demand in the Pennsylvania state legislature and in 1822 from Ken-

tucky's anger at the Supreme Court's *Green v. Biddle* decision; the third in a letter to the president from a former senator. B. Friedman, "Countermajoritarian," 359–63, 370, 379–81, 407.

28. L. Friedman, *History of American Law,* 322–26.

29. B. Friedman, "Countermajoritarian," 407–8.

30. Ibid., 360 n. 140.

31. Ibid., 400 n. 269. Jackson, famed as a fighter against the Indians, notoriously sympathized with Georgia against the Cherokee, so was not inclined to send the troops anyway. Ibid, 398–401, nn. 264–69.

32. Alter, "Who Are the 'Masters'?," 131–33, citing Pierson, "Path to European Integration."

33. B. Friedman, "Countermajoritarian," 386 n.203.

34. Pollack, "Delegation, Agency," 118.

35. Seurin, "Towards a European Constitution?," 633–34; Shaw, "European Union: Legal Studies"; Alter, "Court's Political Power," 476.

36. Moravcsik, "Explaining International Human Rights."

37. Weiler, "Transformation," 2426. Among the later-joining countries, judicial review was exercised prior to joining the EC by a high court in Denmark and in Ireland. Caldeira and Gibson, "Legitimacy of Transnational Institutions," 464.

38. Burley and Mattli, "Political Theory," 63–64.

39. While an earlier version of this section of this book was in press, Karen Alter made a similar point in "Court's Political Power," 471. See Goldstein, "State Resistance to Authority."

40. Burley and Mattli, "Political Theory," 62–65.

41. Carl Kaestle, *Pillars of the Republic,* 6–7, 71, 99–100.

42. David Deudney, "Binding Sovereigns," 206.

43. The Reporter's Act of 1817 was drafted by Supreme Court justice Joseph Story, who also worked with the reporter Henry Wheaton to produce a digest of U.S. Supreme Court opinions for publication and nationwide sale. (They were to be published under Wheaton's name.) White, *American Judicial Tradition,* 44–45.

44. In the thinking of James Wilson, one of the influential framers of the U.S. Constitution, Americans would come to feel a loyalty to that which they chose for themselves—their own product. The democratic elections for federal officials, he argued, would promote a federal sense of loyalty. Beer "Federalism and the Nation-State," 231.

45. E.g., Weiler, "Transformation," 2428–31; Lenaerts, "Some Thoughts"; Rasmussen, *On Law,* 288–91; Burley and Mattli, "Political Theory," 67–68.

46. According to Bowler et al., "Eurobarometer survey after Eurobarometer survey document[s] the . . . generally low levels of enthusiasm for European unification" in European public opinion ("Building," 16).

47. Rasmussen, *On Law,* 289, 291.

48. This conclusion is based on the reported mass *perception* of not seeing or reading anything "recently" "in the papers, on the radio, or on television" about the European Court of Justice, as compared to the mass perception on similar questions about other institutions of the European Union. While 82 percent had heard or read something about the European Community, 55 percent about the European Parliament, 51 percent about the European Commission, 59 percent about their national court, and 85 percent about the Maastricht Treaty, only 34.4 percent claimed to have heard or seen anything recently about the European Court of Justice. Caldeira and Gibson, "Legitimacy of the Court," 362, 373–74.

49. Burley and Mattli, "Political Theory," 67–68, citing Rasmussen, *On Law* (emphasis in original).

50. Scharpf, "Joint-Decision Trap," 268.

51. Karen Alter, for instance, (in "Who Are the 'Masters'?") argues that leaders of a number of member states in the EC did not want the tighter union that the ECJ created but were somewhat helpless to correct the situation because on any one issue where a member state lost at the ECJ it was difficult or impossible to build the near-unanimity consensus needed to pass a new Euro-rule or amend the treaty on that particular point. Henry Schermers has pointed out that on at least some occasions national-level executive branch politicians in Europe acted in a more anti-EC direction than was favored by public or parliamentary opinion in their country ("Comment," 2527–28). Regardless of the nuances of difference among scholars on the question of how much the member-state political leadership wanted the degree of integration that the ECJ imposed, it is clear that their willingness to embrace the tactic of official public declamations of the illegitimacy of union authority was exhibited at a lower frequency than took place in the American union.

52. Wood, *Creation of the American Republic.*

53. Scharpf, "Joint-Decision Trap," 269.

54. Weiler, "Transformation," 2425; Weiler, "Journey," 424–25. Burley and Mattli, too, endorse his proposition, in "Political Theory," 67.

55. White, *American Judicial Tradition,* 45.

56. Warren, "Attacks," 6–12, 15–19, 175; Tipton, *Nullification,* 25–27, 36–39; McDougall, *Fugitive Slaves,* 68; McDonald, *History,* 98–103, 106–9; Kelly et al., *American Constitution,* 150–53; Powell, *Languages,* 230, 239–48, 287–89, 296–309.

57. Weiler, "Journey," 423–27.

58. Burley and Mattli, "Political Theory," 65–73.

59. B. Friedman, "Countermajoritarian," 388–89 with n. 217, 405 with n. 289, and 414 with n. 325.

60. Burley and Mattli, "Political Theory," 58–65; Weiler, "Journey," 424; Scheingold, *Political Integration.*

61. For a history of the stratification of the professional bar in the early United States and a history of legal education in the period, see L. Friedman, *History of American Law,* chap. 7. For an account of the evolution of an alliance between an increasingly professionalized bench and bar in the 1790–1820 United States and commercial interests, all of whom came to prefer that nationally uniform rules of commerce replace locally idiosyncratic laws and juries, see Morton Horwitz, *Transformation of American Law,* chap. 5. Thomas Hueglin, too, notes that in the nineteenth-century United States, as in Switzerland, "the modernizing forces of economic liberalism . . . of the new bourgeois elites" provided political pressures toward federal consolidation ("New Wine in Old Bottles?," 206).

62. Garrett and Weingast, "Ideas, Interests"; Garrett, "International Cooperation and Institutional Choice."

63. Alter, "Who Are the 'Masters'?," 136–40, citing at length Scharpf, "Joint-Decision Trap," and also citing Pollack, "Delegation, Agency."

64. *Parliamentary Debates (Hansard)* 6th Series, Commons, vol. 265, col. 12–13 (Nov. 1995) (emphasis added). For discussion of the two Barber decisions (*Barber v. Guardian Royal Exchange Assurance Group* and *Tenover Case* [*Barber II*]) and of the Barber Protocol to the Maastricht Treaty, see Rasmussen, *European Court of Justice,* 219–20, 294, 302–4.

65. Forsyth, *Unions of States,* chaps. 4–6; Merriam, *Theory of Sovereignty,* chaps. 9–10; Borel, *Etude.*

CHAPTER 3: THE SEVENTEENTH-CENTURY DUTCH REPUBLIC AND THE EUROPEAN UNION

1. Lister, *Early Security Confederations;* Tromp, "European Unity," 5–7; Prokhovnik, "Sovereignty"; Forsyth, *Unions of States.* See also Aubert, "Observations," 16–17 (arguing that the evolution of Dutch federalism offers a helpful comparison for understanding the evolution of the Swiss federal union, the subject of the next chapter in this study).

2. On the provinces' role within this centralized government see Leach, "Provinces."

3. Reitsma, *Centrifugal and Centripetal,* 171, 205, and chap. 5.

4. Haley, *Dutch,* 72.

5. Rowen and Losskey, *Political Ideas,* 8–10; Israel, *Dutch Republic,* 219–224, 301; Haley, *Dutch,* 75, 101.

6. Kossman, "Dutch Republic," 19; Price, *Holland,* 112, 236; 't Hart, *Bourgeois State,* 77–225; te Brake, "Provincial Histories," 67.

7. Israel, *Dutch Republic,* 302–3.

8. Ibid., 298–300.

9. Ibid., 304. Friesland, by contrast, had a stadholder continuously from 1521 until 1795.

10. Daalder, "Consociationalism," 189; Haley, *Dutch,* 78; and Huizinga, *Dutch Civilisation,* 32, are rather typical in crediting the Prince of Orange with aiming at the good of the Republic as a whole; but cf. Price, *Holland,* 250, 283, for the view that the Prince of Orange sometimes simply favored different sectional interests—those of the inland provinces—or else his own dynastic interests.

11. Israel, *Dutch Republic,* 240; Price, *Holland,* 3; Huizinga, *Dutch Civilization,* 31; but cf. Hoetjeś, "Federalism," 128, for a contrasting assessment.

12. Israel, *Dutch Republic,* 804.

13. Ibid., 784–828.

14. Kossman and Mellink, *Texts,* 166.

15. Israel, *Dutch Republic,* 295. In addition to the separate mints that functioned in every province, Zeeland also had its own measuring system—a "pound" that weighed six times what a "pound" did in the other provinces. 'T Hart, *Bourgeois State,* 200. And Holland and Zeeland employed a dating system different from those of the other provinces. Haley, *Dutch,* 69.

16. Kossman and Mellink, *Texts,* 169–71.

17. Israel, *Dutch Republic,* 217.

18. Ibid., 423–64, 468–69; Price, *Holland,* 234.

19. Currently in the United States, one can still hear such phrases as "the sovereign state of South Carolina." In contrast to the discourse of the seventeenth-century Dutch union, such talk generally involves rhetorical flourish geared to appeal to local pride; it generally does not mean that the speaker believes the entity to be "sovereign" in the sense that the U.S. government lacks supreme authority over it, as per the Supremacy Clause of the U.S. Constitution.

20. Price, *Holland,* 221.

21. I have discovered only one scholar who agrees with this depiction of the decision-making process: Frederick Lister, *Early Security Confederations,* 111–16.

22. Israel, *Dutch Republic,* 753–54.

23. Reitsma, *Centrifugal,* 238–39; Israel, *Dutch Republic,* 223; 293; 403–5; 287; 541; 596–97; Price, *Holland,* 213; Haley, *Dutch,* 112; Lister, *Early Security Confederations,* 127; Israel, *Dutch Republic,* 753–54, 835; Price, *Holland,* 241.

24. The Zeeland States, indecisively breaking with Holland and like-minded provinces, in 1652 named the baby William III of Orange (age two) as its stadholder and William Frederick (then stadholder of Friesland and Groningen) as lieutenant general of the army and acting admiral of the navy "provided other provinces [agree]." Israel, *Dutch Republic,* 718–19.

25. Ibid., 540–41; Price, *Holland*, 235–46; Kossman, "Dutch Republic," 22.

26. Israel, *Dutch Republic*, 794.

27. Ibid., 722–34, 750–51.

28. Chesterfield, *Letters*, 2:607.

29. 'T Hart, *Bourgeois State*, 20; te Brake, "Provincial Histories," 71; Worst, "Constitution," 147–48; Daalder, "Consociationalism," 186; Rowen and Jensen, *Dutch Republic*, 5; Haley, *Dutch*, 67; Huizinga, *Dutch Civilisation*, 30; Temple, *Observations*, 56.

30. Kossman, "Dutch Republic," 22; Price, *Holland*, 214, 285.

31. I have found no other scholars as blunt on this point. Israel writes, for instance, "The rule about unanimity turned out to be largely academic . . . hardly any major decisions of the United Provinces in the seventeenth century were taken unanimously—the decision to back William III in invading England in 1688, being a notable and almost unique exception—it frequently happened that principal decisions were taken over the opposition of more than one province" (*Dutch Republic*, 276). Also, "Provincial sovereignty—a half-truth [until 1618]—was an almost total fiction after 1618" (540–41). And, "the claim [put forth by Holland in a 1656–57 controversy] . . . that each province of the United Provinces was sovereign . . . was a manifest fiction and everyone knew it to be a manifest fiction. There had always been majority voting in the States General and this was unavoidable if the Republic was to function. Holland regularly participated in majority votes in the Generality. But this was when Holland was in the majority" (733).

32. Ibid., 220–24, 301–2. Israel offers two somewhat conflicting versions of Holland's sovereignty arguments on this issue, without noting the conflict. Citing van Deursen ("Maurits," 88), he says that Holland claimed that the provincial states and the States General had received sovereignty once they renounced the King of Spain and therefore these bodies, not the Earl and his Council of State, had authority to appoint stadholders. Ibid., 224. Elsewhere, citing Wernham ("English Policy," 36–38), he says that Holland's argument was that each province, rather than the Generality, was heir to the erstwhile sovereignty of the King of Spain, and that provincial states therefore held this sovereign appointment power. Ibid., 301.

33. Ibid., 304.

34. Ibid., 304, 450–60, 467–68; Price, *Holland*, 39–40, 142–44, 216.

35. Israel, *Dutch Republic*, 703–7.

36. Kossman and Mellink, *Texts*, 171–72.

37. 'T Hart, "Rules."

38. 'T Hart, *Bourgeois State*, 78.

39. Israel, *Dutch Republic*, 285.

40. 'T Hart, *Bourgeois State*, 80-83, 169.

41. Ibid., 79.

42. Israel, *Dutch Republic*, 286-87.

43. 'T Hart, *Bourgeois State*, 82-83.

44. Israel, *Dutch Republic*, 289-90; 't Hart, *Bourgeois State*, 145, 135-36, 146-47.

45. 'T Hart, *Bourgeois State*, 146.

46. Israel, *Dutch Republic*, 756; 't Hart, *Bourgeois State*, 142-43, 146.

47. 'T Hart, *Bourgeois State*, 79-80, 145; Israel, *Dutch Republic*, 287.

48. 'T Hart, *Bourgeois State*, 135-36, 146-47.

49. Price, *Holland*, 184.

50. Israel, *Dutch Republic*, 423-24.

51. Ibid., 424-28.

52. 'T Hart, *Bourgeois State*, 32-36.

53. Israel, *Dutch Republic*, 423-41.

54. Kossman and Mellink, *Texts*, 166-68.

55. 'T Hart, *Bourgeois State*, 34-35, 38, 62, 86; Israel, *Dutch Republic*, 294-95.

56. Israel, *Dutch Republic*, 294-95.

57. Ibid., 441-44.

58. Ibid., 444-47.

59. J. L. Price does cite some later additional cases tried by specially created Generality courts but notes that the practice declined by the end of the century (*Holland*, 285).

60. Israel, *Dutch Republic*, 448-61.

61. Ibid., 662-69.

62. Ibid., 761-66.

63. Kossman and Mellink, *Texts*, 168 n.8.

64. 'T Hart, *Bourgeois State*, 35, 43, 45-46.

65. Ibid., 48, 147.

66. Ibid., 47.

67. Price, *Holland*, 128, 236.

68. Israel, *Dutch Republic*, 602-3.

69. Rowen, 65-67; Israel, *Dutch Republic*, 603-6.

70. Israel, *Dutch Republic.*, 606; Rowen, *Rhyme and Reason*, 66-67.

71. Israel, *Dutch Republic*, 606; Rowen, *Rhyme and Reason*, 68-69.

72. Israel, *Dutch Republic*, 606-7; Rowen, *Rhyme and Reason*, 70-77.

73. 'T Hart, *Bourgeois State*, 62.

74. Rowen, *Rhyme and Reason*, 67; Price, *Holland*, 237.

75. Huizinga, *Dutch Civilisation*, 23-29, 33, 109; Price, *Holland*, 209-10.

76. Kossman "Popular Sovereignty"; see also Hinsley, *Sovereignty;* De Jouvenal, *Sovereignty.*

77. Horwitz, *Transformation of American Law.*

78. Burley and Mattli, "Political Theory," 58–65.

79. Scheingold, *Political Integration,* chap. 3.

80. England, for instance, one of the more stable states in Europe, experienced in this century a civil war, a revolution (Cromwellian), a counterrevolution (the Restoration), and then another revolution (the Glorious).

81. Wincott, "Law, and the European Union," 181; see also Alter, "Court's Political Power."

82. Golub, "Politics of Judicial Discretion," 377–81; see also Alter, "Court's Political Power."

83. Karen Alter has generalized from the observation by Buffet-Tchakaloff (*France devant la Cour,* 24–25) of differential rates at which lower and higher courts of France referred cases to the ECJ to assert that not just in France but throughout the EU, courts of last resort, in contrast to lower courts, felt disempowered by the ECJ and therefore passively resisted by failing to refer preliminary questions cases for European judgment. Thus Alter claims that specifically lower courts were the motor of integration for the EC/EU, but she does acknowledge that her generalization does not apply equally well across all six original member states or even across the category "courts of last resort" ("Court's Political Power," 464–69). So perhaps one should qualify the point to a claim that lower courts had an especially strong role in furthering EC integration.

84. 'T Hart, "Rules."

CHAPTER 4: THE FIRST HALF-CENTURY OF THE MODERN SWISS FEDERATION

1. Beaufrays, "Observations"; Eschet-Schwarz, "Swiss Federal Experience"; Forsyth, *Unions of States,* 18–30; Hicks, *Federalism,* 156–68; Hughes, "Cantonalism," 155; Landau, "Language Problem"; McKay, "Political Legitimacy"; Pfeiffer and Weber, "Fédéralisme"; Thürer, "Switzerland"; but cf. Hueglin, "New Wine," 205–9, for argument that it is a poor model.

2. For an English translation of the oath covenant see Vincent, *State and Federal,* 191–93.

3. One scholar would dispute the label, "voluntary." He claims, "The consolidation of the Swiss Union in 1848 was based exclusively upon the military defeat of the Catholic (Sonderbund) cantons by Protestant cantons in 1847" (Preston King, *Federalism and Federation,* 88–89). While it is true that most of the Sonderbund cantons did vote against ratification of the 1848 Constitution (the only exception being Fribourg), it is also true that the goal of the Sonderbund league

was not secession from the Swiss union. (The Sonderbund cantons were content to be members of the union, but preferred different terms of union.) The Pact of 1815 that bound the union together was formed as a voluntary act of equal and independent cantons. Hans Daalder describes the origins of the post–Sonderbund War constitution: "Immediately after the end of hostilities, the conqueror and the conquered sat down together at the same table to design the Constitution of 1848" ("Formation," 394 n.1).

Moreover, the Swiss federation of 1848 had evolved out of a voluntary confederation rooted in a history of some six centuries—one that varied over time in degrees of voluntariness, degrees of confederalness (vs. centralization), and degrees of inclusiveness of the twenty-two cantons (Forsyth, *Unions of States,* 18–30).

4. Linder, *Swiss Democracy,* 5. But cf. Hughes's claim that despite their lengthy history of "acting as states do," the cantons were never really sovereign ("Cantonalism," 157). For accounts of the various transitions of intercantonal arrangements between the thirteenth and nineteenth centuries see Luck, *History;* Forsyth, *Unions of States,* 30; Eschet-Schwarz, "Swiss Federal Experience." Both of the latter end where this study begins, in 1848.

5. The popular majority in favor of ratifying the Constitution was greater than two-thirds (170,000 to 72,000, according to Forsyth; 140,000 to 60,000, according to Grisel). According to the latter, it is an error to view the acceptance of the 1848 Constitution as coming from the procedure that the document specifies for its own amendment. Cf. Forsyth, *Unions of States,* 29. Grisel describes the Diet as having decided that the procedure for replacing the 1815 Pact would be to let each cantonal government determine its own method for the decision whether to ratify, as a canton, the new Constitution, and also to hold a national popular vote on ratification. One and a half cantons let their popular assembly of the citizenry (the "Landsgemeinde") decide on ratification, and in one canton (Fribourg) the decision was made by the cantonal legislature. All the others simply counted the popular vote. Then the Diet decided to declare the Constitution ratified in consideration of the fact that, while the cantons had not unanimously accepted it, the cantons representing 1.9 million people had done so, while cantons containing only 300,000 opposed it (Grisel, *Première,* 58–60).

6. See discussion below of the protests of Uri, Nidwald, and Obwald against the validity of the Diet's decision that the Constitution had been ratified.

7. In the United States, Rhode Island and North Carolina refused ratification until after the first Congress began meeting. North Carolina ratified in 1789 and Rhode Island in 1790.

8. Bryce, *Modern Democracies,* 356.

9. Aubert, *Traité,* vol. 1, para. 784–85, pp. 297–98; Aubert, *Petite,* para. 115,

pp. 106–7; Adams and Cunningham, *Swiss Confederation,* 72–74; Frowein, "Integration," 596–97; Rappard, *Government,* 88–90; Rice, *Two Courts,* 6, 9–10, 20–24; Tripp, *Swiss,* 107 n. 175.

10. Grisel, *Première,* 59–60; Tripp, *Swiss,* 74.

11. Tripp, *Swiss,* 74, makes a similar suggestion. The term "civil war" is set in quotation marks because if the cantons were truly independent sovereign bodies in 1847, a war amongst them was not, strictly speaking, a civil war. From the perspective of the post-1848 Confederation it is a civil war, but this is an anachronistic perspective. The Federal Tribunal ruled in 1858 that the secession that provoked the war, while contrary to federal law, had not been a criminal act. Ullmer, *Droit,* 1:374–75; ATF, 3 July 1858. Secession in the nineteenth-century United States was treated much more harshly.

12. Tripp, *Swiss,* 75.

13. Ibid., 130; Aubert, *Traité,* 1:305; Grisel, *Deuxième,* 47–49.

14. Luck, *History,* 390–94; see also Ruffieux, "Radicaux," 611–13; Eschet-Schwarz, "Processus," 164–66.

15. FF 1861, 2:109, cited in Ullmer, *Droit,* 1864, 1:vi at n. 2. Bracketed language added simply to smooth the transition to English. Translations from French sources herein are my own.

16. Adams and Cunningham, *Swiss Confederation,* 62–63.

17. Article 4 of the Transition Provisions of the 1848 Constitution says simply that the Federal Constitution "abrogates" any provisions that are contrary to it in cantonal constitutions. It makes no mention of cantonal statutes, but the Federal Assembly ruled in 1852 that this silence was of no consequence: under Article 4 any cantonal statutes contrary to the Federal Constitution were immediately abrogated when the Federal Constitution took effect on September 12, 1848. FF 1852 1:433ff.

18. Linder, *Swiss Democracy,* 71–72.

19. The cantonal archives are, variously, kept in one of three different languages (French, Italian, German), as are opinions of the Federal Tribunal. Moreover, the bulk of the opinions of the Federal Tribunal remain in unpublished archives (Rice, *Two Courts,* xii–xv). To date no Swiss historian or political scientist has published any comprehensive account of cantonal resistance to federal authority. (This last assertion is based on author's conversation with Pia Caroni, Swiss legal historian, and Roland Ruffieux, Swiss political scientist.)

20. Luck, *History,* 390–94; Eschet-Schwarz, "Processus," 164–66.

21. The 1866 constitutional revision clarifying the citizenship rights of the Jewish Swiss, according to J. F. Aubert, was necessary "in order to overcome the unwillingness of some of the cantons" to cooperate on federal policy in this matter. *Petite,* para. 34, pp. 35–36.

22. Adams and Cunningham, *Swiss Confederation*, 63.

23. A copy of the Constitution of 1848 appears in the first pages of volume one of the *Recueil Officiel* (RO).

24. Luck, *History*, 363–65.

25. FF 1848–49, 1:183; 1852, 1:23; 1858, 2:272; Ullmer, *Droit*, 1864, 1, para. 322–23, pp. 330–31.

26. Droz, "Histoire," 270–71, 350–55; Luck, *History*, 388–90; Ullmer, *Droit*, 1864, 1, para. 537, pp. 461–63.

27. Myron Tripp (*Swiss*, 77–82), commenting on the first century of the Federation, omits any discussion of cantonal involvement with foreign revolutions and identifies a different pattern. He suggests that cantonal loyalty tended to be the foundation of "states' rights" disputes in Switzerland, whereas regional economic interests dominated such disputes in the United States. But his analysis may have been focusing on the more recent three quarters of the century, after revolutionary fervor had died down. Cf. also Baudouin who asserts, in a study of political opposition by leaders of Vaud against the centralization of federal power within Switzerland in the second half of the nineteenth century, that allegations of concern for the principle of cantonal sovereignty sometimes thinly disguised the motive of cantonal material self-interest. *Vaud*, 214–15. One should probably conclude that cantonal resistance to federal policies over the fifty-year period stemmed from a variety of motivations.

28. Ullmer, *Droit*, 1:349–54 and FF 1857, 2:547–63.

29. ATF 5 (1880): 520–27; Ruffieux, "Radicaux," 631.

30. Ullmer, *Droit*, 2:58–59, para. 748.

31. Ibid., 2:45–46, para. 733; 1:198{endash}201, para. 208; 1:207–9, para. 213–14.

32. Ibid., 2:152–54, para. 853.

33. Hughes, *Federal Constitution*, 77–79.

34. RO 2:205.

35. Ullmer, *Droit*, 1, para. 98, pp. 78–85; 1, para. 100, pp. 86–87.

36. FF 1859, 1:397–410.

37. Ullmer, *Droit*, 1, para. 98, pp. 84–85; para. 583, pp. 534–35; FF 1859, 1:406–8, 410; Salis, *Droit*, 1, para. 82–84, pp. 344–75; Vincent, *State and Federal*, 36–37; Droz, "Histoire," 339–47.

38. Salis, *Droit*, 1, para. 74, pp. 328–29; Ruffieux, "Radicaux", 622–23.

39. Ullmer, *Droit*, 1, para. 30, pp. 27–28.

40. Ibid., 1, para. 35, pp. 36–37.

41. For a few such examples from the late 1850s and early 1860s, see ibid., 1, para. 36, pp. 37; and 2:, para. 715–16, pp. 36–37.

42. Salis, *Droit*, 1, para. 44, p. 206.

43. Ibid., vol. 1, para. 56, pp. 229–36; para. 57, pp. 242–44; Ullmer, *Droit,* 1, para. 27–29, pp. 23–27. Federal level opposition to the establishment of new Catholic religious orders in Switzerland dated back to the Sonderbund War in which the Catholic cantons had attempted to secede, and also to the perception that the pontifical Church authorities agitated in a pro-monarchist, antidemocratic direction. Aubert, *Traité,* 1, para. 57ff., para. 106 and 112ff.; 2, para. 2054 and 2056ff.; 2:1, para. 2051 bis.

44. Salis, *Droit,* 1, para. 57, pp. 242–47.

45. Ibid., 1, para. 59–60, pp. 271–75.

46. In the United States, for instance, the constitution of the state of Delaware mandated "separate [public] schools for white and colored children" until 1995, although such official separation of the races became contrary to the U.S. Constitution in 1954. Actual governmental practice in Delaware stopped separating the races in public schools in the 1960s. Thus, actual state-level resistance continued for about a decade, but from the looks of the state constitution, it would have appeared to have gone on for some forty years. Sacks, "Education," 172–73.

47. RO 5:33–34; 6:543–44.

48. Adams and Cunningham, *Swiss Confederation,* 62–63; see also Salis, *Droit,* 1, para. 82–84, pp. 344–75; Vincent, *State and Federal,* 36–37; Droz, "Histoire," 339–47.

49. Droz, "Histoire," 270.

50. Luck, *History,* 388–90; Droz, ibid., 271. Droz reports the number of expelled Ticinese at "more than 5,000," while Luck puts the number at 10,000.

51. Droz, "Histoire," 271.

52. Ullmer, *Droit,* vol. 1, para. 537, pp. 461–63; Droz, "Histoire," 350–55.

53. Droz, "Histoire," 350–55.

54. Material on this incident comes from Ullmer, *Droit,* 1:349–54; and FF 1857, 2:547–63. References to the Vaud government throughout this section refer to its Conseil d'État (Council of State), its executive council.

55. Ullmer, *Droit,* 1:351.

56. Ibid., 1:352.

57. All sections of the 1874 Constitution quoted here in English use Hughes, *Federal Constitution.* Material in this and in the following two paragraphs was drawn from ATF 5 (1880): 520–27. See also Ruffieux, "Radicaux," 631.

58. Ullmer, *Droit,* 2:58–59, para. 748.

59. Ibid., 2, para. 733, pp. 45–46.

60. Ibid., 1, para. 208, pp. 198–201.

61. Ibid., 1, para. 213, pp. 207–8.

62. Ibid., 1, para. 214, pp. 208–9.

63. Ibid., 1, para. 218–19, pp. 212–13; para. 46–47, pp. 45–46.

64. Ibid., 1, para. 47, pp. 46–47 (emphasis in original). The Federal Tribunal in 1861 offered a further refinement of these guidelines, in a case brought by a Jewish Swiss citizen of the canton Aargau who was employed and resided in the canton of St. Gall. The latter charged Jews a fee twenty-five times as high for a residence license as it charged non-Jews, and the aggrieved litigant took his constitutional challenge all the way to the high court, where he won. The Federal Tribunal explained that the canton was indeed free to exclude Jews as citizens or as long-term residents, but once they were in the canton, they were entitled to be treated in a manner guided by the general principle of equality before the law. This principle, enshrined in Article 4 of the Constitution, meant at least, specifically, that law had to apply to Swiss Jews the same "forms and taxes" as to other Swiss. *Journal des Tribuneaux* 9 (July 10, 1861): 361–64.

65. Ullmer, *Droit*, 2, para. 853, pp. 151–52.

66. Ibid., 2, para. 853, pp. 152–53.

67. Ibid.

68. FF 1864, 2:340–454, 756–57.

69. Ullmer, *Droit*, 1, para. 98, pp. 78–85.

70. Ibid., 1, para. 100, pp. 86–87.

71. RO vol. 1, no. 2, pp. 130–39.

72. RO vol. 1, no. 2, p. 135.

73. Ibid., 131–32; see also Hughes, *Federal Constitution,* 77–79.

74. FF 1859, 1, 394.

75. Ullmer, *Droit,* 1, introduction to chap. 10, p. 430.

76. Ibid., 1, para. 500, pp. 437–38.

77. Ibid., 1, para. 488, 502, 510–12; pp. 493–521; FF 1859, 1, 394.

78. Ullmer, *Droit,* 2, para. 1040, pp. 365–66.

79. FF 1859, 1, pp. 397–410.

80. Ullmer, *Droit,* 1, para. 98, pp. 84–85; para. 583, pp. 534–35; FF 1859, 1, pp. 406–8.

81. FF 1859 1, p. 410.

82. Salis, *Droit,* 1, para. 82–84, pp. 344–75; Vincent, *State and Federal,* 36–37.

83. Vincent, *State and Federal,* 36–37; Droz, "Histoire," 339–47.

84. Vincent, *State and Federal;* Droz, "Histoire"; Salis, *Droit,* 1, para. 82, p. 345; Brooks, *Government,* 56–57; Grisel, *Deuxième,* 41–47.

85. Salis, *Droit,* 1, para. 82–84, pp. 344–75.

86. Adams and Cunningham, *Swiss Confederation,* 62–63.

87. In terms of defiance of federal law, Ticino's repeated presence in this table certainly marks it as a standout. Researcher Roger Baudouin focused instead on political leadership in mobilizing sentiment against the centralization of power

into the hands of federal authorities, and from this perspective concluded that the canton of Vaud occupied a "predominant place" in Swiss history of the second half of the nineteenth century as the voice of cantonal "resistance" to increased federal power (*Vaud,* v, 210).

88. Aubert, from another vantage point, also notes the dominance of the theme of cantonal citizen rights in Swiss nineteenth-century constitutional politics. With a focus on constitutional alteration, he identifies the dominant theme of the individual constitutional amendments of the nineteenth century as the adding of powers to the federal government, but in the wholesale constitutional revisions/replacements of 1848, 1866, and 1874, he judges the dominant concern to have been the progressive strengthening of the freedom of all Swiss to establish themselves as citizens with full rights in any of the cantons of Switzerland. "Observations," 12–13, 18–19.

89. E.g., Moravcsik, *Choice for Europe;* Mattli, *Logic of Regional Integration.*

90. Rappard, *Government,* 79.

91. Ullmer, *Droit,* 1:viii-ix.

92. See, e.g., discussion of the treatment of convents in the Uri Constitution in Salis, *Droit,* 1, para. 56, pp. 229–32.

93. Such a transformation of judicial power did take place with respect to relations between the U.S. president and Supreme Court. In the 1860s the Supreme Court refrained from confronting President Lincoln over what it viewed as unconstitutional behavior in a situation where his defiance of the Court was predictable, but in the 1950s successfully ordered President Truman to cease an unconstitutional policy and in the 1970s issued an order that resulted in the resignation of President Nixon.

94. Salis, *Droit,* 1, para. 82, p. 345; Brooks, *Government,* 56–57; Vincent, *State and Federal,* 36–37; Droz, "Histoire," 347; Grisel, *Deuxième,* 41–47.

95. Burley and Mattli, "Political Theory"; Moravcsik, *Choice for Europe;* Mattli, *Logic of Regional Integration;* Stone[-]Sweet and Brunell, "Supranational Constitution."

96. Tripp, *Swiss,* 77, 84; Hueglin, "New Wine," 205–6.

97. Eschet-Schwarz, "Swiss Federal Experience," 174–75; Aubert, "Observations," 11, briefly makes the same point.

98. Tripp, *Swiss,* 77, 84.

CHAPTER 5: CONCLUSIONS

1. Forsyth, *Unions of States,* 208.

2. Hughes, "Cantonalism," 167. William Riker, on the basis of a multicountry comparison, flatly contradicts this assertion (*Federalism: Origin, Operation, Significance,* 136).

3. Riker, "European Federalism," 24.

4. Cf. Elazar, "The New Europe"; Ferry, "La Communauté Européenne." See also analysis in Chryssochoou, *Theory and Reform*, 10–52, and Taylor, *European Union*, 79–97.

5. Cram, "Integration Theory"; Schmitter, "Some Alternative Futures"; Cafrany and Lankowski, "Europe's Ambiguous Unity," 8; Hooghe and Marks, "Contending Models of Governance," 39; Chryssochoou, *Theory and Reform*, 52; Banchoff and Smith, *Legitimacy and the EU*.

6. Elazar, *Constitutionalizing Globalization;* Volcansek, *Law above Nations.*

7. On domestic economic groups see Moravcsik, *Choice for Europe;* on transstate economic groups, Stone[-]Sweet and Caporaso, "Free Trade to Supranational"; on both, Close and Ohki-Close, *Supranationalism;* Mattli and Slaughter, "Revisiting"; Mattli, *Logic of Regional Integration.*

8. Mills, *Human Rights;* Krasner, *Sovereignty,* 30–33, 75, chap. 4. Krasner makes a point of emphasizing historic precedents that bore certain similarities to the late-twentieth-century conventions on human rights, such as the protection of religious toleration for Protestants and Catholics in the Peace of Westphalia and protections of ethnic minorities, announced but never enforced in various League of Nations rules. But even Krasner acknowledges that the concern with human rights as such is a phenomenon of the late twentieth century and that the regime of the European Human Rights Convention enforced in fact by a transstate court is "perhaps [the] only example" of a giving away of ["Westphalian"] sovereign power by domestic authorities for the sake of protecting human rights (118–19).

9. E.g., Moravcsik, *Choice for Europe;* Mattli, *Logic of Regional Integration;* Close and Ohki-Close, *Supranationalism;* Mills, *Human Rights;* Krasner, *Sovereignty.*

10. Riker, *Federalism: Origin, Operation, Significance* and *Development of American Federalism;* Wheare, *Federal Governments;* Watts, *New Federations.*

11. Close and Ohki-Close, *Supranationalism,* 62–63.

12. Walter Mattli's recent book, *Logic of Regional Integration,* also takes up this topic, but he does so by comparing the EC not to other multistate political unions where elements of sovereignty have been significantly pooled (such that states abandon their veto power over decisions that shape their own policies) or have been delegated (such that designated central authorities can command member-state obedience). Instead he compares the EC to other customs unions or free trade areas. His goal is to understand both the motive for joining and what contributes to successful maintenance. Not surprisingly, since he has selected economic partnerships to study, he finds that economic forces predominate in determining both initial motivation and lasting success. However, he acknowledges that the EC's system of enforcement power delegated to the ECJ and European Commission is

uniquely powerful among his set of cases. This fact would seem to indicate that he is in fact comparing a group of cases that are in a fundamental respect dissimilar, and therefore not usefully comparable.

13. *Politics*, bk. 2, chap. 8, para. 1269a.

14. Krasner, *Sovereignty*, 7.

15. Pierson, "Path to European Integration." Other scholars cut up the pie in somewhat differing configurations. See, e.g., Chryssochoou, *Theory and Reform*, chaps. 1–2, dividing the theorists of European integration among fourteen different categories.

16. See also discussion of Garrett and Weingast scholarship in Chapter 2. As of 1998, Garrett, at least, appears to have modified his approach, and now asserts that his earlier intergovernmentalism benefits by being supplemented with insights that are more attentive to institutional particularities (and thus arguably derive from historical institutionalism). Garrett et al., "European Court of Justice," 175.

17. See discussion of their arguments about interest groups in Chapter 2 (Burley and Mattli, "Political Theory," 58–65; Mattli and Slaughter, "Law and Politics"). Moravcsik (*Choice for Europe*) produces a kind of hybrid of neofunctionalism and intergovernmentalism by arguing that the power of interest groups within a given member state has driven the policy-making of its governmental leaders, who then operate more or less as the intergovernmentalism model suggests.

18. Pierson, "Path to European Integration," 123–31, 147.

19. Alter, "Who Are the 'Masters'?" (citing Pierson, ibid., and Pollack, "Delegation, Agency.")

20. Mattli and Slaughter, "Revisiting."

21. Bulmer, "New Institutionalist"; Shaw and More, "Introduction," 5; Armstrong, "Institutions and Institutional Change"; Wincott, "Law and the European Union" and "Court of Justice."

22. Moravcsik, *Choice for Europe*, 494, 68.

23. Scharpf, "Joint-Decision Trap."

24. De Vree, *Political Integration*, 10–15, 22–37, 371–76; see also Lister, *European Union*, for a similar argument.

25. A notable exception is Murray Forsyth's *Unions of States*. Where he focuses on the epoch immediately preceding the formation of a truly federal union in order to understand the process leading to federation, and does so for the cases examined here plus the German Bund of the nineteenth century, this work has focused on the question of resistance in the epoch immediately following formation of the union, to determine which elements make member-state resistance to central authority more likely or less likely.

26. For a sampling of the extensive comparative federalism literature see works

in the bibliography by Burgess and Gagnon, Elazar, Ferry, Forsyth, Friedrich, Hesse and Wright, Hicks, King, Knop et al., Lemco, Riker, Sawer, Watts, and Wheare.

27. Mattli and Slaughter, "Revisiting," 183, 189.

28. Riker, *Development of American Federalism,* 119–26.

29. In addition, in both Italy and Germany national-level courts have issued what might be thought of as warnings to the ECJ, which very fact might be read as implying that these member-state (constitutional) courts consider their own authority to be above that of the ECJ. These warnings concern the need for the ECJ to respect fundamental rights of the member-state citizens. It is difficult to treat such warnings simply as member-state defiance, however, since it is ECJ doctrine that the ECJ does and will respect the fundamental rights of EC citizens.

30. Volcansek, *Law above Nations.*

31. Such assertions are made by Weiler, "Journey," 423–27, and Burley and Mattli, "Political Theory," 65–73.

32. Riker, *Federalism: Origin, Operation, Significance,* 129–35.

33. Pufendorf, *De Jure Naturae et Gentium Libri Octo* (The Law of Nature and Nations), bk. 7, chap. 5, Sect. 20.

34. Moravcsik, "Explaining International Human Rights."

APPENDIX A: STATE RESISTANCE TO FEDERAL AUTHORITY IN THE UNITED STATES

1. Warren, "Attacks," 5.

2. Warren ("Attacks," 23) indicates that Supreme Court records show *Green v. Biddle* to have been a 4–1 decision (one of the justices having been absent when it was argued, and one of the original six absent when it was handed down).

3. This clause states: "No person held to service or labor in one state under the laws thereof, escaping into another, shall, in consequence of any law or regulation therein be discharged from such service or labor, but shall be delivered up on claim of the party to whom such service or labor may be due."

Cases Cited

Ableman v. Booth. 1857; 1859. 18 Howard 476; 21 Howard 506.

Bank of the United States v. Halstead. 1825. 10 Wheaton 1.

Barber v. Guardian Royal Exchange Assurance Group. (Barber I) 1990. ECJ Case C-262/88. (1990) ECR I-1889.

Bodley v. Gaither. 1828. (Kentucky) 3 T.B.Mun. 57.

Boisdet. 1990. Fr. Cons.d'E. Sept. 24, 1990, *Recueil Lebon,* 250.

Cherokee Nation v. Georgia. 1831. 5 Peters 1.

Chisolm v. Georgia. 1793. 2 Dallas 419.

C.I.L.F.I.T. v. Ministro della Sanita. 1982. ECJ Case 283/81, (1983) 1 CMLR 472.

Cohens v. Virginia. 1824. 6 Wheaton 264.

Commission v. Denmark. 1988. ECJ Case 302/86, (1988) ECR 4607.

Commission v. France (Mutton War cases). 1979. ECJ Case 239/78. (1979) ECR 2729. Also Cases 24/80 and 97/80.

Commission v. France (tobacco pricing cases), ECJ June 21, 1983; French Cons.d'E., Dec. 13, 1985, *Recueil Lebon,* 377; ECJ Case 169/87, July 13, 1988.

Costa v. ENEL. 1964. Ital.Const.Ct. (1964) CMLR 425.

Costa v. ENEL. 1964. ECJ Case 6/64. (1964) ECR 585.

Defrenne I (DeFrenne v. Belgium). 1971. ECJ Case No. 80/71. (1974) 1 CMLR 494.

D.G.V. 1979. ECJ Cases 241, 245–250/78. (1979) ECR 3017.

Dodge v. Woolsey. 1856. 18 Howard 331.

Dred Scott v. Sandford. 1857. 60 U.S. 393.

Elkinson v. DeLiesseline. 1823. Fed. Cases, No. 4366.

ERTA Commission v. Council. 1972. ECJ Case 22/70. March 31, 1971. (1971) ECR 263.

Ets.Petitjean. 1967. Fr.Cons.d'E. No.5/1967, 23 Droit Administratif 284–7.

Ex Parte Young. 1908. 209 U.S. 123.

Fairfax's Devisee v. Hunter's Lessee. 1813. 7 Cranch 603.

Fragd v. Amministrazione delle Finanze. 1989. Ital.Const.Ct. No. 232. April 21, 1989, 72 *Revista di Dirito Internationale* 103.

Francovich v. Italy. 1991. ECJ Case No. 6/90. Nov. 19, 1991. (1991) ECR 5357.

Frontini v. Ministero delle Finanze. 1973. Ital.Const.Ct. (1974) 2 CMLR 381.

Grad v. Finanzamt Traustein. 1970. ECJ Case 9/70. (1970) ECR 825.

Granital. 1984. Ital.Const.Ct. June 8, 1984 (1984) CMLR 756.

Green v. Biddle. 1823. 8 Wheaton 1.

Hans v. Louisiana. 1890. 134 U.S.1.

Hunter's Lessee v. Martin. 1815. (Virginia) 4 Munf. 1.

International Handelsgesellschaft v. EVGF. 1970. ECJ Case 11/70. (1970) ECR 1125.

Jackson v. Rose. 1815. 2 Va. Cas. 34.

Jacques Vabré case: *Administration des Douanes v. Société Café Jacques Vabré.* 1975. Fr.C.Cass. (1975) 2 CMLR 336.

Johnson v. Gordon. 1854. 4 Cal. 368 (California).

Lutticke v. Hauptzollamt Saarlois (1966) ECJ Case 55/65, June 16, 1966. ECR 205.

McCulloch v. Maryland. 1819. 4 Wheaton 316.

Maastricht II. 1993. German Const.Ct. 1993 Europäische Grundrechte Zeitschrift 429; 1994 International Legal Materials 388.

Martin v. Hunter's Lessee. 1816. 1 Wheaton (14 U.S.) 304.

Minister of the Interior v. Cohn-Bendit. 1978. (1980) 1 CMLR 543.

Molkerie Zentrale Westphalen v. Hauptzollamt Paderborn (1967) ECJ Case 28/67, March 3 (1968) ECR 143.

Mutton War. See Commission v. France 1979.

New Jersey v. New York. 1830. 28 U.S. 461.

Nicolo. 1989. Fr. Cons.d'E. Oct. 20, 1989, *Recueil Lebon,* 190, concl. Frydman.

Office Nationale Interprofessional de Céréales (ONIC). 1980. Fr. Cons.d'E. 9 May 1980, *Recueil Lebon,* 220; 3 *Revue trimestrielle de droit européen* 1980, 578.

Olmstead et al. v. Rittenhouse's Executrices (cited without citation number in *United States v. Peters*).

Osborn v. Bank of the United States 1824. 9 Wheaton 738.

Padelford v. Savannah. 1854. 14 Georgia 440.

Prigg v. Pennsylvania. 1842. 16 Peters 539.

Ramel case: *Administration des Contributions indirectes et Comité Interprofessionel des vins doux naturels v. P. Ramel.* 1970. Fr.C.Cass. (1971) CMLR 315–324.

Re: The Draft Treaty on a European Economic Area (No.2). 1992. ECJ Case 1/92 (1992) 2 CMLR 217.

Respublica v. Cobbett. 1798. 3 Dallas 462.

Semoules decision: *Syndicat Général de Fabricants de Semoules.* 1968. Fr.Cons.d'E. (1970) CMLR 395.

Shell Barre case. 1964. Fr.Cons.d'E. (1964) CMLR 462.

Simmenthal II. 1978. ECJ Case 106/77. (1978) ECR 629.

Société civile Centre international dentaire. 1981. Fr.Cons d'E. Feb. 25, 1981, No. 1587, 1981 *Revue Droit Fiscal* 31–32.

Société Sovincast. 1980. Fr.Cons.d'E. Nov. 20, 1980, No. 1113, 1981 *Revue Droit Fiscal* 21.

Sociétés de protection des animaux. 1984. Fr. Cons.d'E. Sept. 28, 1984, *Recueil Lebon* 512.

Society for the Protection of Unborn Children v. Grogan. 1991. ECJ Case C-159/90. (1992) CMLR 29:585.

Solange I decision, *Internationale Handelsgesellschaft v. Einfuhr-und Vor-ratsstelle.* 1974. German Const.Ct. (1974) 2 CMLR 540.

Solange II decision, *Wunsche Handelsgesellschaft.* 1986. German Const. Ct. 73 Entscheidungen des Bundesverfassungsgerichts 339 (English [1987], 3) CMLR 225.

Stunt v. The Steamboat Ohio. 1855. 3 Ohio Decision Reprint 362.

Tassel v. Georgia. 1829. (unreported).

Tenover Case. 1993. (*Barber II*). Case C-109/91. (1993) ECR I-4879).

Tyler v. Magwire. 1872. 84 U.S. 243.

United States v. Peters. 1809. 5 Cranch 136.

United States v. The William. 1808. 28 Fed. Cases 614.

Value-Added Tax Directive Case ("VAT I"). 1981. German Sup. Tax Court. (1982) 1 CMLR 527.

Value Added Tax II ("VAT II"). 1985. German Sup. Tax Ct. 143 Entscheidungen des Bundesfinanzhof 383 (1985); 75 Entscheidungen des Bundesverfassungsgerichts 223 (1986); German Const. Ct. 2 Bundesverfassungsgerichts (R category) 687/85.

Van Duyn v. Home Office. 1974. ECJ Case 41/74 (1974) ECR 1337.

Van Gend en Loos v. Netherlandse Administratie. 1963. ECJ Case 26/62. (1963) ECR 1.

Ware v. Hylton. 1796. 3 Dallas 171.

Wayman v. Southard. 1825. 10 Wheaton 1.

Wetherbee v. Johnson. 1817. 14 Mass. 417.

Worcester v. Georgia. 1832. 5 Peters 515.

Works Cited

Adams, Francis O. and Cunningham, C. D. *The Swiss Confederation*. London: Macmillan, 1889.

Adinolfi, Adelina. "The Judicial Application of Community Law in Italy (1981– 1997)." *Common Market Law Review* 35 (1998): 1313–69.

Aggestam, Lisbeth. "The European Union at the Crossroads: Sovereignty and Integration." In Alice Landau and Richard Whitman, eds., *Rethinking the European Union: Institutions, Interests, and Identities,* 75–92. New York: St. Martin's, 1997.

Albors-Llorens, Albertina. "Changes in the Jurisdiction of the European Court of Justice under the Treaty of Amsterdam." *Common Market Law Review* 35 (1998): 1273–94.

Alter, Karen. "The European Court's Political Power." *West European Politics* 19 (1996): 458–87.

———. "Explaining National Court Acceptance of European Court Jurisprudence: A Critical Evaluation of Theories of Legal Integration." In Slaughter et al., *The European Court and the National Courts.*

———. "Who Are the 'Masters of the Treaty'? European Governments and the European Court of Justice." *International Organization* 52 (1998): 121– 48.

Arendt, Hannah. *Between Past and Future*. New York: Penguin Books, 1980.

Armstrong, Kenneth. "Regulating the Free Movement of Goods: Institutions and Institutional Change." In Shaw and More, *New Legal Dynamics,* 165– 191.

Ashe, Samuel A'Court. *History of North Carolina*. Raleigh: Edwards & Broughton, 1925.

Aubert, Jean-François. "Observations sur le Développement de notre Fédéralisme." *Annuaire Suisse de Science Politique* 4 (1964): 7–22.

———. *Petite Histoire Constitutionelle de la Suisse*. Berne: Francke, 1975.

————. *Traité de Droit Constitutionel Suisse.* Vols. 1 and 2. Neuchâtel: Editions Ides et Calendes, 1967. Vol. 3. Neuchâtel: Editions Ides et Calendes, 1982.

Audeod, O. "The Application of Community Law in France: Review of French Court Decisions from 1974 to 1981." *Common Market Law Review* 19 (1982): 289–309.

Badie, Bertrand. *Un Monde sans Souveraineté.* Paris: Fayard, 1999.

Banchoff, Thomas, and Mitchell Smith, eds. *Legitimacy and the EU: The Contested Polity.* New York: Routledge, 1999.

Baudouin, Roger. *Le Canton de Vaud et l'Autonomie Cantonale en Suisse.* Orléans: Auguste Gout, 1906.

Beaufrays, Jean. "Observations on Switzerland: A Model for Belgium?" In Lloyd-Brown, *Federal-Type Solutions and European Integration,* 365–74.

Bebr, Gerhard. "The Rambling Ghost of *Cohn-Bendit: Acte Clair* and the Court of Justice." *Common Market Law Review* 20 (1983): 439–72.

Beer, Samuel H. "Federalism and the Nation-State: What Can Be Learned from the American Experience?" In Knop et al., *Rethinking Federalism,* 224–49.

Bibas, Steven. "The European Court of Justice and the U.S. Supreme Court: Parallels in Fundamental Rights Jurisprudence." *Hastings International and Comparative Law Review* 15 (1992): 253–95.

Biersteker, Thomas J., and Cynthia Weber, eds. *State Sovereignty as Social Construct.* Cambridge: Cambridge University Press, 1996.

Black, Antony J. *Monarchy and Community: Political Ideas in the Later Conciliar Controversy, 1430–1450.* Cambridge: Cambridge University Press, 1970.

Bobbitt, Philip. *Constitutional Fate.* New York: Oxford University Press, 1982.

Bodin, Jean. *On Sovereignty:* Four chapters from *The Six Books of the Commonwealth.* 1583. Reprint, Cambridge: Cambridge University Press, 1992.

Borel, Eugène. *Etude sur la Souveraineté et l'Etat Fédératif.* Berne: Imprimerie Staempfli, 1886.

Bowler, Shaun, David Farrell, and Ian Holliday. "Building a European Union: Euro-federalism and the ECJ." Paper presented at annual meeting of American Political Science Association, New York, Sept. 1, 1994.

Brake, Wayne Ph. te. "Provincial Histories and National Revolution." In Jacob and Mijnhardt, eds., *The Dutch Republic in the Eighteenth Century,* 60–90.

Brecht, Arnold. "Sovereignty." In Hans Speier and Alfred Kahler, eds., *War in Our Time,* 58–78. New York: W. W. Norton, 1939.

Bribosia, Hervé. "Report on Belgium." In Slaughter et al., *The European Court and the National Courts.*

Brooks, Robert C. *Government and Politics of Switzerland.* Yonkers: World Book, 1918.

Brunsson, Nils. *The Organization of Hypocrisy: Talk, Decisions, and Actions in Organizations.* Chichester: John Wiley & Sons, 1989.

Bryce, James. *Modern Democracies.* New York: Macmillan, 1921.

Buffet-Tchakaloff, Marie-France. *La France Devant La Cour de Justice des Communautés Européennes.* Paris: Économica, 1985.

Bulmer, Simon. "The Governance of the EU: A New Institutionalist Approach." *Journal of Public Policy* 13 (1993): 351–80.

Burch, Kurt. *Property and the Making of the International System: Constituting Sovereignty, Political Economy, and the Modern Era.* Boulder: Lynne Rienner, 1997.

Burgess, Michael, and Alain-G. Gagnon. *Comparative Federalism and Federation: Competing Traditions and Future Directions* London: Harvester Wheatsheaf, 1993.

Burley [Slaughter], Anne-Marie, and Walter Mattli. "Europe Before the Court: A Political Theory of Legal Integration." *International Organization* 47 (1993): 41–76.

Cafrany, Alan W., and Carl Lankowski, eds. *Europe's Ambiguous Unity: Conflict and Consensus in the Post-Maastricht Era.* Boulder: Lynne Rienner, 1997.

Caldeira, Greg, and James Gibson. "The Legitimacy of the Court of Justice in the European Union: Models of Diffuse Support." *American Political Science Review* 89 (1995): 356–76.

———. "The Legitimacy of Transnational Institutions: Compliance, Support, and the European Court of Justice." *American Journal of Political Science* 39 (1995): 459–89.

Calhoun, John C. *Disquisition on Government.* 1848. Reprint, New York: P. Smith, 1963.

Camilleri, Joseph A. "Rethinking Sovereignty in a Shrinking World." In R. B. J. Walker and Saul Mendlovitz, eds., *Contending Sovereignties: Redefining Political Community.* Boulder: Lynne Rienner, 1990.

Campbell, Stanley. *The Slave Catchers: Enforcement of the Fugitive Slave Law, 1850–1860.* New York: W. W. Norton, 1970.

Cappelletti, Mauro. "Is the European Court of Justice 'Running Wild'?" *European Law Review* 12 (1987): 3–17.

Cappelletti, Mauro, and David Golay. "The Judicial Branch in the Federal and Transnational Union: Its Impact on Integration." In Cappelletti et al., *Integration through Law,* 1:3: 261–51.

Cappelletti, Mauro, Monica Secombe and Joseph Weiler, eds. *Integration through*

Law: Europe and the American Federal Experience. Berlin and New York: Walter de Gruyter, 1986.

Cartabia, Marta. "The Italian Constitutional Court and the Relationship between the Italian Legal System and the European Union." Paper presented at workshop on the European Court and National Courts, June 27–29, 1994, European University Institute, Florence.

Casey, Lee A., and David Rivkin, Jr. "Against an International Criminal Court." *Commentary* 105 (May 1998): 56–58.

Chesterfield, Philip Dormer Stanhope, Earl of. *Letters Written . . . to His Son,* ed. Bonamy Dobrée, 6 vols. 1774. Reprint, New York: Viking, 1932.

Chryssochoou, Dimitris et al. *Theory and Reform in the European Union.* Manchester: Manchester University Press, 1999.

Close, Paul, and Emiko Ohki-Close. *Supranationalism in the New World Order: Global Processes Reviewed.* London: Macmillan, 1999.

Coppel, Jason, and Aidan O'Neill. "The European Court of Justice: Taking Rights Seriously?" *Common Market Law Review* 29 (1992): 669–92.

Corwin, Edward S. "National Power and State Interposition 1787–1861." *Michigan Law Review* 10 (1911): 535–51.

Craig, P. P. "Report on the United Kingdom." In Slaughter et al., *The European Court and the National Courts.*

Cram, Laura. "Integration Theory and the Study of European Policy Process." In Jeremy Richardson, ed., *European Union: Power and Policy-Making,* 40–58. London and New York: Routledge, 1996.

Daalder, Hans. "Consociationalism, Center, and Periphery in the Netherlands." In Per Torsvik, ed., *Mobilization, Center-Periphery Structures, and Nation-Building,* 181–240. Bergen, Norway: Universitetsforlaget, 1981.

———. "La Formation des nations par 'Consociatio': Le Cas des Pays-Bas and de la Suisse." *Revue Internationale des Science Sociales* 23 (1971): 384–99.

De Jouvenal, Bertrand. *Sovereignty: An Inquiry into the Political Good.* Trans. J. F. Huntington. Chicago: University of Chicago Press, 1957.

Dehousse, Renaud. "Community Competences: Are There Limits to Growth?" In Renaud Dehousse, ed., *Europe after Maastricht: An Ever Closer Union,* 103–25. Munich: C. H. Beck, 1994.

Delsol, Chantal [Millon]. "Souveraineté et Subsidiarité ou l'Europe contre Bodin." *The Tocqueville Review* 19 (1998): 49–56.

Deudney, Daniel. "Binding Sovereigns: Authorities, Structures, and Geopolitics in Philadelphia Systems." In Biersteker and Weber, *State Sovereignty as Social Construct,* 190–239.

Deursen, A. Th. van. "Maurits." In C. A. Tamse, ed., *Nassau en Orange in de Nederlandse geschiedenis,* 83–109. Alpen aan de Rijn: A. W. Sijthoff, 1979.

Droz, Numa. "Histoire Politique de la Suisse au XIXième Siècle." In Paul Seippel et al., ed., *La Suisse au XIXième Siècle,* 1: 251–378. Lausanne: Payot, 1899.

Dutheil de la Rochère, Jacqueline. "*Société . . . Rothmans* and *Société . . . Philip Morris France,* Two Decisions by the Conseil d'État. . . ." *Common Market Law Review* 30 (1993): 187–98.

Ehlermann, Claus, D. "Différenciation, Flexibilité, Coopération Renforcée: Les Nouvelles Dispositions du Traité d'Amsterdam." Trans. from German by L. Duhannoy. *Revue du Marché Unique* 3 (1997): 53–90.

Elazar, Daniel. *Constitutionalizing Globalization: The Postmodern Revival of Confederal Arrangements.* Lanham, Md.: Rowman & Littlefield, 1998.

———. *Exploring Federalism.* Tuscaloosa: University of Alabama Press, 1987.

———. *Federalism and Political Integration.* Ramat Gan, Israel: Turtledove, 1979.

———. "The New Europe: A Federal State or a Confederation of States?" *Swiss Political Science Review* 4 (1998): 119–38.

Elazar, Daniel, and Ilan Greilshammer. "Federal Democracy: The U.S.A. and Europe Compared, A Political Science Perspective." In Cappelletti, Secombe, and Weiler, *Integration through Law,* 1:1: 71–168.

Elshtain, Jean Bethke. "Rethinking Sovereignty." In Francis A. Beer and Robert Harriman, eds., *Post-Realism: The Rhetorical Turn in International Relations,* 171–91. East Lansing: Michigan State University Press, 1996.

Empel, M. van, H. G. Schermers, et al., eds. *Leading Cases on the Law of the European Communities.* 5th ed. Deventer and Boston: Kluwer, 1990.

Eschet-Schwarz, Andre. "Can the Swiss Federal Experience Serve as a Model of Integration?" In Daniel J. Elazar, ed., *Constitutional Design and Power-Sharing in the Post-Modern Epoch,* 161–83. Lanham, Md.: University Press of America, 1991.

———. "Le Processus de l'Intégration du Canton de Neuchâtel à la Confédération Suisse (1866–1975)." *Annuaire Suisse de Science Politique* 1976: 163–80.

Ferry, Jean-Marc. "La Communauté Européenne, entre Etat Fédéral et Fédération d'États." *Swiss Political Science Review* 4 (1998): 11–31.

Forsyth, Murray. *Federalism and Nationalism.* Leicester: Leicester University Press, 1989.

———. "Political Science, Federalism and Europe." No. FS95/2 Leicester University Discussion Papers in Federal Studies, 1995.

———. *Unions of States: The Theory and Practice of Confederation.* New York: Holmes & Meier, 1981.

Fowler, Michael Ross, and Julie Marie Bunck. *Law, Power, and the Sovereign*

State: The Evolution and Application of the Concept of Sovereignty. University Park: Pennsylvania State University Press, 1995.

Fox, Gregory. "New Approaches to International Human Rights: The Sovereign State Revisited." In Hashmi, *State Sovereignty*, 105–30.

Freestone, David, and Scott Davidson. *The Institutional Framework of the European Communities*. London and New York: Croon Helm, 1988.

Friedman, Barry. "The History of the Countermajoritarian Difficulty, Part One: The Road to Judicial Supremacy." *New York University Law Review* 73 (1998): 333–433.

———. "'Things Forgotten' in the Debate over Judicial Independence." *Georgia State University Law Review* 14 (1998): 737–53.

———. "Valuing Federalism." *Minnesota Law Review* 82 (1997): 317–412.

Friedman, Lawrence M. *A History of American Law*. New York: Simon and Schuster, 1985.

Friedrich, Carl J. *Trends in Federalism: Theory and Practice*. New York: Praeger, 1968.

Frowein, Jochen Abr. "Integration and the Federal Experience in Germany and Switzerland." In Cappelletti, Secombe, and Weiler, *Integration through Law*, 1:1: 572–600.

———. "Solange II (BVerfGE 73, 339). Constitutional complaint Firma W." *Common Market Law Review* 25 (1988): 201–06.

Gaja, Giorgio. "Annotation" to *S.p.a. Granital v. Amministrazione delle Finanze dello Stato, Common Market Law Review* 21 (1985): 764–72.

Garrett, Geoffrey. "International Cooperation and Institutional Choice: The European Community's Internal Market." *International Organization* 46, 2 (1992): 533–60.

Garrett, Geoffrey, and Barry Weingast. "Ideas, Interests, and Institutions: Constituting the EC's Internal Market." In Judith Goldstein and Robert Keohane, eds., *Ideas and Foreign Policy: Beliefs, Institutions, and Political Change*, 173–206. Ithaca: Cornell University Press, 1993.

Garrett, Geoffrey, et al. "The European Court of Justice, National Governments, and Legal Integration in the European Union." *International Organization* 52 (1998): 149–76.

Gierke, Otto von. *Political Theories of the Middle Ages*. Trans. F. W. Maitland. Cambridge: Cambridge University Press, 1927.

Goldstein, Leslie. "State Resistance to Authority in Federal Unions: The Early United States (1790–1860) and the European Community (1958–1994)." *Studies in American Political Development* 11 (Spring 1997): 149–89.

Golub, Jonathan. "The Politics of Judicial Discretion: Rethinking the Interaction between National Courts and the European Court of Justice." *West European Politics* 19 (1996): 360–85.

Gow, James. "Shared Sovereignty, Enhanced Security, Lessons from the Yugoslav War." In Hashmi, *State Sovereignty,* 152–79.

Grisel, Etienne. *Droit Constitutionnel, Première Partie: Les Sources, Cours Donné à l'Université de Lausanne.* Lausanne: Université de Lausanne Polycopies, 1997.

———. *Droit Constitutionnel, Deuxième Partie: La Structure de l'État et le Fédéralisme, Cours Donné a l'Université de Lausanne.* Lausanne: Université de Lausanne Polycopies, 1994.

Gunther, Gerald. *Constitutional Law.* 12th ed. Westbury, N.Y.: Foundation Press, 1991.

Habermas, Jürgen. "The European Nation-State: Its Achievements and Its Limits: On the Past and Future of Sovereignty and Citizenship." *European Journal of Law, Philosophy and Computer Science* 7 (1995): 27–36.

Haley, K. D. H. *The Dutch in the Seventeenth Century.* New York: Harcourt, Brace, Jovanovich, 1972.

Hart, Marjolein 't. *The Making of a Bourgeois State.* Manchester: Manchester University Press, 1993.

———. "Rules and Repertoires: The Revolt of a Farmer's Republic in the Early Modern Netherlands." In Michael P. Hanagan et al., eds., *Challenging Authority: The Historical Study of Contentious Politics,* 197–212. Minneapolis: University of Minnesota Press, 1998.

Hashmi, Sohail, ed. *State Sovereignty: Change and Persistence in International Relations.* University Park: Pennsylvania State University Press, 1997.

Henshall, Nicholas. *The Myth of Absolutism: Change and Continuity in Early Modern European Monarchy.* London and New York: Longman, 1992.

Herdegen, Matthias. "Maastricht and the German Constitutional Court: Constitutional Restraints for an 'Ever Closer Union.'" *Common Market Law Review* 31 (1994): 235–49.

Hesse, Joachim Jens and Vincent Wright. *Federalizing Europe? The Costs, Benefits, and Preconditions of Federal Political Systems* Oxford: Oxford University Press, 1996.

Hicks, Ursula K. *Federalism: Failure and Success, A Comparative Study.* New York: Oxford University Press, and London: Macmillan, 1978.

Hinsley, F. H. *Sovereignty.* New York: Basic Books, 1966.

Hoetjeś, Bernard J. S. "The European Tradition of Federalism: The Protestant Dimension." In Burgess and Gagnon, *Comparative Federalism and Federation,* 117–37.

Hooghe, Liesbet, and Gary Marks. "Contending Models of Governance in the EU." In Cafrany and Lankowski, *Europe's Ambiguous Unity*, 21–44.

Horwitz, Morton J. *The Transformation of American Law, 1780–1860*. Cambridge: Harvard University Press, 1977.

Hueglin, Thomas O. "New Wine in Old Bottles? Federalism and Nation States in the Twenty-First Century: A Conceptual Overview." In Knop et al., *Rethinking Federalism*, 203–21.

Hughes, Christopher. "Cantonalism: Federation and Confederacy in the Golden Epoch of Switzerland." In Burgess and Gagnon, *Comparative Federalism and Federation*, 154–67.

———. *The Federal Constitution of Switzerland*. 1954. Reprint, Westport, Conn.: Greenwood, 1970.

Huizinga, J. A. *Dutch Civilisation in the Seventeenth Century and other essays*, eds. Pieter Geyl and F. W. N. Hugenholtz. London: Collins, 1968.

Ionescu, Ghita, ed. *Between Sovereignty and Integration*. New York: John Wiley & Sons, 1974.

Israel, Jonathan. *The Dutch Republic: Its Rise, Greatness, and Fall, 1477–1806*. Oxford: Oxford University Press, 1995.

Jackson, Robert. "International Community beyond the Cold War." In Gene M. Lyons and Michael Mastanduno, eds., *Beyond Westphalia: State Sovereignty and International Intervention*, 59–83. Baltimore: Johns Hopkins University Press, 1995.

Jackson, Vicki. "The Supreme Court, the Eleventh Amendment, and State Sovereign Immunity." *Yale Law Journal* 98 (1988): 1–126.

Jacob, Margaret C., and Wijnard W. Mijnhardt. *The Dutch Republic in the Eighteenth Century: Decline, Enlightenment and Revolution*. Ithaca: Cornell University Press, 1992.

Jessup, Dwight Wiley. *Reaction and Accommodation: The United States Supreme Court and Political Conflict*. New York: Garland, 1987.

Kaestle, Karl. *Pillars of the Republic: Common Schools and American Society, 1780–1860*. New York: Hill and Wang, 1983.

Kantrowicz, E. H. *The King's Two Bodies*. Princeton: Princeton University Press, 1957.

Kavanagh, Dennis. "Beyond Autonomy? The Politics of Corporations." In Ionescu, *Between Sovereignty and Integration*, 46–64.

Kelly, Alfred H., Winfred Harbison, and Herman Belz. *The American Constitution: Its Origin and Development*. 6th ed. New York: W. W. Norton, 1983.

Kelsen, Hans. *Law and Peace in International Relations*. Cambridge: Harvard University Press, 1942.

Kent, Penelope. *European Community Law*. London: Longman, 1992.

King, Preston. *Federalism and Federation*. London: Croon Helm, 1985.

Klein, Robert A. *Sovereign Equality Among States: The History of an Idea*. Toronto: University of Toronto Press, 1971.

Knop, Karen, et al. *Rethinking Federalism: Citizens, Markets, and Governments in a Changing World*. Vancouver: University of British Columbia Press, 1995.

Kokott, Juliane. "Report on Germany." In Slaughter et al., *The European Court and the National Courts*.

Kossman, E. H. "The Dutch Republic in the Eighteenth Century." In Jacob and Mijnhardt, *The Dutch Republic in the Eighteenth Century*, 19–32.

———. "Popular Sovereignty at the Beginning of the Dutch Ancien Régime." *The Low Countries History Yearbook, Acta Historiae Neerlandicae* 14: 1–28. The Hague: Martinus Nijhoff, 1981.

Kossman, E. H., and A. F. Mellink. *Texts Concerning the Revolt of the Netherlands*. London: Cambridge University Press, 1974.

Krasner, Stephen. "Sovereignty: An Institutional Perspective." *Comparative Political Studies* 21 (1988): 66–94.

———. *Sovereignty: Organized Hypocrisy*. Princeton: Princeton University Press, 1999.

Krislov, Samuel, Claus-Dieter Ehlermann, and Joseph Weiler. "The Political Organs in the Decision-Making Process in the United States and the European Community." In Cappelletti, Secombe, and Weiler, *Integration through Law*, 1:2: 3–108.

Landau, Jacob M. "The Language Problem in European Integration: The Lesson of Other Federal-Type Solutions." In Lloyd-Brown, *Federal-Type Solutions and European Integration*, 501–13.

Laski, Harold J. *Authority in the Modern State*. New Haven: Yale University Press, 1927.

Leach, Richard. "The Provinces in the Dutch System of Government." *South Atlantic Quarterly* 69 (1970): 327–45.

Lemco, Jonathan. *Political Stability in Federal Governments*. New York: Praeger, 1991.

Lenaerts, Koen. "Constitutionalism and the Many Faces of Federalism." *American Journal of Comparative Law* 38 (1990): 205–63.

———. "Some Thoughts about the Interaction between Judges and Politicians." *University of Chicago Legal Forum* (1992): 93–133.

Levitan, David. "The Foreign Relations Powers: An Analysis of Mr. Justice Sutherland's Theory." *Yale Law Journal* 55 (1946): 467–97.

Linder, Wolf. *Swiss Democracy Possible Solutions to Conflict in Multicultural Societies*. New York: St. Martin's Press, 1994.

Lister, Frederick. *The Early Security Confederations: From the Ancient Greeks to the United Colonies of New England.* Westport, Conn.: Praeger, 1999.

———. *The European Union, the United Nations, and the Revival of Confederal Governance.* Westport, Conn.: Greenwood, 1996.

Lloyd-Brown, C., ed. *Federal-Type Solutions and European Integration.* Lanham, Md.: University Press of America, 1995.

Luck, J. Murray. *A History of Switzerland. The First 100,000 Years: Before the Beginning to the Days of the Present.* Palo Alto, Calif.: Society for the Promotion of Science and Scholarship, 1985.

Luxemburgensis. "The Emergence of a European Sovereignty." In Ionescu, *Between Sovereignty and Integration,* 118–34.

MacCormick, Neil. "Beyond the Sovereign State." *The Modern Law Review* 56 (1993): 1–18.

———. *Questioning Sovereignty.* Oxford: Oxford University Press, 1999.

Madison, James. "Number 39." In Alexander Hamilton, John Jay, and James Madison, *The Federalist Papers.* 1787–88. Reprint, New York: Mentor, 1961.

Malcolm, Noel. "Sense on Sovereignty." In Martin Holmes, ed., *The Eurosceptical Reader,* 342–67. New York: St. Martin's, 1996.

Mattli, Walter. *The Logic of Regional Integration: Europe and Beyond.* Cambridge: Cambridge University Press, 1999.

Mattli, Walter, and Anne-Marie [Burley]Slaughter. "Law and Politics in the European Union: A Reply to Garrett." *International Organization* 49 (1995): 183–90.

———. "Revisiting the European Court of Justice." *International Organization* 52 (1998): 177–209.

McDonald, Forrest. 1982. *A Constitutional History of the United States.* New York: Franklin Watts.

McDougall, Marion Gleason. *Fugitive Slaves, 1619–1865.* 1891. Reprint, New York: Bergman, 1967.

McKay, David. "Policy Legitimacy and Institutional Design." *Journal of Common Market Studies* 38 (2000): 25–44.

Merriam, Charles E. *History of the Theory of Sovereignty Since Rousseau.* New York: Columbia University Press, 1900.

Mills, Kurt. *Human Rights in the Emerging Global Order: A New Sovereignty?* New York: St. Martin's Press, 1998.

Moravcsik, Andrew. *The Choice for Europe: Social Purpose and State Power from Messina to Maastricht.* Ithaca: Cornell University Press, 1998.

———. "Explaining International Human Rights Regimes: Liberal Theory and

Western Europe." *European Journal of International Relations* 1 (1995): 157–89.

Morris, Richard B. *The Forging of the American Union, 1781–1789.* New York: Harper & Row, 1987.

Murphy, Alexander. "The Sovereign State as Political-Territorial Ideal." In Biersteker and Weber, *State Sovereignty as Social Construct,* 81–120.

Myers, Henry A., with Herwig Wolfram. *Medieval Kingship.* Chicago: Nelson-Hall, 1982.

Nathan, James A. "A New World Order That Meant Something." *Aspen Institute Quarterly* (1994): 109–36.

North, Douglass C. *Structure and Change in Economic History.* New York: W. W. Norton, 1981.

O'Connor, Karen, and Larry Sabato. *American Government Roots and Reform.* New York: Macmillan, 1993.

Pfeiffer, Katrin, and Luc Weber. "Le Fédéralisme Suisse à l'Epreuve du Temps: Un Modèle pour l'Europe?" *Politiques et Management Public* (Paris) 9 (1991): 103–38.

Philpott, Daniel. "Sovereignty: An Introduction and Brief History." *Journal of International Affairs* 48 (1995): 353–68.

Pierson, Paul. "The Path to European Integration: A Historical Institutionalist Analysis." *Comparative Political Studies* 29 (1996): 123–63.

Pinder, John. "The New European Federalism: The Idea and the Achievements." In Burgess and Gagnon, *Comparative Federalism and Federation,* 45–66.

Plötner, Jens. "Report on France." In Slaughter et al., *The European Court and the National Courts.*

Pollack, Mark. "Delegation, Agency, and Agenda-Setting in the European Community." *International Organization* 51 (1997): 99–134.

Powell, Jefferson. *Languages of Power: A Sourcebook of Early American Constitutional History.* Durham: Carolina Academic Press, 1991.

Powell, William. *North Carolina through Four Centuries.* Chapel Hill: University of North Carolina Press, 1989.

Price, J. L. *Holland and the Dutch Republic in the Seventeenth Century: The Politics of Particularism.* Oxford: Clarendon, 1994.

Prokhovnik, Raia. "Sovereignty in Hobbes, Spinoza and Contemporary Europe." Paper presented at the bi-annual conference of the International Society for the Study of European Ideas, August 1994, Graz, Austria.

Pufendorf, Samuel. *De Jure Naturae et Gentium Libri Octo* [The Law of Nature and Nations]. 1672. Trans. C. H. Oldfather and W. A. Oldfather. New York: Oxford University Press, 1934.

Rabkin, Jeremy. *Why Sovereignty Matters*. Washington: American Enterprise Institute Press, 1998.

Rappard, William. *The Government of Switzerland*. New York: Van Nostrand, 1936.

Rasmussen, Hjalte. *The European Court of Justice*. Copenhagen: Gadjura, 1998.

———. *On Law and Policy in the European Court of Justice*. Dordrecht: Martinus Nijhoff, 1986.

———. "Towards a Normative Theory of Interpretation of Community Law." *University of Chicago Legal Forum* (1992): 135–78.

Reitsma, Rients. *Centrifugal and Centripetal Forces in the Early Dutch Republic: The States of Overijssel 1566–1600*. Amsterdam: Rodopi, 1982.

Rice, William G. *A Tale of Two Courts*. Madison: University of Wisconsin Press, 1967.

Riker, William. *The Development of American Federalism*. Boston: Kluwer Academic Publishers, 1987.

———. "European Federalism: Lessons of Past Experience." In Hesse and Wright, *Federalizing Europe?*, 9–24.

———. *Federalism: Origin, Operation, Significance*. Boston: Little, Brown, 1964.

Rowen, Herbert H. *Rhyme and Reason of Politics in Early Modern Europe: Collected Essays of Herbert Rowen,* ed. Craig Harline. Dordrecht: Kluwer, 1992.

Rowen, Herbert H., and De LaMar Jensen. *The Dutch Republic: A Nation in the Making*. St. Charles, Mo.: Forum Press, 1975.

Rowen, Herbert H., and Andrew Losskey. *Political Ideas and Institutions in the Dutch Republic*. Los Angeles: Williams Andrews Clark Memorial Library, UCLA, 1985.

Ruffieux, Roland. "La Suisse des Radicaux 1848–1914." In Georges Andrey and Jean-Claude Favez, eds., *Nouvelle Histoire de la Suisse et des Suisses,* 599–682. 2d ed. Lausanne: Payot, 1983.

Rutland, Robert et al., eds. *Papers of James Madison*. Chicago: University of Chicago Press, 1975.

Sacks, Edward. "Education Article X." In H. B. Rubenstein et al., eds., *The Delaware Constitution of 1897: The First One Hundred Years,* 167–75. Wilmington: Delaware State Bar Association, 1997.

Salis, L. R. von, ed. *Le Droit Fédéral Suisse, Jurisprudence du Conseil Fédéral et de l'Assemblée Fédérale en Matière de Droit Public et de Droit Administratif Depuis le 29 Mai 1874*. Trans. Eugène Borel, 2d ed. Berne: K.-J. Wyss, 1904–7.

Sawer, Geoffrey F. *Modern Federalism*. Carlton, Australia: Pitman, 1976.

Scharpf, Fritz. "The Joint Decision Trap: Lessons from German Federalism and European Integration." *Public Administration* 66 (1988): 239–78.

Scheingold, Stuart A. *The Law in Political Integration.* Cambridge: Center for International Affairs of Harvard University, 1971.

Schermers, Henry G. "Comment on Weiler's 'The Transformation of Europe.'" *Yale Law Journal* 100 (1991): 2525–36.

Schermers, Henry G., and Denis Waelbroeck. *Judicial Protection in the European Communities.* Deventer and Boston: Kluwer, 1992.

Schmitter, Phillipe C. "Some Alternative Futures for the European Polity and Their Implications for European Public Policy." In Yves Mény et al., eds., *Adjusting to Europe: The Impact of the European Union on National Institutions and Policies,* 25–31. London and New York: Routledge, 1996.

Seurin, J. L. "Towards a European Constitution? Problems of Political Integration." *Public Law* (1994): 625–36.

Shapiro, Martin. "The European Court of Justice." In Alberta Sbragia, ed., *Europolitics: Institutions and Policymaking in the "New" European Community,* 123–156. Washington, D.C.: Brookings Institute, 1992.

Shaw, Jo. "European Union: Legal Studies in Crisis? Towards a New Dynamic." *Oxford Journal of Legal Studies* 16 (1996): 231–54.

Shaw, Jo, and Gillian More. "Introduction." In Jo Shaw and Gillian More, eds., *New Legal Dynamics of European Union,* 1–14. Oxford: Clarendon Press, 1995.

Shaw, Martin. "Toward a Theory of State Transformation." *Review of International Political Economy* 4 (1997): 497–513.

Sherry, Suzanna. "The Eleventh Amendment and Stare Decisis: Overruling *Hans v. Louisiana.*" *University of Chicago Law Review* 57 (1990): 1260–72.

Skidelsky, Robert. "The House of Rothschild: The World's Banker, 1849–1999." *New York Review of Books* 46: 20 (Dec. 16, 1999): 24–27.

Slaughter, Anne-Marie [Burley], Alec Stone[-]Sweet, and Joseph Weiler, eds. *The European Court and the National Courts: Doctrine and Jurisprudence: Legal Change in Its Social Context.* Oxford: Hart; Evanston: Northwestern University Press, 1997. Previously published as EUI Working Papers. Florence: European University Institute, 1995.

Snyder, Francis. "The Effectiveness of European Community Law: Institutions, Processes, Tools, and Techniques." *Modern Law Review* 56 (1993): 19–54.

Stein, Eric. "Lawyers, Judges, and the Making of a Transnational Constitution." *American Journal of International Law* 75 (1981): 1–27.

Stein, Torsten. "Case VR 123/84, Decision of the *Bundesfinanzhof* of 25 April 1985, (1985) DB 1443." *Common Market Law Review* 23 (1986): 727–36.

Stone, Alec. "Ratifying *Maastricht:* France Debates European Union." *French Politics & Society* 11 (1993): 70–88.

Stone[-]Sweet, Alec. "Constitutional Dialogues in the European Community." In Slaughter et al., *The European Court and the National Courts.*

Stone[-]Sweet, Alec, and James Caporaso. "From Free Trade to Supranational Polity: The European Court and Integration." Working Paper 2.45, Center for German and European Studies, University of California, Berkeley, 1996.

Stone[-]Sweet Alec, and Thomas Brunell. "Constructing a Supranational Constitution: Dispute Resolution and Governance in the European Community." *American Political Science Review* 92 (March 1998): 63–81.

Strayer, Joseph R. *On the Medieval Origins of the Modern State.* Princeton: Princeton University Press, 1970.

Taylor, Paul. *The European Union in the 1990s.* Oxford: Oxford University Press, 1996.

Temple, William. *Observations upon the United Provinces of the Netherlands.* 1690. Cambridge: Cambridge University Press, 1932.

Thelen, K., and S. Steinmo. "Historical Institutionalism in Comparative Analysis." In K. Thelen et al., eds., *Structuring Politics,* 1–32. New York: Cambridge University Press, 1992.

Thürer, Daniel. "Switzerland: The Model in Need of Adaptation?" In Hesse and Wright, *Federalizing Europe?,* 219–39.

Tilly, Charles. "Warmaking and Statemaking as Organized Crime." In Peter Evans, Dietrich Rueschemeyer, Theda Skocpol, eds., *Bringing the State Back In,* 169–91. Cambridge: Cambridge University Press, 1985.

Tipton, Diane. *Nullification and Interposition in American Political Thought.* Albuquerque: University of New Mexico Institute for Social Research and Development, 1969.

Tripp, Myron L. *The Swiss and the U.S. Federal Constitutional Systems: A Comparative Study.* Ph.D. dissertation, University of Zurich. Paris: Librairie Sociale et Economique, 1940.

Tromp, Bart. "European Unity in Historical Perspective." Paper presented at biannual conference of the International Society for the Study of European Ideas, August 1994, Graz, Austria.

Tyne, Claude Van. "Sovereignty in the American Revolution: An Historical Study." *American Historical Review* 12 (1906–7): 529–45.

Ullmer, R. E., ed. *Droit Public Suisse ou Jurisprudence des Arrets des Autorités Fédérales Suisses.* Trans. Eugène Borel. Vol. 1. Neuchâtel: Imprimerie Montandon Frères, 1864. Vol. 2. Neuchâtel: Imprimerie Sandoz, 1867.

Vincent, J. M. *State and Federal Government of Switzerland.* Baltimore: John Hopkins Press, 1891.

Volcansek, Mary. *Judicial Politics in Europe.* New York: Peter Lang, 1986.

———, ed. *Law above Nations: Supranational Courts and the Legalization of Politics.* Gainesville: Universities of Florida Press, 1997.

Vree, Johan de. *Political Integration: The Formation of Theory and Its Problems.* The Hague: Mouton, 1972.

Ward, Ian. "Identity and Difference: The European Union and Postmodernism." In Shaw and More, *New Legal Dynamics,* 15–28.

Warren, Charles. "Legislative and Judicial Attacks on the Supreme Court of the United States: A History of the Twenty-fifth Section of the Judiciary Act." *The American Law Review* 47 (1913): 1–34, 161–89.

Watts, Ronald L. *New Federations: Experiments in the Commonwealth.* Oxford: Clarendon Press, 1966.

Weiler, Joseph. "Journey to an Unknown Destination: A Retrospective and Prospective of the European Court of Justice in the Arena of Political Integration." *Journal of Common Market Studies* 31 (1993): 417–46.

———. "The Transformation of Europe." *Yale Law Journal* 100 (1991): 2403–83.

Wernham, R. B. "English Policy and the Revolt of the Netherlands." *Britain and the Netherlands* 1 (1960): 29–40.

Wheare, Kenneth C. *Federal Governments.* 4th ed. Oxford: Oxford University Press, 1963.

White, G. Edward. *The American Judicial Tradition Profiles of Leading American Judges.* New York: Oxford University Press, 1976.

Wilks, Michael. *The Problem of Sovereignty in the Later Middle Ages: The Papal Monarchy with Augustinus Triumphus and the Publicists.* Cambridge: Cambridge University Press, 1963.

Wincott, Daniel. "The Court of Justice and the European Policy Process." In Jeremy J. Richardson, ed., *European Union: Power and Policy-Making,* 170–84. London and New York: Routledge, 1996.

———. "Political Theory, Law, and the European Union." In Shaw and More, *New Legal Dynamics,* 165–91.

Wood, Gordon. *The Creation of the American Republic, 1776–1787.* Chapel Hill: University of North Carolina Press, 1969.

Worst, I. J. H. "Constitution, History, and Natural Law: An Eighteenth Century Political Debate in the Dutch Republic." In Jacob and Mijnhardt, *The Dutch Republic in the Eighteenth Century,* 147–69.

Index

Fugitive Slave Act (1793), 23, 26–27, 30
Fugitive Slave Act (1850), 27, 28, 30
fundamental rights: ECJ doctrine on, 33–34; German and Italian Constitutional Courts on, 33–34, 95, 205n. 29; provision in Treaty of Amsterdam, 34

Garibaldi, Guiseppi, 108
Garrett, Geoffrey, 59, 60–61, 144, 204n. 16
GATT, 4, 179–80n. 12
Gelderland, 68, 69, 70, 75, 76, 80, 82, 84, 85, 87
Generality (Dutch). See Dutch Republic
Generality Lands (Dutch), 69
Geneva, 108
Georgia, 11, 16, 30, 32, 58, 190n. 31
German Bund, 204n. 25
German Bundestag, 33, 35
German Constitutional Court, 22, 33–34, 35, 37, 42, 43
German Empire of 1871, 181n. 37
German Finance Ministry, 20, 34–35, 37, 150
German Supreme Tax Court, 20, 33, 35, 37, 150
Germany, 22, 34, 35, 43, 120, 150, 160
Gibbons v. Ogden, 60
Golub, Jonathan, 95, 156
Gomarist, 83, 84, 86
governor-general (Dutch), 69, 79
Granges, 119
Granital, 39, 184–85n. 23
Graubunden, 108
Greece, 184n. 20; ancient, 5
Green v. Biddle, 189–90n. 27, 205n. 2

Grisel, Etienne, 197n. 5
Groningen, 68, 69, 70, 80, 82, 84
Grotius, Hugo, 85–86

Habermas, Jürgen, 2
half-cantons, 99
Hartford Convention, 25, 32
Heath, Sir Edward, 3
heimatlosen, rights violated, 111, 128–30
Henry III, King of France, 69
heterogeneity, ethnic, 18–19, 65, 148
historical institutionalism, 144–45, 204n. 16
Hobbes, Thomas, 65
Hogerbeets, 85–86
Holland: armed forces reductions promoted by, 88–89; in Council of State, 69; dominance: —political, 76; —in population, 70, 76; —over taxes, 70, 76; leadership role in Dutch Republic, 70–72; merchant class in, 70–71, 91–92; out-voted in States-General, 76–77; pensionary of, 70–72; policy tendencies of, 71–72; pro-peace, 72; religion in, 74, 83–86; stadholder of, 70–72, 79; veto power (sovereignty) claimed by, 194n. 31
Horowitz, Morton, 91
Hueglin, Thomas, 140
Hughes, Christopher, 141, 197n. 4
human rights conventions, 4, 8, 64, 142–43, 159, 203n. 8. See also European Court of Human Rights; multilateral normative commitments
human rights regimes, suprastate, 159
Hunter's Lessee v. Martin, 46, 48